Allegory and Violence

Eugène Delacroix. *Dante and Virgil in Hell*. Louvre, Paris. Alinari/Art Resource, New York.

ALLEGORY

AND

VIOLENCE

GORDON TESKEY

Cornell University Press

ITHACA AND LONDON

THIS BOOK HAS BEEN PUBLISHED WITH THE AID
OF A GRANT FROM THE HULL MEMORIAL
PUBLICATION FUND OF CORNELL UNIVERSITY.

First published 1996 by Cornell University Press.

Printed in the United States of America

⊗ The paper in this book meets the minimum requirements
of the American National Standard for Information Sciences—
Permanence of Paper for Printed Library Materials, ANSI Z39.48-1984.

Library of Congress Cataloging-in-Publication Data

Teskey, Gordon, 1953–
    Allegory and violence / Gordon Teskey.
      p.   cm.
    Includes bibliographical references and index.
    ISBN 0-8014-2995-1 (cloth : alk. paper)
      1. Allegory.   2. Violence in literature.   3. Literature—History and
criticism.   I. Title.
PN56.A5T47   1996
809'.915—dc20   96-26917

For Mary Ann Radzinowicz

Mens hebes ad verum per materialia surgit.

—Abbot Suger

C'est la violence elle-même qui valorise les objets.

—René Girard

CONTENTS

ILLUSTRATIONS

PREFACE

T his book had its beginning in an article on allegory I con-
tributed to *The Spenser Encyclopedia*, edited by A. C. Hamilton, Donald Cheney, W. F. Blissett, David Richardson, and
William W. Barker (Toronto: University of Toronto Press, 1990).
A. Kent Hieatt persuaded me to write on the subject, and the editors,
especially Bert Hamilton, warmly encouraged me to pursue my own line
of thought. I attempted in that article to construct a poetics of allegory,
offering a definition of the genre, an analysis of its elements and their
relative functions, an outline of its historical development, and an orga-
nizing hypothesis within which the transactions of the allegorical work
with its culture might be understood.

In Aristotle's *Poetics*, the model for any such exercise, the organiz-
ing hypothesis is taken from medicine and the transaction accomplished
by the tragic drama is a therapeutic purgation, a catharsis. My organiz-
ing hypothesis was taken largely from information theory and from the
criticism of idealism in Wittgenstein's later philosophy; and the transaction of the work with its culture which I saw allegory performing was
that ritualized form of information processing we call interpretation.
It occurred to me that allegorical expression develops its imaginative
structures by exaggerating those aspects of an eidetic theory of language
most vulnerable to criticism on logical grounds and most likely to be
undermined by processes that belong to becoming. I worked on the assumption that the cultural purpose allegory serves is to call forth from

the reader, through interpretation, a continual translation of human experience into an arrangement of visual forms, an ideology.

The present study takes a somewhat different approach. Rather than itself engaging in the translation of experience (the experience of art) into a technical arrangement of forms, it seeks to open up the field of allegory studies by asking questions about what lies beneath the phenomenon under analysis. What broader human problems motivate allegorical expression? What deeper, religious concerns, and what intractable conceptual dilemmas, lie behind the impulse to personification? What cultural circumstances made possible, and perhaps even required, the emergence of allegorical writing in late antiquity? What is the relation of allegory to irony, and to what extent are they incompatible expressions of meaning as force—of meaning, that is, at the point of its encounter with chaos? What problems are raised by the transactions of allegorical expression with the sacred? How are these transactions exploited politically in the Renaissance, making a sort of religion of power? And how are they at length secularized, in the Enlightenment, as instrumental knowledge enslaved to desire? What can a questioning of allegory, and especially of secretive language, tell us about political risk and political care? What can the allegorical poet's engagement with the material remains of the past tell us about the larger relations between creative work and cultural change, that is, about literary history? Finally, what do the allegorical poets themselves, preëminently Dante and Spenser, reveal about the darker motives of allegorical expression, about allegory and radical violence? My aim is not so much to answer these questions as to try to understand what they mean—to ask them *at length*. In the more speculative method of inquiry I undertake here I can only hope that my findings will afford some guidance to further reflection on the cultural practices that have, in the twentieth century, succeeded to allegory, chief among which are literary history and critical theory.

I wish to thank the staffs of the Fisher, Robarts, and Renaissance and Reformation Institute libraries at the University of Toronto, of the Olin and Kroch libraries at Cornell University, and of the National Humanities Center. It is a pleasure to thank for their support the Cornell Society for the Humanities; the Mellon Foundation, which supported a year of research at the National Humanities Center; the National Humanities Center itself; the Cornell University Department of English; and the National Endowment for the Humanities, from which I received a summer research fellowship. I wish also to thank the Social Sciences and

Humanities Research Council of Canada, which long ago made it possible to do the reading necessary for the article for *The Spenser Encyclopedia*.

My indebtedness to persons is extensive and, I regret to say, impossible to rehearse in detail. I am grateful to those who have assisted me in various ways with this project, not omitting those anonymous scholars who read it at several stages. I have received valuable advice from Paul J. Alpers, Elizabeth Jane Bellamy, William Blissett, Cynthia Chase, Ann Baynes Coiro, Andrew Galloway, Steven Goldsmith, Kenneth Gross, Nicholas Halmi, A. C. Hamilton, A. Kent Hieatt, Sean Kane, Carol Kaske, Carol Krumhansl, Robert Lamberton, Charles Mahoney, David Lee Miller, Michael Murrin, John Najemy, Alan Nussbaum, Patricia Parker, Annabel Patterson, Hayden Pelliccia, Maureen Quilligan, Thomas P. Roche, Neil Saccamano, Danuta Shanzer, Fiona Somerset, Elizabeth Teskey, Winthrop Wetherbee, and Joseph Anthony Wittreich Jr. These readers and others have prevented me from making many mistakes. I am responsible for those that remain. I am grateful for the intellectual community of Cornell University, and especially for the stimulating example of my colleagues in the department of English. For research assistance I thank Timothy Billings, Susan Bruce, Michelle Marie Stern, and Patricia Welze. Susan Foster took charge of the index. I am very much indebted, for patience among other things, to Bernhard Kendler and the staff of Cornell University Press. I would also thank for their hospitality the staff of the Residenz, Würzburg; Gian Maria Erbesato of the Palazzo Te; Marina Turchetti, who took me to see the Taddeo Zuccaro allegories at Caprarola; and Sarah Poyntz, who took me to Spenser's Kilcolman. I regret I am no longer able to thank Denton Fox, Robert Finch, Northrop Frye, James Winny, and especially Donald Strathdee.

An earlier version of Chapter 1 appeared, under the title "Allegory, Materialism, Violence," in *The Production of English Renaissance Culture*, ed. David Lee Miller (Ithaca: Cornell University Press, 1994), pp. 293–318. Chapter 3 appeared in an earlier version, though under the same title, in *PMLA* (May 1994); and Chapter 8 appeared in an earlier version, under the title "Mutabilitie, Genealogy, and the Authority of Forms," in *Representations* 41 (Winter 1993): 104–22. Some phrases from the following have found their way into this book: "The Making of the Culture of the Sign," *University of Toronto Quarterly* 52 (1983): 209–13; "From Allegory to Dialectic: Imagining Error in Spenser and Milton," *PMLA* 101

(January 1986): 9–23; and my *Spenser Encyclopedia* article on allegory. I thank the editors and the presses involved for permission to redeploy these materials here. "Leda and the Swan" is reprinted with the permission of Simon and Schuster from *The Poems of W.B. Yeats: A New Edition*, edited by Richard J. Finneran. Copyright 1928 by Macmillan Publishing Company; Copyright © renewed 1956 by Georgie Yeats.

References to classical texts are taken from the Loeb Classical Library. References to Dante are from *The Divine Comedy*, translated, with a commentary, by Charles S. Singleton, 6 vols. (Princeton: Princeton University Press, 1970–75). References to Spenser, including the "Letter to Raleigh," are from *The Faerie Queene*, ed. A. C. Hamilton (London: Longman, 1977). Unattributed translations are mine.

Perhaps the happiest moment I spent in researching this book was the occasion of its second beginning. It was the morning I spent alone in the Room of Eros and Psyche in the Palazzo Te, observing the vertiginous movement of the bodies on the walls and, on the ceiling, the labyrinthine ascent of the soul. I thought of how the room was invaded by a deadly fever from the city nearby and of Giulio Romano's anonymous assistants who died of it. Like Spenser's *Mutabilitie*, the glory of that room evoked everything allegory is trying to conceal and everything it is trying to be.

GORDON TESKEY

Ithaca, New York

Allegory and Violence

I

Personification and Capture:
Francesca da Rimini

T he word *allegory*, from *allo* "other" and *agoria* "speaking," has been used in many ways. Keats said that a man's life of any worth is a continual allegory, of which very few eyes can see the mystery. He may have meant that the events of a worthy life are, after the fashion of a traditional allegory such as *Pilgrim's Progress*, both exemplary in themselves and indications of a higher, remoter ideal. Or, as is more likely, he may have meant that the mind of a worthy man has an absolute value to which his achievements are only the traces and signs, unreadable to all but the like-minded few. This would throw some light on Keats's further, stranger remark that Shakespeare led a life of allegory, on which his works are the comments.[1] Shakespeare's works did not of course stand outside his life, as a commentary on it; they were for more than twenty years the center of his life, as the labor in which, as he put it, his nature was subdued. Even if we suppose that the life can be separated from the works, those works are not of less but of more value to us, and doubtless were of more value to Shakespeare himself, than the "continual allegory" they are supposed to be a commentary on. But perhaps to Keats they were not. Perhaps Keats wished to subordinate Shakespeare's depressingly unsurpassable achievement to something he could share with the bard: the mystery of a poet's mind. In any event,

---

1   John Keats, *The Letters of John Keats, 1814–1821*, ed. Hyder Edward Rollins (Cambridge: Harvard University Press, 1958) 2: 67; 18 February 1819.

Keats's remarks indicate the extent to which the usefulness of the term *allegory* may depend on its not having any very precise meaning, allowing it to do psychological work of which we are hardly aware.

In this psychological work there appear to be two operations: to use meaning as a wedge to split a unity into two things and to yoke together heterogeneous things by force of meaning. Meaning at this level is not a simple object or goal; it is not an adequation of thought to its object; it is not a representation of any kind. Meaning is an instrument used to exert force on the world as we find it, imposing on the intolerable, chaotic otherness of nature a hierarchical order in which objects will appear to have inherent "meanings." At the same time the otherness of nature is placed by the mind outside the world altogether, as an ideal toward which we can ascend by discovering those inherent meanings in things. The very word *allegory* evokes a schism in consciousness—between a life and a mystery, between the real and the ideal, between a literal tale and its moral—which is repaired, or at least concealed, by imagining a hierarchy on which we ascend toward truth. The opening of a schism or, as I shall call it, a rift, and the subsequent effort to repair it by imaginative means lie behind many of our commonest uses of the term. On the whole, when we speak of *allegory* we refer to an enlightening or witty analogy between two things, both of some complexity, but one of less importance than the other.

Literary criticism and theory do not always use *allegory* more precisely than that. Poems are commonly referred to as "allegories" of something in which the critic, but probably not the poet, is interested. This practice goes back to the earliest interpreters of Homer, that is, to the beginnings of western literary criticism in *hermeneia* "interpretation." In more recent critical practice the issue of intention, which is crucial to allegory, and by no means as simple as might be supposed, is avoided by reference to the autonomous power of literary language. The result is a tendency to confuse allegorical interpretation with the making of allegories, subsuming a general concern with heterogeneity under the spacious term, "the allegorical."[2] However valuable the results of allegorical interpretation may be, to *allegorize* a poem—to say it says something other than what it does say—does not make that poem an allegory. The Christian Fathers' interpretation of the Song of Songs as an allegory of Christ's love for his

2   See Fredric Jameson, *Postmodernism, or, the Cultural Logic of Late Capitalism* (Durham, North Carolina: Duke University Press, 1991), p. 168.

church (following Jewish interpretations of the Song of Songs as an allegory of God's love for Israel) and Porphyry's Neoplatonic interpretation of the cave of the nymphs episode in the *Odyssey* are of cultural value in their own right; and they have in turn inspired great art. But neither of the works on which they comment is an allegory; for neither work, to put it simply at the outset, contains instructions for its own interpretation.

Of more taxonomical difficulty are the numerous personifications that we see on official buildings (I recommend the totemically ideological figures of the continents, by Daniel Chester French, in front of the old customs house in lower Manhattan) or that we encounter in otherwise nonallegorical works of art and literature, for example, Rumour, "painted full of tongues," who speaks the prologue to the second part of Shakespeare's *Henry the Fourth*. Perhaps the most famous of these is the Statue of Liberty. Liberty is represented almost as famously in Delacroix's "Liberty Leading the People" (see Figure 1), where an abstract universal appears in a realistic setting, leading very realistic people. Such figures, when they do not appear in a work that invites us to combine them with similar figures in a comprehensive structure of meaning, may still be termed *allegorical*; but neither they nor the works in which they appear are allegories. When, however, we encounter in the opening episode of Spenser's *Faerie Queene* a monstrous, book-vomiting serpent named *Error*, we have been given more than a set of instructions in how to interpret her. We have been told to interpret in a similar way every other figure we encounter in the poem. Error tells us not only what she means but what sort of book we are reading, what conventions apply.

The most important of these conventions is that the book we are reading is, like nature itself, secondary to a primary, but ultimately ineffable meaning, as Shakespeare's works are said by Keats to be comments on a life that is secondary to a mystery that surpasses all expression. In an allegory the search for meaning is cast in the form of a ritual initiation in which higher but still expressible truths lead to the inexpressible presence of absolute truth. And in the manner of a ritual initiation the work of art that leads to this goal functions as a sort of labyrinth, though in the end the work is reduced to the status of a *text*, a thing that has been woven, a veil. Metaphorically, the allegorical work functions both as a labyrinth and as a veil, these being traditional figures of deferral. In Derridean terms, allegory is the logocentric genre par excellence, the genre that depends more explicitly than any other on the notion of a centered structure in which differences infold into the One. (The post-

1. Eugène Delacroix. *Liberty Leading the People*, the 28th of July 1830. Louvre, Paris. Alinari/Art Resource, New York

modern use of "the allegorical" in the opposite sense, as a discourse that acknowledges incommensurable registers in itself, derives from Walter Benjamin's initial use of the term in a historically specific context, when the hierarchical transcendentalism of the Renaissance gave way to what Benjamin regarded as the dialectical transcendentalism of the baroque; but in Benjamin the term remains deeply theological and has not been freed of the theological since.) Just as a tragedy, as part of the total effect it is designed to achieve, raises the emotions of pity and terror, so allegory elicits continual interpretation as its primary aesthetic effect, giving us the feeling that we are moving at once inward and upward toward the transcendental "other." To bring about this consistently theological movement an allegory must be, unlike a parable or a fable, incoherent on the narrative level, forcing us to unify the work by imposing meaning on it. An allegory is an incoherent narrative (or, in the visual arts, an incoherent picture) that makes us interpret throughout.

My remarks so far (excepting those on instrumental meaning and schism) belong to what may be termed a poetics of allegory—whence the comparison with Aristotle's analysis of tragedy.[3] By "poetics" I mean the technical analysis of how works within a genre are designed to call forth a specific response in the reader. A poetics of allegory can achieve stability only by grounding itself on an unambiguous determination of the "other" in the word *allegory* as that to which the discourse refers, the ideal "meaning." This determination is formalized in poetics as what I call the *singularity*, the ineffable presence into which, it is supposed, everything in the allegorical work ultimately is drawn. The singularity operates in an allegory as does the vanishing point in a linear perspective: it is never visible itself, but everything that *is* visible directs the eye toward it. The singularity is also the point of contact between a specific allegorical work, such as Dante's *Commedia*, and absolute meaning, the logos. Hence a poetics of allegory is itself logocentrically grounded. Although such a poetics is not, as is sometimes supposed, itself an allegory, it stands on the same ground as what it explains. To recognize this is not, however, to reject the task of poetics as worthless: on the contrary. But the recognition does draw attention to limits. Although a poetics of allegory is indispensable to our understanding of how allegories work and of what, in an immediate sense, allegories are, it must close off a more open questioning of the phenomenon under its eye. In particular, a poetics of allegory cannot reflect on the deeper motives for allegorical expression, any more than Aristotle's analysis of tragic form could reflect on what Nietzsche explored in the more open, speculative project undertaken in *The Birth of Tragedy*.

At the root of the motives for allegorical expression is what I referred to a moment ago as instrumental meaning, meaning not as a representation of what already is but as the creative exertion of force. We saw that meaning exerts force by driving a wedge into some part of nature in order to make two opposed things, two "others," or by yoking heterogeneous

---

3 I attempt such a poetics in "Allegory," in *The Spenser Encyclopedia*, ed. A. C. Hamilton et al. (Toronto: University of Toronto Press, 1990).

things together so that one may be thought to refer to the other or both may be thought to refer to different aspects of a single, invisible truth. In every case, however, the object on which the force is exerted belongs to a realm that is intolerably "other" before it is raised to the position of the transcendental "other." This archaic, negative other marks the point at which instrumental meaning exerts force on what is to that meaning a chaos. And just as the transcendental other is the point of contact between allegory and the logos, so this moment of instrumental meaning— of what I shall refer to as "capture"—is the point of contact between allegory and violence. By concealing the underlying, originative work of instrumental meaning allegory reinterprets the noise beneath the things ·we can see as the inner desire of those things to return to their origin in the One.

If we look closely at the word *allegory* we see an oscillating movement between these negative and positive others, between a meaning that is other to its speaking and a speaking that is other to its meaning. An allegory means something other than what it says and says something other than it means. The former, positive sense of the "other" as a higher, abstract meaning reflects back on a literal narrative that is "other" in a negative sense, one that implies the inability of instrumental meaning entirely to assimilate a realm that it distinguishes as "literal." (We shall see this negative otherness in the person of Francesca da Rimini, whose passion is unassimilable to the allegorical project of Dante's *Inferno*, a project in which, nevertheless, she is captured in order to act as a sign.) From the tension between these opposite "others" the various approaches to allegory have been generated, inclining to either side of the rift at the heart of the word. There can, however, be no "true account," no *etymos logos* of allegory that does not look into this rift, which runs as deep as any in the philosophical tradition, separating the categories of the material and the ideal.

The master metaphor of allegorical expression concerns the self and its negative "other," the world. This metaphor is the analogy of microcosm and macrocosm, of man as a little world and the world as a large man. Just as the perceiving subject of eighteenth-century psychology, when looking into himself, sees a smaller man inside him, a homunculus who receives and coordinates sense impressions, so the macrocosm looks into himself (there being nothing for him to look at outside) and sees another world, which is in the form of a man identical to him. Both models, the perceiving homunculus inside the perceiving subject and the microcosm-macrocosm analogy, betray their absurdity by opening an infinite regression. By locating this absurdity more precisely we may see where the rift which we have discerned already in the word *allegory* is to be found in allegory's most comprehensive metaphorical structure. The rift at its deepest lies between our awareness of the imponderable otherness of nature and our equally imponderable embeddedness in nature. For nature remains alien to a consciousness that is the product of natural forces. (This does not mean that nature is alien to knowledge, which is not the same thing as consciousness, but the knowledge of nature is knowledge, as Vico said, from the outside.[4] We have knowledge of nature but not consciousness of it.)

Instrumental meaning creates consciousness by concealing the presence of this rift between the self and the world, transforming the otherness of nature into a hierarchy of anagogic (upward-moving) meanings. But the final imaginative resolution of the dilemma of a consciousness that is produced by what is alien to it is to affirm the identity of those opposites: to think of the self as the world and the world as the self. The rift in the word *allegory* between the negative and the positive senses of the "other" is thus existentially present as the rift between the chaotic otherness of the world and the transcendental otherness that we situate above the world in order to make that world, as the macrocosm, coincide with the self. This is what lies behind our feeling that everything the hero of an allegory encounters is a manifestation of his or her internal nature in an external form.

Now the microcosm-macrocosm analogy is more than a purely formal structure, allegory's most comprehensive imaginative form. It is also an expression of desire, the desire of the organism to master its environment by placing that environment inside itself. This image has been explained in the past in less predatory terms, as the goal of human creativity or of struggle for a libidinal utopia, where the body is in a state of pure pleasure because nothing is any longer outside it. For this goal Northrop Frye borrows the theological term *anagogy*, literally a "going

---

4 Giambattista Vico, *Princìpi di Scienza Nuova*, ed. Fausto Nicolini (Milan: Mondadori, 1992), sections 236 and 331, pp. 100 and 121–22. See also Thomas Goddard Bergin and Max Harold Fisch, "Introduction," *The New Science of Giambattisto Vico*, 3d ed. (Ithaca: Cornell University Press, 1970), xxxvi; and Isaiah Berlin, *Vico and Herder: Two Studies in the History of Ideas* (New York: Viking, 1976) pp. 12, 25–26, and 103.

up" to the highest plane of human destiny, where the universe will take the form of a giant man who builds his cities out of stars.[5] But when we consider that something like this is the desire of every body, the reality of enviousness and competitiveness, of what René Girard calls mimetic desire, comes into view. We desire what others desire not for itself but because they desire it. (When Rimbaud, in "Fêtes de faim," describes himself eating rocks, his voracity is terrifying because we sense it has been directed away from other bodies. It is a poem about the horror of absolute hunger.) Every body wants to include the universe inside it; but every body, seeing others like it, knows that these others desire the same. They represent alternative worlds. The existence of other bodies therefore represents the most serious impediment to the hope of including the world in the self. The body of the other must therefore be annihilated in the only way possible: by devouring it.

The radical form of this confrontation is of two bodies engaged in mutual devouring as each strives to enclose the other in itself. This is the radical structure underlying the microcosm-macrocosm analogy, as it underlies the ancient image of the serpent swallowing itself by the tail. It is an image of fundamental, violent contradiction from which everything in an allegory is raised by the decisive intervention of instrumental meaning. For mutual devouring—or, as I shall call it, *allelophagy*—is the corporeal expression of the symmetrical otherness we have seen in the word *allegory*, each body being radically other to the other. If instrumental meaning is the point of contact between allegory and violence, allelophagy is the violence itself. When our horizon is expanded beyond the limits of poetics, we see how allegory as a means of expression does not simply refer upwards, anagogically, toward the absolute other. Allegory oscillates between a project of reference and a project of capture.

Violence is also a divided word, although, unlike *allegory*, its division is not etymologically apparent; the division lies instead in the different spheres in which words denoting violence are used: physical law and human relations. In Greek physics "violence," *bia*, means the forcing of something to act against its nature, as when a fire is extinguished and so kept from rising to its home above the air, or when a stone is held high

5 Northrop Frye, *Anatomy of Criticism: Four Essays* (Princeton: Princeton University Press, 1957), pp. 113 and 119; and Fredric Jameson, *Marxism and Form: Twentieth-Century Dialectical Theories of Literature* (Princeton: Princeton University Press, 1971), p. 402.

and so kept from sinking to earth, its home below the air.[6] This sense of violence as the interruption of natural rights migrates from Greek to Latin science and from Aristotelian to Newtonian physics, where *vis* "force," interrupts the natural tendency of objects to continue at rest or in linear motion. But in the course of this transition the violence is purified of personal or moral sentiments and becomes indifferent force. When the stone and the fire are kept from their "homes" above the air and under it, we feel that they are suffering violence in our sense of the word, that their rights are being abrogated and that they have cause to be indignant. We think of them as persons.

Little of this imaginary consciousness survives explicitly in Aristotelian physics; but it is more apparent in earlier Greek physical thought, notably at the beginning, in the extant fragment of Anaximander, which says that things in the system of nature "pay penalty and retribution to each other for their injustice, according to the assessment of time." This statement is preserved in a later author, Simplicius, who adds, "as [Anaximander] describes it in these rather poetical terms."[7] It is now "poetical" to speak of natural things being subject to the injustice of violence. Simplicius's editorial remark shows the direction of scientific thought in the West toward the moral neutralization of violence as impersonal force.

In the sphere of human relations, however, words such as *force, power,* and of course *violence* have a much different impact on us than they do in the abstract, quantifiable realm of physics. In that realm power is an objective force to be harnessed; it is drawn from flowing rivers, fossil fuel, and uranium to be converted into electricity, motion, and heat. Yet all these manifestations of power are directed at the natural world with the aim of transforming it into the fulfillment of human desire. And the end of that desire is, as we saw, to give the universe the form of a body that will, like Saturn, strive to include in itself anything that is other than itself.

Even the most impersonal sense of power, as available energy, is con-

6 See Martin Heidegger, *Die Frage nach dem Ding: Zu Kants Lehre von den Transzendentalen Grundsätzen*, Gesamtausgabe 41 (Frankfurt am Main: Klostermann, 1984), pp. 81–89, esp. p. 84. Trans.: "Modern Science, Metaphysics, and Mathematics," in Heidegger, *Basic Writings, from "Being and Time" (1927) to "The Task of Thinking" (1964)*, ed. David Farrell Krell (New York: Harper and Row, 1977), pp. 247–82; excerpted from *What is a Thing?*, trans. W. B. Barton, Jr. and Vera Deutsch (Chicago: Regnery, 1967).
7   G. S. Kirk, J. E. Raven, and M. Schofield, *The Presocratic Philosophers: A Critical History with a Selection of Texts*, 2d ed. (Cambridge: Cambridge University Press, 1983), p. 117.

nected to the older, Anaximandrian sense of natural force as violence or injustice (*adikia*). The most cursory reflection on the uses of stored power—of gasoline and uranium in the Second World War, for example—reveals the extent to which such power increases our capacity for the destruction of bodies, for it is bodies that "pay penalty and retribution to each other for their injustice, according to the assessment of time." Human violence, being directed at other bodies that desire equally to be worlds unto themselves, has two phases: 1. the catastrophic invasion of the interior of a body (for example, by piercing with a weapon) and 2. the annihilation of a body (for example, by burning or burying). But the second has its fullest measure of horror in devouring. That prospect is raised in the greatest literary study of bodily violence, the *Iliad*, where the annihilation of an enemy by devouring him is usually transferred to another agent, as when, for example, Asteropaios is eviscerated by Achilles (first phase) and thrown into the river (second phase), where the eels and fish tear at his kidneys. More striking still is Achilles' regret that his anger against Hector is not strong enough to drive him to eat his foe, a task that must be left instead to the dogs and the birds.[8] In these moments in the *Iliad* we are given a vision of life that allegory conceals when it makes bodies significant parts of one world. It is the vision of a contest for being itself, in which bodies are separate worlds to one another. The one allegorical work that opens such a vision on the conceptual plane, Spenser's *Mutabilitie* (which I discuss in chapter 8), pushes allegory beyond the limit it imposes on itself.

The various critical approaches to allegory reflect the division we have seen in the word between discourse and meaning. Of these approaches the most familiar raises the question whether allegory is, in Northrop Frye's terminology, a mode or a genre, a means of encoding any discourse whatever or an altogether separate category of discourse. Whereas the modal approach claims that any narrative structure is open to adventitious allegorizing, the generic approach observes how ideological structures, determined more or less in advance, are inserted into narratives by adventitious encoding in such a way that those narratives become formally distinct from all others.[9] Even the notion, still impor-

8   *Iliad* 21.179–204, 22.346–54.
9   See Angus Fletcher, *Allegory: The Theory of a Symbolic Mode* (Ithaca: Cornell University Press, 1964), pp. 6–8 and 365–67; Maureen Quilligan, *The Language of Allegory: Defining the Genre* (Ithaca: Cornell University Press, 1979), pp. 14 and 20–21; and Northrop Frye,

tant in Dante studies, of figural realism as a kind of allegory that is superior to personification can be seen as inclining toward the material register of the poet's "earthly world," to use Erich Auerbach's phrase, as opposed to the ideal register of its meaning, where Beatrice is Theology and Virgil is Reason.[10] Similarly, the question whether allegory is a means of expression that reveals the translucency of material things to the logos, as in the encyclopedic allegories of the medieval cathedrals, or whether it is one that forces on our attention the difference between what it refers *to* and what it refers *with*, can be seen as proceeding from the dissonance of the radicals in the word *allegory* itself.

It would be rash to suppose that every approach to allegory can be reduced to one or the other extreme; all make allowances for what they are required to forget. For example, the philological critics, for whom allegory marries the substance of ancient epic and the ideals of medieval philosophy, are not unaware of the rift that is opened by that conjunction, though they acknowledge it only by a certain dryness of tone when recounting absurdities.[11] It was left to Paul de Man to find in such absurdities indications not of incompetence in the poets but of fundamental instability in the project of marrying figurative language and thought. He could therefore put the question concerning allegory in the most direct way: "Why is it that the furthest reaching truths about ourselves and the world have to be stated in such a lopsided, referentially indirect mode?"[12]

Anatomy of Criticism: Four Essays (Princeton: Princeton University Press, 1957), pp. 53–54 and 89–91. See also Joel D. Black, "Allegory Unveiled," *Poetics Today* 4, no. 1 (1983): 109–26.

10   For Charles S. Singleton's influential theory of figural realism, see " 'In Exitu Israel de Aegypto,' " in *Dante: A Collection of Critical Essays*, ed. John Freccero (Englewood Cliffs, N.J.: Prentice-Hall, 1960), pp. 102–21. Singleton follows the work of Erich Auerbach in "Figura," in *Scenes from the Drama of European Literature* (1959; reprint, Minneapolis: University of Minnesota Press, 1984), pp. 11–76, and in *Dante: Poet of the Secular World*, trans. Ralph Manheim (Chicago: University of Chicago Press, 1961).

11   For the philological perspective on allegory, see Ernst Robert Curtius, *European Literature and the Latin Middle Ages* (Princeton: Princeton University Press, 1953), pp. 360–62; and Hans Robert Jauss and Uda Ebel's valuable "Entstehung und Strukturwandel der allegorischen Dichtung," in *La littérature didactique, allégorique, et satirique*, ed. Jürgen Beyer, vol. 6 of *Grundriss der Romanischen Literaturen des Mittelalters* (Heidelberg: Winter, 1968), 1:146–244 and 2:203–80. The philological tradition in German scholarship on allegory has borne fruit in a wide-ranging, interdisciplinary approach to the subject, witnessed in the remarkable papers in *Formen und Funktionen der Allegorie, Symposion Wolfenbüttel 1978*, ed. Walter Haug (Stuttgart: Metzler, 1979). Also of interest is James J. Paxson's *The Poetics of Personification* (Cambridge: Cambridge University Press, 1994).

12   Paul de Man, "Pascal's Allegory of Persuasion," in *Allegory and Representation*, ed. Stephen J. Greenblatt (Baltimore: Johns Hopkins University Press, 1981), p. 2.

No one forgets altogether that there are two sides to the problem of allegory, as there are two parts to the word. Nor is it apparent that a correct approach would try to hold them in balance. They cannot be balanced. Extreme approaches have led to insights that would never have been obtained by more apparently responsible ones. Perhaps the most that can be asked, therefore, of any effort to understand allegory is that it acknowledge the terms within which it inclines to either extreme and that it recognize the inevitability of a confrontation with what it denies. For what is most deeply denied in the various approaches to allegory is not just the other side of the question but the rift at its center, the very rift that it is the purpose of an allegorical work to conceal. If the rift at the center of the various approaches to allegory is also at the center of allegory itself, it runs deeper than both. The rift reaches down through the foundations of an eidetic metaphysics the absurdities of which allegory tries to repair by imaginative means, logical ones being inadequate to the task.

Of the extreme approaches to which I referred the most influential is the neo-Hegelian discussion of allegory in Walter Benjamin's *Origin of German Tragic Drama*, which revived what in the 1920s was the unfashionably allegorical court drama of seventeenth-century Germany.[13] By reversing the aesthetic valuation of the symbol over allegory, which had dominated German aesthetics since Goethe, Benjamin argued that the almost surrealistic character of allegorical imagery in German baroque drama forced the mind, in its quest for meaning, to abandon the realm of sense and perception for that of theological truth. The impossibility of accommodating the allegorical signs within any coherent structure of meaning impelled the mind to an act of negation whose movement was dialectical and theological, but whose immediate effect was to encourage the production of signs that emphasize their dead materiality. The harmonious worldview promoted, largely for political ends, by Renaissance allegory, as in the great triumph of the Emperor Maximilian, executed by Dürer, no longer carried conviction.[14] And while affirmative allegory,

13 Walter Benjamin, *The Origin of German Tragic Drama*, trans. John Osborne (London: Verso, 1985), pp. 159-235; *Ursprung des deutschen Trauerspiels*, in *Gesammelte Schriften*, vol. 1, ed. Rolf Tiedemann and Hermann Schweppenhäuser (Frankfurt am Main: Suhrkamp, 1974), pp. 336-409.
14 See Erwin Panofsky, *The Life and Art of Albrecht Dürer*, 4th ed. (Princeton: Princeton University Press, 1955), pp. 172-81, and Joseph A. Mazzeo, "Allegorical Interpretation and History," *Comparative Literature* 30 (1978): 9. Like Panofsky, Benjamin draws on Karl Giehlow's *Die Hieroglyphenkunde des Humanismus in der Allegorie der Renaissance, besonders*

2. Pompeo Girolamo Batoni. *The Triumph of Venice*. 1737. North Carolina Museum of Art, Raleigh, Gift of the Samuel H. Kress Foundation

in which signs appear to have a vigorous life of their own, survived into the eighteenth century in the visual arts (for example, in Batoni's *Triumph of Venice;* see figure 2), the allegory that Benjamin saw in German tragic drama represented to him a moment of historical crisis when the power of the imagination to represent its ideals was lost.

For Benjamin the figure presiding over this new sort of allegory was Death personified, a figure that makes personification itself possible by cutting a line of demarcation between "meaning" (*Bedeutung*) and "nature" (*Physis*). Benjamin uses the latter, Greek term, which implies life and growth, to indicate a nature that is not so much an organized cosmos as it is an anarchic region of struggle, a forest of entangled, urgent, competitive growth. In this forest meaning, and even order, is possible only when the life is destroyed: "the greater the significance,"

der Ehrenpforte Kaisers Maximilian I, in *Jahrbuch der kunsthistorischen Sammlungen des allerhöchsten Kaiserhauses* 32 (1915): 1–232.

Benjamin writes, "the greater the subjection to death, because death digs most deeply the jagged line of demarcation between physical nature and significance."[15] In Benjamin's argument Renaissance allegory had concealed this rift between actual life and abstract truth, insisting that the two coincide, whereas in German tragic drama the rift is exposed as the action of a first allegorical personification, Death, who stands near the beginning of a genealogical tree, like the god Saturn. If it is somewhat unsatisfactory to find the origin of allegory, as Benjamin does, in an allegorical figure, his statement does raise the issue of personification in a context that emphasizes the alienation of the material from the ideal. In my opinion allegory has its origin in that process of hierarchical ordering which is in reaction to the chaos of Saturnian, allelophagic desire. But this ordering has its initial expression in the problem of personification as the problem of the presence of abstraction in the world.

At the heart of what allegory is trying to conceal—that is, at the heart of a more general, metaphysical disorder—is the problem of *methexis*, or "participation" (literally, a "having across"), by which abstractions are predicated of individual things only after being predicated of themselves through the trope of personification, as when Justice is said to be just.[16] The absurd supposition that a universal can be predicated of itself, its absurdity concealed behind tautological phrases such as "Justice is just," goes back to Plato. That he was aware of its presence in the theory of forms, even if he could not identify its character precisely, is indicated by his deployment in the *Parmenides* of an argument against him to which he seems not to have had any answer. This argument, commonly referred to as the "Third Man," purports to show that the theory of the forms involves an infinite regression. The form Man is connected to a particular man by the two sharing something that is separate from each. This thing can be nothing other than a Third Man, which must in turn share something with the first two, and so on.[17] It should be pointed out that in

15 "Soviel Bedeutung, soviel Todverfallenheit, weil am tiefsten der Tod die zackige Demarkationslinie zwischen Physis und Bedeutung eingräbt." Benjamin, *Origin of German Tragic Drama*, p. 166; *Ursprung des deutschen Trauerspiels*, p. 343.
16 Plato, *Parmenides* 132d; Aristotle, *Metaphysics* 987b10–15. Cf. Plato, *Parmenides* 131a and *Phaedo* 100d.
17 Gregory Vlastos, "The Third Man Argument in the *Parmenides*," in *Studies in Plato's Metaphysics*, ed. R. E. Allen (London: Routledge, 1965), pp. 231–63. See also John Malcolm, *Plato on the Self-Predication of Forms: Early and Middle Dialogues* (Oxford: Clarendon Press, 1991), pp. 47–52. For ancient references to "Third Man" arguments, see Francis Mac-

the *Parmenides* the form Largeness is used, not the form Man, and that the phrase "Third Man" first appears in Aristotle's version of the same argument as a technical abbreviation, although a particularly apt one, for it is clear that it is the concept Man that is principally at stake in any attack on or defense of the theory of the forms. We thus find Aristotle's attack on Platonic idealism brilliantly parodied in Milton's Latin poem "On the Platonic Idea as Aristotle Understood It," where what is ridiculed is the notion that the form Man must itself be a particular man, though perhaps somewhat larger.

The strictly logical sense of the argument in the *Parmenides* is the same no matter which form is invoked, but the human consequences of the difference are obviously great. Whereas Largeness is a concept sufficiently airless to stifle distraction, Man carries with it more than a few associations that are hard to disentangle from the logical issue at hand. That issue is instead transferred to, not to say lost in, the relation of the concept Man to a feminine other it encloses as an internal difference necessary to its self-propagation. As a father stands to his sons, so form stands to its instances, which are begotten in and propagated through an alien subject, matter-as-woman.

Although the most striking formulation of this alien subject as feminine is presented in the *Timaeus* (to which I shall turn in a moment), its implications are brought out with particular clarity in Aristotle's treatise on the generation of animals, in which the female is presented as the material receptacle for masculine form, which is contained in the sperm: "The male provides the form and the principle of movement, the female provides the body, in other words the material." As the analysis unfolds, the identification of form with movement and of matter with passivity becomes more sexually explicit: "If the male is the active partner, the one which originates the movement, and the female *qua* female is the passive one, surely what the female contributes to the semen of the male will not be semen but material. And this is in fact what we find happening; for the natural substance of the menstrual fluid is to be classed as 'prime matter.' "[18] The problem of how form participates in matter is transferred to

---

Donald Cornford, *Plato and Parmenides* (London: Routledge, 1939), pp. 87–90. For Aristotle in particular, see Vlastos, "Third Man Argument," pp. 241 n. 2, 246 n. 5, and 250–51 n. 3.

18 Aristotle, *De generatione animalium* 729a10; see also 729a24. The menstrual fluid is "prime matter" only relatively, that is, only with respect to the living animal to which it is prior.

the alien context of gender, where it can appear to be solved under the image of sexual congress. Consequently, sexual relations in allegory are invested with metaphysical significance and metaphysical problems are "solved" in imaginary, sexual terms.

We may see what is implied by these sexual terms by examining those used in the *Timaeus* to account for the relations of matter and form, in particular the featureless "mother" or "receptacle" through which the father propagates his seed in the world of things. The receptacle is designated literally as "that which receives from below," the *hypodoche*, a substantive formed from the verb *hypodechomai*, one meaning of which is simply "to become pregnant."[19] Matter is made pregnant with form by assuming a "subject" (*sub-iectum* "cast down") position with respect to the male. It is unnecessary here to enter into the question whether this "receptacle" can be simply identified with the Aristotelian term for matter, *hypokeimenon*, "that which lies underneath." What is important is that both words indicate matter as assuming the proper position for the wife in intercourse. Nor is the significance of this identification just that philosophical idealism was from its inception entangled with older, mythical notions of the generation of the world from sexual congress. If the case were that simple, the metaphorics of gender would scarcely have adhered so tenaciously to idealism. The confusion has survived because it is psychologically resonant and politically useful: it is an ideology, a way of seeing the world as unified whole. In Althusserian terms it is also, because it is an ideology, a practice, one taking the form of a strangely ritualized kind of reading we call interpretation, whereby we participate in the work of universalizing relations of authority in the family so that these may be discovered in the natural world and prescribed in the state.[20] Considered as the basis of a social practice, allegory categorizes bodies as the material basis of an order of signs.

Through what they imply about the inferior position of matter when receiving the imprint of form, the Greek and Latin words for matter— *hypokeimenon, hypodoche, subiectum, substratum*—are metaphorical indications of the function of idealism as a cultural force, which is to maintain

---

19 Plato, *Timaeus* 50c–51b. On the metaphorics of paternity and generation in Platonic metaphysics, see Jacques Derrida, "The Father of the Logos," in *Plato's Pharmacy*, in *Dissemination*, trans. Barbara Johnson (Chicago: University of Chicago Press, 1981), pp. 75–84.

20 Louis Althusser, "Ideology and Ideological State Apparatuses," in *Lenin and Philosophy and Other Essays*, trans. Ben Brewster (New York: Monthly Review Press, 1971), p. 169.

stability in knowledge, in politics, and in sexual relations. Idealism in this sense is not motivated by the will to discover the truth behind appearances, for such a truth would be entirely different from what, in Platonic terms, we already know and therefore need only remember. Idealism is driven instead by a will-to-power that subjects what it does not understand, the realm of *physis* or growth, to a knowledge it imagines it already has. Hence a form such as Justice reduces to indifferent substance an other that it still needs as a place to occur outside itself. Like its symbol, the goddess Astraea, Justice has removed to the heavens, though justice is still done in the world. That justice is always imperfectly done is the fault of that world, in particular of the resistance of matter to form.

To summarize the discussion so far, the logical concepts at the basis of Platonic idealism, *methexis* and *chorismos*, "participation" and "separation," enter into a metaphorics of insemination and parturition respectively, by which a form such as Justice can multiply itself through a featureless, alien mother—even as it continues, in the empyrean, to father itself. One result of this translation of metaphysical problems into the structure of the family is the Neoplatonic illusion of incorporeal intelligences; we may call this hierarchical, animated idealism. A certain agency is attributed to abstractions that, in predicating themselves, overflow their limits and cascade into the world, where they take up a partial residence in things. Allegory is more than the literary representation of this ideological order. As the basis of the social practice of interpretation, allegory actively sustains that order. The integrity of the hierarchy is repeatedly affirmed while everything else is reduced to the status of a substance imprinted by form.

Now when we consider the concept of matter apart from its ideological identification with the female, it functions as a logical instrument for establishing the principle of individuation beneath the lowest order of abstractions, the *infima species*.[21] It allows us to distinguish, under the form Justice, one just man from another, thus separating individuals within an abstract class that unites them. Logically speaking, there can be nothing material, nothing alive, and certainly nothing masculine about

<hr />

21 For an overview of the concept of matter in ancient philosophy, see *hyle* in F. E. Peters, *Greek Philosophical Terms: A Historical Lexicon* (New York: New York University Press, 1967), pp. 88–91. Technically the principle of individuation belongs to secondary, not primary, matter. See Toshimitsu Hasumi, "Le problème du concept de matière et la théorie de la valeur," in *L'Homme et son univers au moyen âge*, ed. Christian Wenin (Paris: Vrin, 1986), 1:328.

any abstract class considered apart from its members. Nor can there be anything material, alive, or masculine about the highest abstraction from which all others are supposedly derived. The Father as the conscious, immaterial agent of form does not exist, which is why he has to be hidden behind subordinate agents—*daemons* or *intelligences* in hierarchical, animated idealism generally, *personifications* in allegory—who are abstractions themselves but who seem nevertheless to have something substantial about them: they instantiate what they abstract.[22] In hierarchical, animated idealism agents need matter in order to act, for which reason Aquinas supposed that angels, being insubstantial and therefore invisible, had to put on bodies of compressed air to be visible to humans.[23] The grand metaphorics of paternity, with its hierarchy of agents, cannot survive so long as matter is kept out of its reach, beneath the lowest order of species. It is necessary, therefore, that allegory somehow capture the substantiality of beings and raise it to the conceptual plane. But for this to occur any integrity those beings may have must be negated. The negation of the integrity of the other, of the living, is the first moment of allegory's exertion of its power to seize and to tear. It is the moment of what may be called prevenient violence, a power that comes invisibly beforehand to soften the ground, converting all things before it into substance.

In the more powerful allegorical works this prevenient violence is unexpectedly revealed at moments that are so shocking in their honesty that they are consistently misread as departures from allegorical expression. Such moments literalize a metaphor from Neoplatonism, the moment of *raptio*, or "seizing," in which Matter, perversely resisting the desire of the male, must be ravished by form before being converted and returned to the Father. To be ravished is what Matter secretly wants, so that it may bear in its substance the imprint of beautiful forms.[24] At such moments we see violence being committed on an unwilling woman in such a way that the usual fantasy of her conversion to the rapist's desire is

22   For Neoplatonic daemons and the repetitive behavior of personifications, see Fletcher, *Allegory*, pp. 25–69, and Roger Hinks, "Daemon and Personification," in *Myth and Allegory in Ancient Art* (London: Warburg Institute, 1939), pp. 106–13.
23   Aquinas, *Summa theologica* 1.51.2; cited in A. J. Smith's commentary on ll. 23–24 of "Air and Angels," in *John Donne: The Complete English Poems* (Harmondsworth: Penguin, 1973), p. 354.
24   See Edgar Wind, *Pagan Mysteries in the Renaissance* (New Haven: Yale University Press, 1958), p. 48 n. 1 and p. 40 nn. 4 and 5. Wind notes that the verb *rapere* is a literal translation of *harpazein* in the Chaldean Oracles and in Proclus's commentary on the *Parmenides*, where it denotes an act of violent seizing by which beings are returned to the One. See *In Parmenidem* V, col. 1033.27, in Proclus, *Opera*, ed. Victor Cousin (Paris, 1864).

abandoned. Nor is there, however, any fantasy of releasing her from that desire. We are confronted instead with a struggle in which the rift between heterogeneous others is forced into view. The woman continues forever to resist being converted into an embodiment of the meaning that is imprinted on her.

In Spenser's *Faerie Queene* that scene is revealed in the torture of Amoret, who is bound to the pillar of bronze as the enchanter Busyrane writes in her blood. Nor is that blood, though it comes from her heart, to be very clearly distinguished from that to which Aristotle refers as prime matter:

> And her before the vile Enchaunter sate,
>   Figuring straunge characters of his arte,
>   With living bloud he those characters wrate,
>   Dreadfully dropping from her dying hart,
>   Seeming transfixed with a cruell dart,
>   And all perforce to make her him to love,
>   Ah who can love the worker of her smart?
>   A thousand charmes he formerly did prove;
> Yet thousand charmes could not her stedfast heart remove.[25]

In a literary genre concerned more than any other with the metaphysical implications of gender, such moments are infrequent. It is more broadly characteristic of allegory—though by no means more true of it—for violence such as this to be concealed so that the female will appear to embody, with her whole body, the meaning that is imprinted on her. When this occurs we have personification. But the violence inside personification is exposed when that figure is, by an act I shall refer to as capture, turned inside out. What the act of capture exhibits is the truth over which allegory is always drawing its veil: the fundamental disorder out of which the illusion of order is raised. For the present, we may define the material in allegory as that which gives meaning a place to occur but which does not become meaning itself.

The scholastic solution to this resistance is to conceive of matter as longing for the imposition of form "as a woman longs for a man" ("Materia appetit formam ut femina virum"). Although this strange notion

---

25 *Faerie Queene* 3.12.31. Cf. the figure of Mirabella at 6.7.28–44, whose capture and punishment by Disdain and Scorn mark her transformation into an allegorical figure.

derives from Aristotle's *Physics* (where it is not approved of), it seems to have entered medieval culture through Calcidius's commentary on the *Timaeus*.[26] From thence it found its way into Bernardus Silvestris's philosophical allegory, the *Cosmographia*, in which Matter, or Silva, is described as follows: "*Silva*, a coagulate mass that is dissonant with herself, chooses in the midst of her crudeness to be united with form, and desiring to leave her ancient tumultuousness demands the embellishment of number and the bonds of musical harmony."[27] It emerges in what follows that Matter is dissonant with herself because her "appetite" for the good, that is, for masculine form, is opposed by another impulse in her to malignity, as a consequence of which any form that is imprinted on her will be imperfect. Again, in Alan of Lille, we are told that Matter begs for the beautiful appearance of form, which it receives by means of a kiss transmitted through intermediary icons.[28] It is not hard to see

26   See Aristotle, *Physics* 192a23. In Richard McKeon's translation, *The Basic Works of Aristotle* (New York: Random House, 1941): "What desires the form is matter, as the female desires the male and the ugly the beautiful—only the ugly or the female not *per se* but *per accidens* [*kata sumbebekos*]." For commentary, see W. Charleton, *Aristotle's "Physics,"* books 1 and 2 (Oxford: Clarendon Press, 1983), pp. 83–85. For the source available to the Platonists of the School of Chartres, see Calcidius, *Platonis Timaeus interprete Calcidio*, ed. Ioh. Wrobel (Leipzig: Teubner, 1876), pp. 317–18, where we are left free to suppose what Aristotle disallows: that matter is essentially female. See also J. C. M. Van Winden, *Calcidius on Matter: His Doctrine and Sources* (Leiden: Brill, 1965). Aquinas notes that Aristotle implies that it is an error of the Platonists simply to identify matter with the female. See *In octo libros physicorum Aristotelis expositio*, ed. P. M. Maggiolo (Turin: Marietti, 1965), pp. 67–68. In Robert Grosseteste's *Commentarius in VIII libros physicorum Aristotelis*, ed. Richard C. Dales (Boulder: University of Colorado Press, 1963), p. 29, impregnation is emphasized: matter longs for form, by which it is impregnated as the mother (*mater*) is by the father. For permutations of the commonplace in popular literature, see Guido de Columnis's *Historia destructionis Troiae*, ed. Nathaniel Edward Griffin (Cambridge: The Medieval Academy of America, 1936), p. 17, and Chaucer's *The Legend of Good Women*, ll. 1582–87, where Jason's promiscuity is likened to the inconstancy of matter with respect to form. I am indebted for this reference to Carolyn Dinshaw.

27   "*Silva . . . sibi dissona massa . . . formam rudis . . . Optat, et a veteri cupiens exire tumultu, / Artifices numeros et musica vincla requirit.*" Bernardus Silvestris, *Cosmographia*, ed. Peter Dronke (Leiden: Brill, 1978), 1.18–22. See Winthrop Wetherbee, trans., *The "Cosmographia" of Bernardus Silvestris* (New York: Columbia University Press, 1973), p. 145 n. 9, and Wetherbee, *Platonism and Poetry in the Twelfth Century: The Literary Influence of the School of Chartres* (Princeton: Princeton University Press, 1972), pp. 28–36. On matter in twelfth-century poetry, see Wetherbee, *Platonism and Poetry*, pp. 158–59, 161 n. 12, and 178–79, and Brian Stock, *Myth and Science in the Twelfth Century: A Study of Bernard Silvester* (Princeton: Princeton University Press, 1972), pp. 97–118, 228 n. 1, and 232.

28   Alan of Lille, *De planctu Naturae* 18.95–97, ed. Nikolaus M. Häring, *Studi medievali*, 3d ser., 19 (1978): 797–879, reading *speciem* for *speculam*. See Danuta R. Shanzer, "Parturition through the Nostrils? Thirty-Three Textual Problems in Alan of Lille's *De planctu Nature*," *Mittellateinisches Jahrbuch* 26 (1991): 147–48.

how this notion of matter is a theological modification of the receptacle in the *Timaeus*, introducing noise into the channel through which form is transmitted. In the twelfth century, at the outset of the main phase of the allegorical tradition, we find the concept of the material explicitly introduced as place of conflict between "ancient tumultuousness" and a metaphysical desire imposed from above. The longing of matter is a version of the fantasy of the suppressed smile of the woman who only appears to resist what is happening to her.

How does this attribution of masculine desire to its object fit into the more general picture of literary history? Curiously enough, it emerges at a time when woman, in the imaginative world of romance, was beginning to be understood in the opposite way—as that which is fleeting, that which resists, that which is desired by the male. Literary romance and scholastic philosophy have sharply opposed notions of the feminine substance on which meaning and form are imprinted. The one regards the feminine as that which resists the desire of the male, the other as that which longs for it. In the *Roman de la rose* we find the notion of woman as that which resists more evident in the first part, which is closer to the traditions of courtly romance, whereas the notion of woman as secretly desiring the male emerges, together with an influx of scholastic philosophy, in the second part of the poem, where the castle of the lady's resistance is burned down by her desire to be taken.[29] As the only literary form that records a sustained effort to unite philosophical and imaginative truth, allegory emerges from the tension between romantic and scholastic perspectives on the origin and place of desire.

I have suggested how this desire is served in allegory through the figure of personification, which raises the logical problem of a universal that is true of itself. But for the study of allegory the logical problem leads to a somewhat different, imaginative one. What is the nature of a subject (literally, "that which is thrown down, or cast underneath") of a predicate that relies on itself? What sort of body does Justice have? Philosophers do not worry about this problem, except to dismiss it as a trick of the imagination. But a body of some kind is there for the poets, for whom the event of self-predication, whereby Justice is said to be just, leaves a residue that is not justice but the thing in which Justice must inhere in order to be true of itself. The logical absurdity is transformed

29   Guillaume de Lorris and Jean de Meun, *Le Roman de la rose*, ed. Daniel Poirion (Paris: Garnier-Flammarion, 1974), ll. 21,228–74.

by the poets into a kind a metaphysical wit, creating a surface noise that we are to suppose the allegory will recuperate at a point farther in: "*Disdayne* he called was, and did disdaine / To be so cald."[30] It appears as if the essence of Spenser's Disdain, disdaining to be Disdain, initiates a movement within the sign to a remoter level of abstraction, where the contradiction at this level is overcome. Spenserian wit typically has this anagogical spin. But the movement to a remoter level of abstraction must pass through an unacknowledged substance that is a *subject* in both senses of the word. It is an underlying, physical substance and a conscious agent who disdains and therefore is.

Whether this substance-as-subject in which Disdain is imprinted is inert, like wax, or something weirdly animate, a consciousness that differs from its name by affirming its identity with its name, the difference between subject and predicate cannot be overcome by being translated to a higher level of abstraction. The word *persona* means "mask," literally a thing "to sound through," *per-sonare*, indicating a sonic essence transpiercing a mask that at once represents and conceals the wearer. But in the figure of personification whatever voice the persona has emerges from the logical dissonance of the mask with itself. Only by not listening too closely is it possible to hear this vibration as the resonance of an underlying truth; and no one is meant to listen as closely as we have just now. Personification has been regarded as the sine qua non of allegorical expression. But if this is so, then it is not because personification reveals what is essential to allegory but because it hides what is essential so well.

One way in which it does this is to give a feminine gender to the figures that confer form, rather than to the female receptacle, so that these "intermediary icons" (to use Alan of Lille's phrase) will already possess Matter's gender.[31] Yet even as they perform this intermediary role feminine agents are both examples of the universals they instantiate and living sources from which those universals cascade into the world: "She is the fountaine of your modestee," Spenser's Alma tells Guyon; "You shamefast are, but *Shamefastnesse* it selfe is shee."[32] At this moment in *The Faerie Queene* a masculine figure, Guyon, is addressed as a lower instance of an abstraction (Shamefastness) which is female. It might well

---

30 *Faerie Queene* 2.7.41.
31 Male personifications in the *Faerie Queene*—for example, Orgoglio, Disdain, Furor, and Corflambo—are demonstrably physical, as if to make up for their relative insubstantiality.
32 *Faerie Queene* 2.9.43.

be asked why, if the project of cultural idealism is typically encoded as the masculine imprinting of a feminine other, the genders in the hierarchy are reversed. A grammatical explanation, that abstract nouns in Latin are feminine, is at best partial. It seems that by conferring on personifications the feminine gender matter is surreptitiously raised up from its logical place, which is beneath the lowest *species*, into the realm of abstractions, giving these something solid to stand on. What is the stuff out of which Shamefastness is made? She is made of her gender.

The figure of personification only distracts us from what the project of allegorical meaning must struggle with immediately as its other: narrative. We see this distraction at work when Addison remarks that allegorical personification mobilizes "a Scheme of Thoughts traced out upon Matter."[33] Addison was following the neoclassical assumption, foreign to Spenser, that allegory should have as little to do with narrative as possible. In Johnson's allegories, for example, the thought represented by a series of personified abstractions is carefully worked out so that only the most rudimentary narrative is required to link the elements of the series together. It seems, then, that in allegory narrative and personification are inversely prominent. In Spenser the narrative is a heuristic instrument through which the poet discovers his thought as he proceeds, such that the poem seems to think on its own instead of merely representing thought. The conventional structure of allegory can accommodate the resistance of narrative to meaning only by reducing narrative to a homogeneous condition, that is, by calling it literal. But because narrative, notwithstanding this reduction, continues to subvert every imposed structure of meaning, it creates a background of resonant noise. Any logocentric reencoding of that noise can never be wholly persuasive because the struggle at the rift can never be wholly concealed. The resulting dissonance is something that the great allegorical poets recognize and exploit while the minor ones do what they can to avoid it. The more powerful the allegory, the more openly violent the moments in which the materials of narrative are shown being actively subdued for the purpose of raising a structure of meaning. This is what I meant when I said that allegory includes in its transcendental movement an opposite project of capture.

33 Joseph Addison, *The Spectator*, ed. Donald F. Bond, 5 vols. (Oxford: Clarendon Press, 1965), 3:577. See also Richard Blackmore, "Preface to *Prince Arthur*," in *Critical Essays of the Seventeenth Century, 1685–1700*, ed. J. E. Spingarn, 3 vols. (Oxford: Clarendon Press, 1908–9), 3:238.

An interesting example of what such a project entails occurs in a work that is not allegorical in general structure, although the political circumstances in which it appeared could be counted on to make it be seen in that way. I refer to the moment in the fourth act of Verdi's *Rigoletto* when the murderer asks Rigoletto the name of the victim he will be paid to dispatch. Rigoletto replies very strangely: "Vuoi saper anche il mio? Egli è Delitto, Punizion son io" [Would you like to know my name, too? He is Crime and I am Punishment]. Rigoletto appears unable to name himself allegorically without naming the diacritical complement that gives his new name its significance. The peculiarly menacing character of the gesture lies in the textualizing violence by which the very life of the persons named — that of the speaker just as much as his victim — is suppressed so that their substance may be raised up onto a table of moral opposites where each thing exists in a diacritical relation to another: "Would you like to know my name, too? He is Crime." The pleasure we normally associate with allegory — of recognizing the aptness and wit of an imaginative presentation of ideas, of building up complex structures of meaning out of a narrative unfolding in time, of seeming to penetrate to the center of a truth that is hidden from view — should not distract us from the most satisfying pleasure of all: that of observing the subjection of what we cannot control to the violence of thought, which we imagine we can.

We may even see the persistence with which students of Dante condemn the reduction of Beatrice to Theology and of Virgil to Reason as an expression of moral aversion to the violent pleasure of thought. Such aversion is an authentic response to what the allegory of the *Commedia*, and not just its allegorizing critics, is doing behind the work of the veil. But it is a mistake to suppose that the violence has nothing to do with Dante, who was, as John Freccero has shown, more a Nietzschean interpreter of the world than is generally supposed, and whose strength as a poet radiates from the primary work of reducing persons to substance. This work is accomplished not so much by an act of abstraction as by, in Nietzsche's words, "a tremendous *expulsion* of the principal features."[34] The greatest allegorical poets do not simply transform life into meaning. They exacerbate the antipathy of the living to the significant by exposing the violence entailed in transforming the one into the other. The

---

34   Friedrich Nietzsche, *"Twilight of the Idols" and "The Anti-Christ,"* trans. R. J. Hollingdale (New York: Viking Penguin, 1990), p. 82. John Freccero, in *Dante: The Poetics of Conversion*, ed. Rachel Jacoff (Cambridge: Harvard University Press, 1986), p. 104, speaks of the *Inferno* as possessing "an artistry that masks its ferocity."

exploitation of this antipathy is what distinguishes an allegorical personification such as Philology from a person, such as Dante's Beatrice, who has been captured in order to mean. The same difference may be observed in the personifications in Deguileville's *Pèlerinage de la vie humaine* as compared to the uncannily familiar characters of Bunyan, who seem to be being turned into writing by a force that bends all their actions to suit what they are called.[35]

The bending of a woman's destiny to suit what she is called is shown with great force—so much that we have yet to learn to read it as allegory—in the most famous episode in allegorical literature. I refer of course to the episode of Francesca da Rimini, in the fifth canto of the *Inferno*, where we are shown a woman in the process of being made, or almost made, into a sign. But it is the incompleteness of this transformation, meeting with resistance from its subject, Francesca, that the poet is setting before us.

The entire structure of the fifth canto of the *Inferno* is designed to expose allegory's primary work, which is to force meaning on beings who are reduced for that purpose to substance. The agent representing this violence is the first figure encountered in hell, Minos, the judge of the dead, who assigns every soul to its place of torment by winding his tail around himself as many times as the soul has to descend levels, an operation he performs with the mechanical relentlessness of the Harrow in Kafka's "In the Penal Colony." Charged with "cotanto officio" [so great an office] (5.18) Minos stands in contrast to Francesca, who, speaking of Lancelot in the romance she and Paolo were reading when they first kissed, utters the answering phrase, "cotanto amante" [so great a lover] (5.134). The tension in the canto is marked by these extremes of punishment and passion, where the former is in the service of a project of meaning that never succeeds in emptying Francesca to the point where she is nothing more than the sign of a vice. In other words, Dante is revealing in this episode the failure of allegory to accomplish, to adapt Nietzsche's phrase, a total expulsion of life. He is reminding us that there is something out there beyond the grasp of the pilgrim's interpreting mind, a negative other that announces itself in real events, real bodies, and real pain. At the end of the episode the narrator's capacity for sympathy with

---

35 For Deguileville and Bunyan, see Rosemond Tuve, *Allegorical Imagery: Some Medieval Books and Their Posterity* (Princeton: Princeton University Press, 1966), pp. 145 and 172.

this realm, sympathy on a level deeper than any act of interpretation, is registered in his body, as he faints: "E caddi come corpo morto cade" [I fell, as a dead body falls] (5.142).

In reading the episode it is of some importance not to mistake which sin is reaching out to Francesca to make her its mask. Given the authority with which the word *lust* has been applied to her, it should be noted that the word *lussuria* is used in the canto only to characterize Semiramis (5.55), a rather special case. Dante describes the sinners in this circle as those who have submitted reason to "desire" or "inclination," *talento:* "I peccator carnali, / che la ragion sommettono al talento" (5.38–39). *Talento* means something quite different from *lussuria* and is placed by Dante at a distance from Francesca to avoid passing direct judgment on her. The first soul that we meet among the damned is remarkably independent of her abstract condition in hell.

Whether we should see Francesca's punishment as an expression of dismay at the justice of God or as a warning against passionate love is a question that cannot be answered, even if the best answer we have, Freccero's, can accommodate both points of view by distinguishing the pilgrim who feels from the poet who thinks. Any indecision is subsumed, says Freccero, in "the dialectical relationship of the pilgrim's view to that of the poet." But if the authoritative view that emerges from this dialectic is finally committed, as Freccero puts it in a phrase as revealing as it is magnificent, to "the crushing exigencies of the poet's structure," it remains in our eyes an extension of Minos's power. Freccero speaks of the poet's global detachment as the perspective to which the anagogical movement of the *Commedia* is directed, ascending, as he says, from "the problematic and humanistic" to what is "certain and transcendent . . . from a synchronic view of the self in a dark wood to a diachronic total view of the entire world as if it were, to use Dante's powerful image, a humble threshing floor upon which a providential history will one day separate the wheat from the chaff."[36] What is most striking about this description is its evocation of the thrilling violence of the *Commedia*, the sheer power with which the crushing exigencies of the poem's intellectual design flatten the complexities of life and of feeling to the plane of a threshing floor—an image that is terrifying just because it is so humble. It is an image that exposes the agent of meaning in the *Inferno* for what it

36 Freccero, *Dante*, pp. 25–26. The places of *synchronic* and *diachronic* in this passage should perhaps be reversed.

is: wrath. Wrath and love are indistinguishable in Christian eschatology (witness the inscription on the gates of hell),[37] just as hatred and eros are indistinguishable in rape. Even at the conclusion of the *Commedia* we cannot think of Francesca's torture as a manifestation of the love that moves the sun and the stars. We have to forget her, which at that point is easy to do. But our forgetting the moment when Francesca stops speaking does not change what Dante has revealed about the limits of his art and of the transcendental design it supports.

Those limits are marked in Francesca's final words: "quel giorno più non vi leggemmo avante" [that day we read in it no farther] (5.138). She is referring, of course, to the book she and Paolo stopped reading when they first kissed: "Galeotto fu 'l libro e chi lo scrisse" [a pander was that book, and he who wrote it] (5.137). But in a larger sense the book represents a realm of textuality set over against life. The book evokes in this way the transcendental design of the *Commedia* through which Francesca is made known to us and into which she has been drawn because of her sin. For Giuseppe Mazzotta, Francesca's sin was that of reading too literally, "according to the flesh," mistaking "the insubstantial shadows of the text for her own self." This mistake, Mazzotta argues, reflects a more general tendency in Francesca to live out her passion neurotically through books, to "lapse into lust," and to enter a state of criminal literariness in which her very speech "resembles both Guinizzelli's and Dante's stilnovistic formulas."[38]

Let us pause to consider this view of Francesca as what Freccero has called a "medieval Emma Bovary."[39] For some time I found that view of her a satisfying corrective to any inclination to sentimentalize the damned. I wanted Francesca to be not only lustful but shallow and to deserve punishment more than I could feel that she does. By assenting unequivocally to the design of the poem as a whole one can feel less remorse for being a voyeuristic party to a fate that as Robert Hollander would have it, "dwells in the memory of almost every literate Western man." But if Francesca's fate dwells in the memory of almost every literate Western man, her voice is as resistant to her becoming such a reminder as it is to her becoming a personification of lust. She remains in the memory of those who read her with attention not as the allegori-

---

37 *Inferno* 3.5–9.
38 Giuseppe Mazzotta, *Dante, Poet of the Desert: History and Allegory in the "Divine Comedy"* (Princeton: Princeton University Press, 1979), pp. 169 and 196.
39 Freccero, *Dante*, p. 25.

cal agent Hollander describes, as one whose "power to seduce is so great and so beautiful," but as a woman whose punishment is simply unjust — a "mal perverso," as she calls it.[40] The discomfort this memory causes has therefore prompted some critics to try to make the criminal fit the punishment. Charles S. Singleton speaks of Boccaccio's account of the legendary circumstances alluded to in Francesca's narrative as "embroidered nicely to exculpate Francesca as much as possible,"[41] without indicating what more reliable account is being so embroidered. It seems to me that Boccaccio's tale of Francesca's being tricked into marrying the deformed brother of the man she loved is more in keeping with the complexity of Dante's treatment of her than is the desire to see her torture smoothly incorporated into the interpretive design of the *Commedia*.

The aggression required to incorporate Francesca into that interpretive design is startlingly apparent in Hollander's discussion, in which the "lustful lady" is little more than a personification of what "the once lustful poet" has overcome. Even Hollander's important interpretive achievement in excavating the Virgilian, Pauline, and Augustinian substructure of allusion in the canto is marred by the gibe that she "loved the wrong Paul."[42] Although the subtexts Hollander exposes are indisputably at work beneath the surface of the canto, their relation to that surface is more complicated than he allows. They provide more than the concealed truth of an episode that is dangerously seductive if read on the surface; they evoke an order of abstract imperatives from which a violent assault on the other is launched.

It is, however, in Francesca's language, rather than in the poet's more recondite allusions, that we may discern the ambiguity of the violence directed against her. A sensitive critic such as Mazzotta, having committed himself to an aggression that Dante anticipates and exposes, must condemn that language as meretriciously literary. But who, we may well ask, is the agent of this literariness, Francesca or Dante? And what justifica-

---

40 Robert Hollander, *Allegory in Dante's "Commedia"* (Princeton: Princeton University Press, 1969), pp. 106-7. Francesca is thankful to the pilgrim because he takes "pity on our perverse misfortune" [poi c'hai pietà del nostro mal perverso, *Inferno* 5.93]. Whether "mal" should be translated here as "ill" (with Singleton) or "misfortune" depends on the extent to which one wants to separate her consciousness from the punishment inflicted on her. Singleton (*"Inferno": Commentary*, p. 89) cites the words "mal perverso" as if they were spoken by the poet in reference to Francesca's love rather than by Francesca in reference to her punishment.

41 Singleton, *"Inferno": Commentary*, p. 84.

42 Hollander, *Allegory*, pp. 107 and 113.

tion is there for transferring that agency to her? A reader who adheres unreservedly to the crushing exigencies of the poem's design may wish to do so. But there is little warrant for characterizing Francesca, a reader of Arthurian romances, as someone who speaks in the cadences of the "sweet new style" of Guinizzelli and Dante. Her passion is represented in literary language because she is a literary creation: "Amor, ch'a nullo amato amar perdona, / mi prese del costui piacer si forte, / che, come vedi, ancor non m'abbandona" [Love, which never spares the loved one from giving love in return, seized me so strongly with joy in him that, as you see, it still does not leave me] (5.103-5). The error of which Francesca stands accused by Mazzotta — of living vicariously, of confusing with life what she reads of in books — is the error that, according to the transcendental standard of the allegory, she should have committed. Morality demanded that she substitute the experience of reading for the experience of love so that she would never love in act but only in fantasy. That is what she refuses to do when she sins. Her sin is to recognize the difference between what happens in a book and what can happen in life, and her crime against allegory — the crime she continues to commit as we read — is to show that there are some things in life that cannot be captured by books, not even by the *Commedia*. She therefore acts on this recognition "according to the flesh," but by no means "literally," because in the moment of passion she knew the rift separating the flesh from the letter, a rift that Pauline and Augustinian violence conceals.

No impasse in the *Commedia*, not even that with which the poem concludes, is so clearly marked as this one. The pilgrim simply wakes up somewhere else. What is the poet showing us by means of it? If the book that prompts Francesca to love is in her eyes a pander, the book that instructs us to make her an object of the Father's eroticized hate is in our eyes, at this moment, a kind of legal rapist — "e chi lo scrisse." Who is the poet who would make such a confession? She is Crime and he is Punishment.

In the foregoing discussion I have supposed that allegorical expression is characterized not by one but by two kinds of figure. The first is personification, as seen, for example, in Spenser's Disdain. The second is the figure of capture, as we have seen it in Dante's Francesca. The figure of personification directs our attention beyond it to allegory's positive other in absolute meaning, on which a cosmos depends. The figure of capture directs our attention to the region of struggle and growth, the forest of life, which the cosmos is always attempting to enclose. Personification and capture thus stand on either side of the rift, marking the extremes between which the rhetorical possibilities of allegory are found: on the one hand is the intensity of meaning in Spenser's Disdain, who seems about to implode; on the other hand is the physical passion of Dante's Francesca, who, when her episode ends, escapes being allegorically named. Beyond personification waits the infinite regression of the Third Man, which would force allegory into a confrontation with philosophy. Beyond capture waits the endless evasions of the material world, which would force allegory into a confrontation with history.

Now this distribution of perils, with the Scylla of philosophy to one side and the Charybdis of history to the other, may remind us of Aristotle's clearing away the confusion of history and philosophy within literature by expelling both. Whether that operation is a legitimate means of establishing for poetics an independent space among the disciplines, it is clearly illegitimate for allegory. For allegory is committed to bringing history and philosophy together by imprinting abstract forms directly on the material of historical life, capturing some portion of what lies on the other side of the rift and holding it up for inspection. For allegory, as for its theory, there can be no balance of extremes or uncontested middle way.

Considered in this light, the figure of personification is a superficial manifestation of what is happening in an allegory, having been thrown up from below by forces obscurely at work in the struggle at the rift. As for capture, it is not so much a literary figure as it is a moment of revelation in which the origin of figures may be seen. To distribute personification and capture at opposite ends of a continuous field within which allegory functions as a system (one that may be analyzed according to a poetics) is to conceal the disorder with which and out of which allegory works. It is to position the rift outside allegory when it is ineradicably there at the center, producing the images and causing them, by its concealment, to shine. The productive work at the rift goes on behind the secondary work of the veil. The technical term for the latter is *polysemy*, multiple meaning, where every opposition arising from the contrast of meaning and life is redistributed hierarchically such that one term is placed over the other. Under the regime of polysemy, anything that appears to escape or to resist the project of meaning—passion, body, irony—is interpreted as a further extension of meaning. The rift that slashes through the center of the field of allegorical expression, opening into chaos, cannot be shown for what it is except by the poets who have the courage, at brief moments, to do so. These are the poets, such as Dante and Spenser, who draw back the veil of an optimistic, metaphysical illusion to reveal the truth of its origin and the certainty of its undoing.

2

A Genealogy of Agents:
Christianity and Classical Culture

I t has been generally observed that as Greek culture moved into the
classical period the Olympian gods were seen less as divinities than
as personifications of natural forces. The Homeric epics, and, more
important, the gods of the Homeric epics, were submitted to a process of
allegorical interpretation that made them less embarrassing to teach to
the young and more amenable to an increasingly philosophical culture.
For example, the adultery of Ares and Aphrodite, which is exposed when
they are caught in Hephaistos's net, was regarded not just as an amusing,
if immoral, tale but as an allegory of the union of concord and discord in
the net of the logos.[1] This process of rationalization could only be accelerated when the Greek gods were translated into Roman culture, where
the highly personalized gods of Homer became the more abstract ones
of Virgil. By the time of the late empire, the educated classes were inclined to regard mythology in a rarified, philosophical light and to regard
philosophy itself in mythical terms.[2] To put it less favorably, philosophy,

1   See Héraclite, *Allégories d'Homère*, ed. and trans. Félix Buffière (Paris: Belles Lettres,
1962), p. 74, and Buffière's *Les mythes d'Homère et la pensée grecque* (Paris: Belles Lettres,
1956), pp. 168–72.
2   The literature on ancient allegorical interpretation is extensive. For guidance through
the primary literature, see Konrad Müller, "Allegorische Dichterklärung," in *Paulys Real-
encyclopädie der classischen Altertumswissenschaft*, ed. Wilhelm Kroll (Stuttgart: Metzler,
1924), supplementary vol. 4, pp. 16–22. The principal studies are Buffière, *Les mythes
d'Homère et la pensée grecque*; Jean Pépin, *Mythe et allégorie: les origines grecques et les con-
testations judéo-chrétiennes*, 2d ed. (Paris: Études Augustiniennes, 1976); and Robert Lam-

religion, and myth were hopelessly confused. What made this confusion not only possible but respectable was allegorical interpretation.

Yet for all the high-minded speculation in which they were enveloped the ancient gods could not be incorporated into fully allegorical works of the kind that arose in the Middle Ages. What prevented, or at least retarded until the Renaissance, the gods' becoming prominent figures in allegory was their divinity or, to put it subjectively, their numinous power, a power that resisted their reduction to signs. Hence while the pagan gods were submitted in the Middle Ages to an ameliorating allegorism, they resisted any direct, systematic accommodation to actual allegorical writing, to a literary form that situates the numinous outside the order of signs, as absolute meaning. Instead, the personified abstractions of medieval allegory secretly absorbed, from the psychological power of a decaying polytheism, the narrative power of agency.

In allegory generally, where narrative and meaning are at variance with each other, this power of agency is at once necessary to personified abstractions and inimical to them.[3] It is from the struggle between a represented conceptual order and a representing narrative action, between static ideas and dynamic agents, that the sense of pervading mystery is created. Allegory thus draws on the power of what it has to repress. What it has to repress is narrative, but narrative as it is associated with the capacity of the gods to act independently as agents. It follows that allegory could appear only under specific historical conditions, when the rationalization of the gods (a practice of long standing in antiquity) was supplemented by a more radical treatment. These conditions were brought about by the convulsive effect of a major ideological change: the

---

berton, *Homer the Theologian: Neoplatonist Allegorical Reading and the Growth of the Epic Tradition* (Berkeley and Los Angeles: University of California Press, 1986). For late Roman religion, see Franz Cumont, *Recherches sur le symbolisme funéraire des romains* (Paris: Librairie Orientaliste Paul Geuthner, 1942), and William M. Green's introduction to the second volume in the Loeb edition of Augustine's *The City of God against the Pagans* (Cambridge: Harvard University Press, 1963), vii–xxxvi. See also Philip Rollinson and Patricia Matsen, *Classical Theories of Allegory and Christian Culture* (Pittsburgh: Duquesne University Press, 1981).

3 Jon Whitman, in *Allegory: The Dynamics of an Ancient and Medieval Technique* (Cambridge: Harvard University Press, 1987), p. 243, speaks of the problem of "the constriction of personifications to a limited sphere of action." See also his "From the *Cosmographia* to the *Divine Comedy*: An Allegorical Dilemma," in *Allegory, Myth, and Symbol*, ed. Morton W. Bloomfield (Cambridge: Harvard University Press, 1981), pp. 63–86 and Elizabeth J. Bellamy, *Translations of Power: Narcissism and the Unconscious in Epic History* (Ithaca: Cornell University Press, 1992), p. 27.

transition from paganism to Christianity, from a culture of the numen to a culture of the sign. Allegory was imaginatively possible only after a violent purging of the classical gods from the world. Prior to that event there is very little that may safely be called allegorical expression; and there are no literary works of any length that are organized allegorically throughout.

This claim contradicts the more familiar notion that allegory developed in a tradition extending from Homer to the Enlightenment. According to that view, which I discuss at greater length in Chapter 7, a fully allegorical literature is supposed to have emerged from the gradual demystification of the gods of antiquity, leading by degrees, without significant interruption, to the deployment of fully allegorical agents. The appearance of these agents, it is supposed, was only the final stage in the rationalization of the classical gods by the ancient interpreters of Homer, allegory itself being an eminently rational form of expression. Such a picture, however, cannot allow for any meaningful distinction between allegorization and allegory, between mere interpretation of the poets—*hermeneia*, as it was called—and allegorical writing by the poets themselves. Nor can it account for the irrational use allegory made of the classical gods.

To be sure, figures that bear at least a superficial resemblance to medieval personifications are already present in Homer, though on a subordinate plane to the gods. Ares, the god of war, is accompanied by Terror and Panic (*Deimos* and *Phobos*), whose names are still with us as the satellites of the planet Mars; Sleep and Death (*Hypnos* and *Thanatos*) are commanded by Zeus to remove Sarpedon's body from the field; *Eris*, or Hate, strides between the armies as battle approaches, growing larger until her head strikes the sky; and the *Litai*, or Prayers, are described as crippled daughters of Zeus who, if spurned, give way to swift *Ate*, or Madness, who brings destruction to the proud.[4] Unlike the Homeric

4 *Iliad* 15.119-20, 16.453-54, 4.439-45, 9.502-19. See Hesiod, *Theogony* ll. 933-36, in which we are told that Deimos and Phobos, the children of Ares by Aphrodite, drive the closed ranks of men in war, assisted by Ares, the sacker of cities; and *Aeneid* 12.336, where Anger and Ambush are the attendants of Mars. For *Ate* as "psychic intervention" by a god, see E. R. Dodds, *The Greeks and the Irrational* (1951; reprint, Berkeley and Los Angeles: University of California Press, 1973), p. 5. For a Virgilian example of a subordinate god being confined to a particular function, see *Aeneid* 1.52-54, where Juno visits Aeolus, the god of the winds. Cf. *Odyssey* 10.19-21, where Aiolos is a king who, having been given power over the winds, presents them to Odysseus tied up in a bag. Although

gods, who perform actions unrelated to the powers with which they are associated (Aphrodite, for example, fights in a battle), these figures' actions are more closely confined to what their names tell us they are.

Angus Fletcher has argued that it is the compulsive behavior of such daemonic figures, rather than any abstract meaning imposed on them, that became the basis of medieval personification.[5] Personification, as we saw in Chapter 1, is a more complicated matter than instantiating an abstract universal in human form. To personify is to capture a resistant substratum behind a conceptual mask. The tension between these heterogeneous sources—abstract thought and compulsive repetition—gives to allegorical persons an unsettling but fascinating power. Personification is not, therefore, the bloodless abstraction that the romantics decried but a conjoining of forces from opposite poles of the mind. While I am inclined to substitute literary narrative for Freudian pathology in Fletcher's account, his argument supports (perhaps inadvertently) the view that allegory emerged under conditions of historical crisis. It is then to be doubted whether we may speak, without better historical grounds, of allegorical personifications in Homer.

A related problem concerns the proliferation in late antiquity of phenomena, processes, and actions that had been raised to the status of gods because of an idealist anxiety about agency itself. These were referred to as the *di minuti*, the "little gods," who ruled, among other things, sewers, beards, and erections. They were entertainingly mocked by Augustine, as when he remarked that the goddess Pertunda, who presides over the breaking of the hymen, should leave the marriage chamber so that the husband, still aided by a host of gods performing such tasks as loosening the girdle, toppling the bride, and pressing down on her, will have at least one thing to do.[6] Nor was the comic potential of such gods apparent only to those who were openly hostile to their cult. Seneca, in a satirical account of the "pumpkinification" of the emperor Claudius, describes the emperor motioning with his feverish hand to have Fever de-

---

Virgil's Aeolus is more closely confined to a function, he is no more allegorical than his counterpart, Allecto, who, roused by Juno, initiates the action in the second half of the *Aeneid* (7.323–29) by rousing the Latins to anger against Aeneas.

5 Angus Fletcher, *Allegory: The Theory of a Symbolic Mode* (Ithaca: Cornell University Press, 1964), pp. 68–69. See also Paul Piehler, *The Visionary Landscape: A Study in Medieval Allegory* (Montreal: McGill/Queen's University Press, 1971), pp. 12–13, who calls these figures "powers," or *potentiae*.

6 Augustine, *City of God* 6.9. For the absurd labor of dividing all human goods into tiny, distinct parts and assigning a minute god to each, see 4.21.

capitated, Fever having abandoned her shrine to accompany Claudius to the heavens, where she accuses him of being a Gaul.[7] Coleridge had episodes of this sort in mind when he noted the difference between minor gods and allegorical personifications:

> Of a People, who raised Altars to Fever, to Sport, to Fright, &c it is impossible to determine, how far they meant a personal power, or personification of a Power. This only is certain, that the introduction of these agents could not have the same unmixed effect, as the same agents used allegorically produce on our minds — but something more nearly resembling the effect produced by the introduction of characteristic Saints in the roman catholic poets, or of Moloch, Belial, and Mammon in the second Book of Paradise Lost compared with his Sin and Death.[8]

Whether Milton's Sin and Death may be distinguished so clearly as Coleridge supposes from analogous figures in Homer remains to be seen. For the present it is enough to insist on the importance of Coleridge's suggestion that personal powers such as Fever are not just abstractions to which human masks have been given.

But the force of that observation is not apparent outside the context of the historical change that was brought about by Christianity. Christianity demonized the gods to the point where their visual forms could not be used, although their energy could be.[9] By their energy I mean the power of linear action within a process, which classical idealism nervously sought to eliminate by referring all events to their originative forms. Augustine's comic description of the crowded marriage chamber is of more speculative interest than might at first be supposed, calling

---

7 Seneca, *Apocolocyntosis*, ed. P. T. Eden (Cambridge: Cambridge University Press, 1984), section 6, p. 39.

8 *Lectures, 1808–1819, On Literature*, ed. R. A. Foakes, vol. 5 (in two parts) of *The Collected Works of Samuel Taylor Coleridge* (Princeton: Princeton University Press, 1987), 2:102. See also Franz Cumont, *The Oriental Religions in Roman Paganism* (New York: Dover, 1956), pp. 32–33 and 202. For Coleridge's formal definition of allegory, which shows the rhetorical bias of eighteenth-century critical theory, see *Lectures, 1808–1819*, 2:99–100. A more openly tendentious definition of allegory ("worthless," "unsubstantial," "shapeless") as contrasted with the symbol appears in Coleridge's *The Statesman's Manual*, in *Lay Sermons*, vol. 6 of *Collected Works* (London: Routledge & Kegan Paul, 1972), ed. R. J. White, p. 30. See N. A. Halmi, "From Hierarchy to Opposition: Allegory and the Sublime," *Comparative Literature* 44 (Fall 1992): 340–41.

9 See Erwin Panofsky, *Renaissance and Renascences in Western Art* (1960: reprint, New York: Harper & Row, 1972), p. 104.

into question the coincidence of any action with any agent. The effort to impose such coincidence by reducing one term to the other, action to agent, leads to an infinite regression. Such a regression is precisely a descent into the rift between a motionless structure of agents, a cosmology of intercourse, and the temporal continuum of life. The effort violently to force the rift closed drives the proliferation of agents that Augustine describes. If classical idealism survived in medieval personification, offering an imaginative solution to a logically insolvable problem, the classical gods did not survive as the visual forms of ideas. They survived rather as allegory's negative other, the imponderable continuum of life, retaining something of their divinity even as their forms underwent cultural decay.

We may observe this development in the first, and perhaps the most dangerous, of the vices that are defeated in Prudentius's *Psychomachia*. This is a figure called "Worship of the Ancient Gods" (*Veterum Cultura Deorum*), who is defiled with sacrificed beasts, and who suffocates in her own blood as her eyes (with which she reads omens) are trampled by Faith.[10] Prudentius evokes in this figure a pagan view of the world, still very much alive in his time, against which Christianity had to fight. It is the view of the world as a system of interlocking but independent regions of power otherwise known as myth. The regions are governed by divinities who inhabit specific places in nature, such as the streams and the groves, and whose intentions may be discerned in oracles, in the flight of birds, and in the configuration of the entrails in animal victims. In the monotheistic world view Prudentius was fighting to establish, however, everything in nature was thought of as belonging to the stable, unchanging order of an omniscient Creator. The world thus became a text, fixed in one state at its creation, from which the presence of the divine has been removed. Milton, in his "Ode on the Morning of Christ's Nativity," evokes the change of sensibility that occurred when the psychological power of an old world order was purged:

> The lonely mountains o'er,
> And the resounding shore
>   A voice of weeping heard, and loud lament;
> From haunted spring, and dale
> Edged with poplar pale,

10 Prudentius, *Psychomachia*, ll. 28–35, in vol. 3 of *Prudence*, ed. and trans. M. Lavarenne (Paris: Belles Lettres, 1948), p. 52.

The parting genius is with sighing sent,
With flower-inwoven tresses torn
The nymphs in twilight shade of tangled thickets mourn.

The vespertinal mood of the passage gives way to an exhilarated fascination with the obscenity, and the horror, of the classical gods, who are revealed to be devils as they are banished to an "infernal jail." [11] But the psychological power of polytheism was not so successfully quarantined. The gods made occasional reappearances in medieval literature; and their energy was drawn on to lend narrative agency to allegorical figures.

The power of a decaying polytheism, even as it gave impetus to narrative, was exploited to lend a certain numinous terror to static allegorical figures, which, when they retained the identity of a classical god, were typically confined to pagan temples, as in Chaucer's "Knight's Tale," with its temples of Venus, Mars, and Diana, and in Spenser's *Faerie Queene*, where the temple of Venus affords an occasion for an elaborate anatomy of love. The figures were drawn, however, not from the classical gods but from the more specialized divinities of late antiquity, such as Claudian's goddess of Nature, an important figure in medieval allegory who reappears in Alan of Lille and in Spenser.[12] When such figures are incorporated in fully allegorical works they are clearly subordinate to a higher, more comprehensive power. They do not possess that numinous, independent force which makes their ancient precursors at once impressive and isolated. Ovid's cave of Sleep, for example, situated at the limit of the world, near the dark land of Cimmerians, is described differently from similar places in allegorical works, for the very landscape surrounding the god is saturated in a power that exists below the plane of intelligible signs. Before the mouth of the cave abundant poppies bloom, and

11 John Milton, "Ode on the Morning of Christ's Nativity," ll. 181–88 and 232–33, in *Complete Shorter Poems*, ed. John Carey (London: Longman, 1971). See Prudentius's exultant account, in *Apotheosis*, ll. 435–48, in Lavarenne, *Prudence*, 2:19, of the cessation of the pagan oracles with the advent of Christ.
12 For Spenser's temple of Venus and goddess of Nature, see *Faerie Queene* 4.10 and 7.7.9. See also Chaucer's "Knight's Tale," ll. 1893–2088, in *The Works of Geoffrey Chaucer*, ed. F. N. Robinson, 2d ed. (Boston: Houghton Mifflin, 1957). For pagan divinities and medieval personifications, see C. S. Lewis, *The Allegory of Love: A Study in Medieval Tradition* (Oxford: Oxford University Press, 1938), pp. 53 and 73, and Aimé Puech, *Prudence: Étude sur la poésie latine chrétienne au IVe siècle* (Paris, 1888), pp. 240–42. For the cave of Nature, see Claudian, *De consulatu Stilichonis* 2.428–48, and George D. Economou, *The Goddess Natura in Medieval Literature* (Cambridge: Harvard University Press, 1972).

innumerable herbs grow, from whose juices Night distills the essence of sleep and sprinkles it over the dark land.[13] In a fully allegorical work, even in an episode as mystical in tone as Spenser's garden of Adonis, any essential power of this kind is incorporated in the system as a whole, as meaning, and is referred ultimately to a singularity that is outside the system. It is this constant referentiality of the numinous to a point outside the system that makes the work as a whole an interpretable text. In classical culture, however, just because it retains in its literature an analogy of polytheism, works organized to elicit a continuous interpretive response do not appear. Fully allegorical works could be created only in a culture that had submitted nature to a violent expulsion of divinity, a catharsis.

It is hard to enter into the mental world of the Homeric epics because that world is so different from what followed in classical Greece and, unexpectedly, so much like our own. Although the similarities have different causes, they are nevertheless striking. Consider the following statements: perception, consciousness, and thought are physical processes occurring in physical organs; emotions are not abstract states of mind causing physical symptoms but physical events preceding our consciousness of them; thought and language are not separate processes but different aspects of a single one; words have meaning only in the stream of life, and language is a part of that stream, not a detached representation of it; there is no absolute self apart from the body and its actions in the social world; and thought itself is indistinguishable from the current of breath moving in and out of the lungs, that is, from the rhythms of the body as a whole.[14] Such beliefs are as rooted in the world of the Homeric epics as ones similar to them are in ours, prompting Guy Davenport to speak of the twentieth century as a "renaissance of the archaic."[15] Homer is our contemporary in a way that Dante and Spenser are not, for he comes before, as we come after, the trajectory of philosophical idealism from its rise in the classical period to its decline in the Enlightenment.

I observed that the central problem for classical idealism was how a primary abstraction such as Justice could participate in the material world,

13   Ovid, *Metamorphoses* 11.605–7. Cf. Statius's Hall of Sleep, *Thebaid* 10.84–117.
14   See Richard Broxton Onians, *The Origins of European Thought about the Body, the Mind, the Soul, the World, Time, and Fate*, 2d ed. (Cambridge: Cambridge University Press, 1954), pp. 75 and 82–83, in which *aisthesis*, "perception," is derived from the Homeric verb "to breathe" (*aistho* "I gasp, breathe in").
15   Guy Davenport, *The Geography of the Imagination* (San Francisco: North Point, 1981), p. 20.

in instances of justice. In Homer the problem is the reverse. How are occasional events such as panic, or headlong flight, and emotional states such as anger derived from the primary evidence of material things? Idealism sought to overcome this problem of the participation of the abstract in its instances by reducing the physical world to another abstraction: indifferent substance. Archaic thought approached the problem of intangibles from the opposite direction by making finer distinctions among observable things, for example by imagining the various emotions as secretions of particular organs. Personification in the strict sense of the term—the appropriation of material agency to a logically prior, metaphysical idea—is impossible in the Homeric epics because such ideas are unknown. What look to us like universals that are merely represented as individuals are, as we see in Hesiod even more clearly than in Homer, individuals first.

A figure such as *Eris*, who, as we saw, strides between the armies and grows taller as they close, is understood as a real, supernatural agent, not as an abstraction to which agency is subsequently given. When she first appears in the *Iliad* she is in the company of the Olympians Athene and Ares, together with Terror and Panic; and while Athene and Ares take sides, inciting the Achaians and the Trojans respectively, Eris is more closely confined to her function: to arouse hatred and strife. But she is never presented as the secondary manifestation, the sign, of a universal. She is more like the prophetic figures of Blake, a supernatural being who determines events in a particular way. Her genealogy, as described by Hesiod, bears this point out. A daughter of Night and a younger sister of Nemesis, *Eris* herself bore "Toil and Forgetfulness and Famine and Tearful Sorrows, Fightings also, Battles, Murders, Manslaughters, Quarrels, Lying Words, Disputes, Lawlessness and Ruin [*Ate*], all of one nature." [16] In the Greek, the last phrase (*sunetheas allelesin*) suggests cohabitation, familiar proximity, as much as it does a common nature or essence. These beings are near to one another in common, human experience. Such relatedness is expressed, however, not by a logically common term or by a metaphysical principle of shared nature, least of all by the participation of forms in one another. (The problem of *methexis* concerns the participation not only of forms in particulars but also of forms in one another.) We are not to suppose that the bad things Hesiod mentions all participate somehow in the form of the Bad or that good things

16   Hesiod, *Theogony* ll. 223–30, trans. Hugh G. Evelyn-White.

participate in the form of the Good. The bad things are related to one another genealogically, that is, on the looser principle of family resemblance, where two members of a group with no traits in common may both share traits independently with a third.[17] There is no common term present in every member but a more complex continuum of overlapping traits, joining elements that, if considered apart from the system, would have nothing in common.

The more cautious of those who see allegory in Homer confine themselves to the episode of the Litai, or Prayers, in the ninth book of the *Iliad*. It seems safe to speak of the Litai as allegorical figures because they are deployed for an explicitly rhetorical purpose—to persuade Achilles to return to the army—and because they are described in enough detail to indicate deliberate thought. We are told that the Litai, who are daughters of Zeus, are lame and wrinkled, and their eyes always glance to one side or the other, avoiding direct visual contact. They follow after swift-footed Ate, the spirit of mad destruction, who outruns them everywhere on the face of the earth. They confer blessings on whoever reveres them; but on those who spurn them they call down the curse of Zeus and the affliction of Ate.[18] Of this passage Rudolf Pfeiffer remarks: "One can hardly deny that [the Litai passage] is a genuine allegory. . . . When rhapsodes of the sixth century started to detect 'hidden meanings' in many parts of the Homeric epics, they were only developing . . . something which the imagination of a great poet had once created."[19]

But perhaps this account is not cautious enough. In the first place, it is insufficiently concerned with the differences between oral and literate cultures. If it may be doubted whether the rhapsodes, the oral performers of the Homeric poems, initiated the practice of allegorical interpretation, it may certainly be asked whether the notion of an "undermeaning" (*hyponoia*) concealed below the surface of a text could have developed out of anything in the epics themselves. Song has no surface. We may indeed deny that the Homeric Prayers constitute a genuine allegory if we suppose that genuineness in this matter cannot be decided by means of a narrow, rhetorical definition. Rhetoric itself, understood as the minute, technical analysis of figures of speech, belongs to a much later age and

17   Ludwig Wittgenstein, *Philosophical Investigations*, 2d ed., trans. G. E. M. Anscombe (New York: Macmillan, 1958), sec. 67, p. 32.
18   *Iliad* 9.502–12.
19   Rudolf Pfeiffer, *History of Classical Scholarship from the Beginnings to the End of the Hellenistic Age* (Oxford: Clarendon Press, 1968), p. 5; see also p. 237.

is the expression of an instrumental relation to language. What sort of beings are the Prayers in the world of the Homeric epics? What is at issue for the speaker who invokes them? Is he concerned merely with the success or failure of his embassy to Achilles or is he genuinely warning Achilles of the danger of offending real supernatural agents?

If one reads the speech concerning the Litai with care, bringing to it a sense of what is due to divinity in Homeric culture, it is impossible to regard the speech merely as an instrument of persuasion, as an artifact composed of figures that are known not to be real. The Prayers have a genealogy linking them to the king of the gods; they aid those who honor and revere them and seek retribution from Zeus against those who do not. Whatever generalizing power the Litai possess is moving in the opposite direction from late classical personification, which seeks to anchor abstractions to one place in the world. The generalizing power of the Litai radiates from, and is secondary to, their primary status as divinities. In giving significant names to such figures the poet is not attempting to anchor an immaterial abstraction in matter. He is extending the reach of physical beings in a world that is so grounded in the sensuous that its gods drink nectar, bleed ichor, and can be recognized by their smell.

This conclusion is not irrelevant to the problem of the supposed allegory of Sin and Death in *Paradise Lost*, which was criticized, most notably by Johnson, for giving too much material agency to personified abstractions, who should not have been permitted to build that bridge across chaos, stupendous though it is. In this matter too, historical reflection on the poet's artistic allegiances and on his conceptual world (in particular, his animated materialism) is of more service than formal definition. Milton's Sin and Death have little in common ontologically with medieval and Renaissance allegorical persons. Their daemonic existence is based on analogous figures in Homer. Sin springs from Satan's head when Satan first conspires to rebel against God; and Death is the product of Satan and Sin's incestuous union.[20] Sin and Death are not signs

20 *Paradise Lost*, ed. Alastair Fowler (London: Longman, 1971), 2.752–89. Cf. *Paradise Lost* 2.965–67 for the Hesiodic figures attending on Chaos: Rumour, Chance, Tumult, Confusion, and Discord. For Samuel Johnson's criticism of Milton's Sin and Death, see *Lives of the English Poets*, ed. George Birbeck Hill (Oxford: Clarendon Press, 1905), 1:185. For other discussions, see Philip J. Gallagher, "'Real or Allegoric': The Ontology of Sin and Death in *Paradise Lost*," *English Literary Renaissance* 6 (1976): 317; Maureen Quilligan, *Milton's Spenser: The Politics of Reading* (Ithaca: Cornell University Press, 1983), p. 126; Steven Knapp, *Personification and the Sublime: Milton to Coleridge* (Cambridge: Harvard

pointing to forces that are more real than they are; they precede and are the causes of what their names tell us they are. She is Sin and he is Death.

If the earliest interpretations of Homer began when literacy was becoming pervasive in Greece, it is not difficult to see how the new technology affected the way literary fictions were to be understood.[21] By mapping an elegantly limited system of graphic signs onto the acoustic field, writing made it possible to think of a text as containing, inside its visible signs, an invisible but more various, more meaningful sound. From this distinction between sign and breath, whereby the breath is authentic and the sign its derived, imperfect container, it is natural to proceed to the distinction between the outer shell of a story, its "literal" meaning, and an invisible "undermeaning." The allegorization of non-allegorical works began when this conception of a poem as a text acted together with the natural tendency of any culture to make earlier literature relevant to present concerns and inoffensive to present morals. In this way Homer became all things to all readers: a Stoic, a Pythagorean, a Neoplatonist, even an oracle to Byzantine Christians, for whom Odysseus at the mast was a figure of Christ on the cross.[22] The material technology of writing was dialectically necessary to the emergence in Greece of the spiritual practice of allegorical interpretation.

By a similar development, in the early Christian era, allegorical expression was at least partly occasioned by the interpretation of the cultural other—the religion of Greek and Roman antiquity—as the material remains of a cultural past. As analogies of the "spoils of Egypt," the relics of classical culture were not to be utterly rejected but seized upon and turned, as Augustine put it, to a better use.[23] Like the fragments of Ro-

---

University Press, 1985), p. 63; Stephen M. Fallon, *Milton among the Philosophers: Poetry and Materialism in Seventeenth-Century England* (Ithaca: Cornell University Press, 1991), p. 180; Mindele Anne Treip, *Allegorical Poetics and the Epic: The Renaissance Tradition to "Paradise Lost"* (Lexington: University of Kentucky Press, 1994), pp. 110-11 and 173-76.

21 For the influence of writing on the emergence of the concept of abstract objects of thought, see Eric A. Havelock, *The Muse Learns to Write: Reflections on Orality and Literacy from Antiquity to the Present* (New Haven: Yale University Press, 1986), p. 97.

22 Hugo Rahner, *Greek Myths and Christian Mystery* (London: Burns & Oates, 1963), p. 353.

23 Augustine, *De doctrina christiana*, bk. 2, sec. 40, in *Aurelii Augustini opera* (Turnhout: Brepols, 1962), 4:1 (pp. 73-74). The captured gold and silver vessels are the liberal arts; the garments, human institutions. The spoils are to be converted to Christian uses for which they were not originally intended. See also Jerome's allegorizing the beautiful captive of Deuteronomy 21:10-13 as classical education, which must be shorn, pared, and stripped of

man architecture that were incorporated in Christian churches as *spolia*, the material remains of the past were torn from their contexts and put to uses that were meant to be seen to be fundamentally at variance with their original purposes. It was the violence of the transformation that was meant to be seen.

The most striking literary example of the spoliation of classical culture is Prudentius's *Psychomachia*, the title of which, indicating a battle of virtues and vices in the soul, alludes to the Homeric *theomachia*, or "battle of the gods." This poem, traditionally regarded as the earliest Christian allegory (it is antedated, however, by the pagan *Tablet of Cebes* and by the Christian *Pastor of Hermas*), is a deliberate Virgilian pastiche. While it is not a *cento* in the strict sense of the word—a poem made up entirely of fragments of other poems—it sets out to achieve an effect similar to the Christian centos, in which verses from Virgil were used to relate biblical tales.[24] Prudentius makes it seem as if the remains of classical culture are being reduced to a material state—to pure sound, in this case—before being put to an alien use. The process of materializing language as writing was carried over to the figures represented in narrative, who were regarded as belonging to a literal level of meaning.

Coleridge's remarks on the *Psychomachia* convey the importance of a change in which narrative agents are known not to be real:

> The most beautiful Allegory ever composed, the Tale of Cupid and Psyche, tho' composed by an Heathen, was subsequent to the general spread of Christianity, and written by one of those Philosophers [Apuleius], who attempted a christianized sort of oriental and Egyptian Platonism enough to set it up against Christianity; but the first Allegory compleatly modern in its form is the Psychomachia or Battle of the Soul, by Prudentius, a Christian Poet of the 5th Century—facts that fully explain both the origin and nature of narrative Allegory, as a substitute for the mythological imagery of Polytheism, and differing from it only in the more obvious

---

all traces of idolatry and pleasure before being used to beget slaves for the house of God, in *Sancti Eusebii Hieronymi epistulae selectae*, ed. Carolus Favez (Brussels: Latomus, 1950), 70.2 (p. 44).

24 See Maclin Smith, *Prudentius' "Psychomachia": A Reexamination* (Princeton: Princeton University Press, 1976), pp. 235–36 and 262–63; and Lavarenne, "Notice," in *Prudence*, 3:12. For the program of the *Psychomachia* in a passage from Tertullian (*De spectaculis* 29), in which the virtues and vices fight for possession of the soul, see Aimé Puech, *Prudence*, pp. 246–47.

and intentional disjunction of the sign from the symbol, and the known unreality of the latter.[25]

It should by now be apparent that allegorical persons are not simply substitutes for the classical gods. It was not the visible imagery of polytheism but its psychological power that was appropriated for allegorical writing. But the "known unreality" of which Coleridge speaks—the primacy of the meaning over the work—ensures that what is supposed to be real will be elevated to a higher plane of being, one that is invisible and "other."

The positiveness of this spiritual other cannot, however, simply be asserted. If it could, Neoplatonism and Pythagoreanism, which simply rejected the material world and sought to escape it, would have been able to produce fully allegorical works, instead of allegorical interpretations. There must be an imaginative movement in the opposite direction, a driving of roots down into the material world—such as we see in the greatest allegorical poets, in Dante, Langland, and Spenser—to propel the imagination to the rarified heights of transcendental vision. The dialectical energy propelling this movement into the spiritual realm extends to the assertion of the materiality of the poem as a text. To this dead materiality all persons represented in the narrative of the poem are assimilated. They are called, as I have said, "literal," but they continue to struggle against their assimilation to the letter.

Allegorical agents are thus more complex than Coleridge allows when, in the sentence following the passage just quoted, he dismisses them as "incapable of exciting any lively interest for any length of time." What excites interest in allegorical agents is their seeming to be built up out of the material remains of the past in a manner that violates the original state of those remains. There thus seems to be a struggle occurring inside such agents. For example, the figure of Sapience in Huon de Meri's *Tourneiment Anticrist* nurses David and Solomon at her breasts, her milk being the source of the psalms and the books of wisdom; her shield displays the liberal arts as they are described by Martianus Capella; the point of her lance is tempered by Reason and filed by Argument; and her helmet is inscribed with the entire text of the Bible.[26] Sapience seems

25 Coleridge, *Lectures, 1808–1819*, 2:102.
26 Huon de Meri, *Le Tourneiment Anticrist*, ed. Margaret O. Bender (University, Miss.: Romance Monographs, 1976), ll. 1867–88. Sapience is recalled in later figures such as Franchise in the *Roman de la rose*, who attacks Dangier "very humbly," her armor being

almost to be made up out of books, like a figure by Arcimboldo. She may with profit be compared to Martianus' Philology, who is informed by the goddess Immortality (Athanasia) that before she may drink from the goddess's cup and ascend to the heavens (for her marriage with Mercury) she must disencumber herself of what is in her stomach, whereupon Philology, with great effort and force, vomits; and the vomit is transformed, as Martianus says, into heaps of every kind of writing. Immortality commands that some of these writings, which contain the figures of beasts, be cut into pillars and situated in caves in the remoter regions of Egypt, to record the genealogies of the gods. Meanwhile, as Philology continues to vomit, she is approached by girls whom some call the arts, others the disciplines, each of whom seizes upon and gathers to herself whatever books are appropriate to her.[27] As with Huon's Sapience, the point of Martianus' figure is to show how all books in the past, whatever their historical contexts, flow from an abstraction that is placed out of time. The obtrusive, nagging constructedness of Sapience and the surreal productiveness of Philology invite us to raise these figures above material things to the realm of ideas. Their impossibility as literal figures arouses hermeneutic anxiety, provoking the reader to cancel the material truth in favor of something more exalted. Absurdity is the trope of sublimity.

Any criticism of the notion of an allegorical tradition extending from antiquity through the Middle Ages should take into account the striking contrast between the status of allegorical interpretation in the two periods. The major classical authors were uniformly contemptuous of allegorical hermeneutics, when they took any notice of it at all.[28] Plato

---

made up entirely of the actions of a seducer. See Guillaume de Lorris and Jean de Meun, *Le Roman de la rose*, ed. Daniel Poirion (Paris: Garnier-Flammarion, 1974), ll. 15, 303–37. See also Marc-René Jung, *Études sur le poème allégorique en France au moyen âge* (Berne: Francke, 1971), pp. 268–89.

27 *Martianus Capella*, ed. James Willis (Leipzig: Teubner, 1983), 2.136 and 138. One is reminded of the serpent-woman in the *Faerie Queene* (1.1.20) whose "vomit full of bookes and papers was." For the complex cultural circumstances from which allegory emerged in late antiquity, see Luciano Lenaz's introduction to *Martiani Capellae de nuptiis Philologiae et Mercurii liber secundus*, ed. and trans. Luciano Lenaz (Padua: Liviana, 1975), and Danuta Shanzer, *A Philosophical and Literary Commentary on Martianus Capella's "De Nuptiis Philologiae et Mercurii"* (Berkeley and Los Angeles: University of California Press, 1986), pp. 1–44. For Martianus's pervasive influence in medieval allegorical art, see Raimond van Marle, *Allegories et symboles*, vol. 2 of *Iconographie de l'art profane au moyen-age et à la renaissance* (The Hague: Nijhoff, 1932), pp. 204–5.

28 Pfeiffer, *History of Classical Scholarship*, p. 237, very plausibly links Aristotle with Plato

and Cicero both regarded allegorization as a practice typical of the intellectually unsophisticated. Even so late a figure as Plutarch, who used allegorical interpretation himself to reconcile Greek and Egyptian mythology, spoke with disdain of those who impose their will on stories "through what used to be termed 'undermeanings' but are now called 'allegories.'"[29]

Whereas Plato mentioned "undermeanings" only in passing,[30] Cicero provided the most extensively critical discussion of the topic before Bacon (who borrows freely from him). In the first book of *De natura deorum*, which is in the form of a dialogue, Velleius the Epicurean accuses Cornutus the Stoic of accommodating the stories of the ancient poets—Orpheus, Musaeus, Hesiod, and Homer—to doctrines they could not have known about.[31] In the second book, Balbus defends the allegorical interpretation of the gods, employing the familiar etymological method to disclose the physical meanings that are hidden in fables: Kronos is *chronos*, or "time"; Hera is an anagram for "air," and so on.[32] Each of Balbus's arguments is set up for destruction by the skeptical academician Cotta, who is Cicero's mask. His criticisms are acute. If the gods are the intelligences behind abstractions, they will multiply indefinitely; it is philosophically crude to suppose that abstractions are gods just because abstractions are intangible and general; and the interpretation of

---

in the rejection of allegorization. In Aristotle's only reference to *hyponoia*, *Ethica Nichomachea* 1128a24, he means something like insinuating irony, which is more gentlemanly than the foul-mouthed *aischrologia* of the old comedy. Plotinus speaks more favorably of riddling undermeanings, in *Enneads* 1.6.17, although he is pointedly subjective: "ainittomenos, dokei moi" [allegorically riddling, as it seems to me]. For the use by the interpreters of myth of the term *ainittomai* (hint at, convey allegorically), see Lamberton, *Homer the Theologian*, p. 41 and "Index of Greek Terms," p. 353 s.v. In *Enneads* 3.5.8 Plotinus allegorizes *Zeus* as *nous*.

29   Plutarch, *Quomodo adolescens poetas audire debeat* 19e–f. The passage is famous for witnessing the supplanting of the term *hyponoia* by *allegoria*. But Plutarch is affirming the superiority of good moral example in literature to allegorical apologies for unedifying episodes. Likewise, the author of the treatise *On the Sublime* (available in the Loeb volume containing Aristotle's *Poetics*), claims at 9.7 that the battle of the gods in the *Iliad*, unless taken allegorically, is sacrilegious and fails to "save propriety." As he remarks shortly after, the battle of the gods is far surpassed by passages in which the divine nature is not confused with the human but is represented in its full majesty.

30   Plato, *Republic* 378d. Plato says that such things as the castration of Cronus and the battles of the gods are not to be admitted into the city, whether they are constructed with undermeanings or without undermeanings, for the young are unable to distinguish which is which.

31   Cicero, *De natura deorum* 1.15.

32   Ibid. 2.23–26.

the gods by their names is nothing more than laborious ingenuity un-checked by any critical spirit—in short, it is illiberal.[33]

The last of these criticisms is repeated in Seneca's moral epistles, where the absurdities of Homeric hermeneutics (together with, it must be admitted, questions of a philological and historical nature) are dis-dained as unworthy of the attention of a free man, whose primary con-cern should be himself.[34] That reading poetry should be chiefly a means of improving the self is a Horatian theme, developed in the epistle in which Horace describes himself at his retreat at Praeneste, away from the world of affairs. While his addressee, Lollius Maximus, is declaim-ing in Rome, Horace is reading the poet of the Trojan War, who tells us what is beautiful, what is evil, what is useful (and what is not), better and more clearly than allegorizers such as Chrysippus and Crantor:

> Troiani belli scriptorem, Maxime Lolli,
> Dum tu declamas Romae, Praeneste relegi;
> qui quid sit pulchrum, quid turpe, quid utile, quid non,
> planius ac melius Chrysippo et Crantore dicit.[35]

Horace goes on to explain (in a passage that would uphold Renaissance commonplaces about Homer's allegorical intentions) how the *Iliad* con-tains a political lesson and the *Odyssey* a moral one. But he never implies that Homer conceals the truth. Just because the moral is plainly there, Homer is a better teacher than Chrysippus or Crantor.

By contrast, even the most classically oriented medieval intellectuals, such as John of Salisbury, revered allegory uncritically, supposing all an-cient literature to conceal truth under the veil of the letter.[36] In this they

33 Ibid. 3.17–25.
34 Seneca, *Epistulae* 88.5–8.
35 Horace, *Epistulae* 1.2.1–4; see also 1.2.17–26, where he notes the moral example of Ulysses. For passages in which Horace uses myth rhetorically to point a moral, see *Carmina* 3.16.1–11 (Danae), *Satirae* 1.1.68–72 (Tantalus), and *Ars poetica*, ll. 391–407 (Orpheus).
36 John of Salisbury, *Entheticus de dogmate philosophorum*, ll. 185–86, in *Entheticus Maior and Minor*, ed. Jan van Laarhoven (Leiden: Brill, 1987), 1:117–18. Referring to Martianus Capella, John says that Mercury is represented as the companion of Philology not so that reverence will be given to false gods but because truths lie under the covering of words. For an overview (with bibliography) of medieval allegorical interpretation, see Stephen L. Wailes, *Medieval Allegories of Jesus' Parables* (Berkeley and Los Angeles: University of California Press, 1987), pp. 9–82. Of theoretical interest is Stephen A. Barney's "Visible Allegory: The *Distinctiones Abel* of Peter the Chanter," in Bloomfield, *Allegory, Myth, and Symbol*, pp. 87–107.

followed the example of the church fathers, especially Augustine and Ambrose, whose methods are inherited through Origen and Philo from the stoic interpreters of Homer. While the Latins, allying themselves with the school of Antioch, claimed to be following the letter rather than condemning it as Origen had done, the very act of isolating the letter and identifying it with narrated events made allegorization inevitable. The phrase "according to the letter" in the title of a work of commentary on Genesis is a guarantee of the most fanciful allegorical speculation. In any event, scruples about the historical truth of Scripture were unnecessary when Christian exegesis was applied to pagan myth, as in the *Ovide moralisé*, where the bull that rapes Europa is Christ.[37]

To understand this elevation of the intellectual status of hermeneutics we must refer to the most general frames of understanding concerning the divine. These could hardly be reasoned about at the time because they constituted not so much objects of thought as the conditions within which thought could take place. If in antiquity the divine impeded the emergence of a fully logocentric view of the world, under Christianity the divine required such a view, reducing the material world to a book, in Hugh of Saint Victor's phrase, written by the finger of God.[38] The concept of the mirror of nature, of the created world as a revelation in things parallel to the Scriptures' revelation in words, is the greatest theme in medieval culture. Its fundamental structure was worked out by Augustine, in the commentaries on Genesis and the treatise on the Trinity. But it was Erigena, commenting on the symbolism of light in the prologue to the Gospel of John, who expressed it most elegantly when he said that the eternal light declares itself in the world in two ways, by the Scriptures and by the creatures ("Dupliciter ergo lux aeterna se ipsam mundo declarat, per Scripturam videlicet et creaturam").[39]

37   For the various forms of the *Ovide moralisé*, see Panofsky, *Renaissance and Renascences*, pp. 78–81.
38   Hugh of Saint Victor, *Didascalion*, in J. P. Migne, *Patrologiae cursus completus, series latina* (Paris, 1844–64), 176:814b. See Henri de Lubac, *Exégèse médiévale: les quatres sens de l'écriture* (Paris: Aubier, 1959), 1:74–75 and 124–25. Cf. 1:121–22, where nature and Scripture are the "two feet of the word" and the two robes, or veils, of Christ.
39   Migne, *Patrologiae cursus completus, series latina*, 122:289c. Erigena goes so far as to identify the four levels of meaning in Scripture with the four elements. See Jean Pépin, *La Tradition de l'allégorie de Philon d'Alexandrie à Dante* (Paris: Études Augustiniennes, 1987), p. 204 n. 25. Pépin's chapter, "La théorie du symbolisme dans la tradition dionysienne," pp. 199–221, shows how a restricted, liturgical concept of the material is broadened by Augustine to include all of nature, such that the created world is an allegory of the Creator. For the expression of this concept in the gothic cathedrals (and the encyclopedic

In the thought-world portrayed in Cicero's treatise on the gods, abstractions cannot be joined in a coherent system so long as each is bound up with an independent, divine power residing within (*vis inest*).[40] Systematic coordination is impossible until that inner power is understood as the rumor not of any proximate divinity but of a singular, transcendent truth. The tendency toward monotheism in Plato, Aristotle, and Plotinus was driven not by a religious but by a philosophical need: to restrict the influence of the divine to a single point, cleansing the system of the uncontrollable power of the sacred, which has gathered in that system's interstices and folds. While the logical expression of this problem concerned itself with how, for example, Justice and Truth, being good, participate in the form of the Good, the drive toward unity was not impeded by logical difficulties alone. The principal obstacle was the psychological effect of polytheism.

Cotta's observation about the Stoics is thus true of classical culture as a whole: it was incapable of mastering plurality, either in religion or in thought. All efforts to achieve systematic unity were frustrated either by a theology that became incontinent when it invaded the realm of thought (*fantastica fornicatio* was Augustine's term for this) or by a thinking that was disrupted by the numinous at every point.[41] Only when we pass from the culture of the numen to the culture of the sign do we encounter appropriate conditions for allegorical expression. For under polytheism the relations among terms in any system of thought, as we saw in Hesiod, were determined genealogically rather than logically. When such thought reached for greater generality, it lost coherence by multiplying gods to fill up the expanding conceptual space; and when such thought focused on a single abstraction, it lost sight of the concept as a concept in the generalized power of the sacred within, as with Claudian's Nature. Under the logocentric conditions of medieval Chris-

---

works that inspired them), see Émile Mâle, *L'art religieux du XIIIe siècle en France: Étude sur l'iconographie du moyen âge et sur ses sources d'inspiration*, 8th ed. (Paris: Armand Colin, 1948), pp. 27–62. See also Brian Stock, *The Implications of Literacy: Written Language and Models of Interpretation in the Eleventh and Twelfth Centuries* (Princeton: Princeton University Press, 1983), p. 320.

40 Cicero, *De natura deorum* 2.23.61–83. On the impossibility of establishing conceptual order in the system of the classical gods, see Augustine's remarkable discussion, in *City of God* 7.5–6, of Varro's vain attempt to obtain for classical theology internal consistency and external unity.

41 Charles Norris Cochrane, *Christianity and Classical Culture: A Study of Thought and Action from Augustus to Augustine* (London: Oxford University Press, 1957), p. 418.

tianity, by contrast, the removal of the divine to a transcendent location, outside the system, guaranteed the articulate coherence of all areas and levels of thought. The result was that ideas could be treated as being at once deeply related to one another and free to exist on their own.

Yet the essential difference between Roman and Christian ideologies is that Rome imagined human life as existence in the world while Christianity imagined human life as existence in time. It was through the dimension of time that Christianity launched its assault on Rome, since time was the empire's only undefended frontier. The world of space over which Rome exerted her power, through roads, armies, and taxes, was thus redefined by Christianity as a tract of time, a *saeculum*.[42] In Roman ideology time is mastered within the space of the world through physical display, representing the past on monumental columns and arches. The Roman triumph, in which towers representing captured cities were carried, is a vindication of civilized space over the disorder of history. In Christian ideology, by contrast, the material world does not attempt to contain history. Instead, the world is enveloped in prophetic time, which progresses toward a city that Augustine, in what would be for a millennium the most influential book outside the Bible, *The City of God Against the Pagans*, explicitly contrasted with Rome. Christianity is the spiritual triumph of time over the civilized space of the world. One is perhaps wrong even to call it a triumph; it is more a procession, from Eden to Apocalypse, which is continually recapitulated in the structure of the Mass and permanently represented in the form of the Bible. The splendid epithet of the Christians as "a shadowy and light-fleeing nation," made by an apologist, Minucius Felix, communicates the uncanniness of the menace they posed to an empire that had confronted all previous opponents in space.[43]

The symbolism of Christian being-in-time is nowhere more powerfully expressed than in the pageant and accompanying political visions in cantos 29 and 32 of the *Purgatorio*, when the pilgrim has entered the Garden of Eden, prefiguring "the Rome whereof Christ is a Roman."[44] It is here, in Eden, that the pilgrim is accorded a vision of history in the form of a procession, led by twenty-four elders representing the books of

42 Ibid., pp. 482–83.
43 Ibid., p. 219.
44 *Purgatorio* 32.102; see also 29.115–17, where the chariot is said to be more splendid than any used in the triumph of an Africanus or an Augustus, more splendid, indeed than the chariot of the sun.

the Old Testament, followed by the four beasts of the gospels enclosing the triumphal car of the church, the two wheels of which represent the active and contemplative life, attended by the four cardinal and the three theological virtues respectively. The car, carrying the veiled Beatrice, is drawn by a griffin, whose double nature indicates that he represents Christ, while the pole by which he is attached to the car represents the cross. The destination of the procession is not, of course, the Capitoline Hill, where the temple of Jupiter stands; but it is the true form of the Capitoline: the tree of the knowledge of good and evil, which in its withered state represents the empire and the principle of righteousness. The griffin, having contemplated the tree and been praised by the others for not tearing fruit from it, attaches the pole to the tree, thus returning the wood of the cross to its origin, whereupon the tree bursts into flower with blooms of imperial purple.[45] In this allegorical vision Dante brings final, conceptual closure to the early Christian translation of imperial space into prophetic time, reconciling them in the Rome of which Christ is a Roman.

As for the classical gods, they lie beyond this culminating vision of the *Purgatorio*, lending their names to the planetary circles of the *Paradiso*. But in being elevated thus, they are cleansed of any independent power, and it is that power with which we are concerned here, not with its luminous, evacuated forms. When the power of the gods was officially driven down into hell, a part of it entered secretly into narrative time, where the gods proved to be as incapable of rebirth as the tree of the empire (being, as Napoleon said of it, neither holy nor Roman) would at length prove incapable of flourishing in the soil of Christian belief. Yet the very decay of the gods was necessary to allegorical meaning, lending the power of corruption to a system that needed a source of disorder if it was to be capable of generating new forms.

Such a system, as it became capable of drawing on and improvising with the power of what it had to repress, acquired something like a consciousness of its own. As we see perhaps most fully in Spenser, the poet and the poem, like the reader and the poem, are engaged in feedback relations that develop the complex characteristics of mind. As Spenser thinks through the constraining dynamics of the unfolding poem, the poem begins thinking through him, using the power of his intelligence to bring its potential for order to light. It seems likely that when allegory

45 *Purgatorio* 32.37–60.

emerged as a literary form and became conscious of itself in this way, as creative work, it recognized the weakness of its absolute claims, together with the impossibility of abandoning those claims. In that moment of recognition allegory relinquished any hope of becoming prophetic and began to improvise instead with the remains of the past. Among those remains classical myth proved to be the most unstable, but also the most imaginatively fertile, of the substances on which allegory seized.

The difficulty of handling the substance of classical myth may be observed in a remarkable passage of *The Faerie Queene*, in which the pagan gods, though confined to hell, have an important role to play in advancing the narrative. From the Christian perspective there were two distinct views of the pagan gods. The first view, which dominated in the Middle Ages, was that the gods are fallen angels or, as Augustine calls them, unclean spirits, who having attracted idolatrous worship to themselves, were confined to hell at the coming of Christ. The second view, which would fully emerge only in the Renaissance, is that the gods are distorted, psychological premonitions of truths that would be seen clearly in the light of revelation. Although the first was the official view of the Church, the second, which took up from the pagans the practice of allegorizing classical myth, was the accommodation Christianity had to make with the imaginative power of the gods. It was the impossibility of deciding between these alternatives which left the gods in a state of decay.

The episode in Spenser to which I refer is the long descent to the underworld in the first book of *The Faerie Queene*.[46] The witch Duessa asks Night to persuade Aesculapius, the god of healing and a son of Apollo, to cure Sans Joy, or *tristitia*, a figure who is akin to Despair and whom we would now call "depression." A son of Aveugle, or "blindness," Sans Joy has been grievously wounded in his combat with Redcross, the knight of holiness. When the episode is thus summarily recounted, the agents involved seem to be purely conceptual in nature, having no existence apart from the train of thought in which they are conjoined. Incurable depression, which is brought about by spiritual blindness, by the failure to accept Christian hope, may be overcome when confronted by faith. But the power of evil will await an opportunity, under cover of night (when faith sleeps), to restore depression to its original state. In

46   *Faerie Queene* 1.5.19–44.

the action of the poem, however, we hardly think of the agents as abstract conceptions that have been merely attached to human forms. They themselves seem to think they are real. And it is in their ability to act as agents, with purpose and forethought, that keeps the narrative open and advances the plot. Yet the divinity of the gods, their numinousness, is also the force with which they continue to resist their fate. Hence Aesculapius's reply to Duessa's request:

> Ah Dame (quoth he) thou temptest me in vaine
>> To dare the thing, which daily yet I rew,
>> And the old cause of my continued paine
>> With like attempt to like end to renew.
>> Is not enough, that thrust from heaven dew
>> Here endlesse penaunce for one fault I pay,
>> But that redoubled crime with vengeance new
>> Thou biddest me to eeke? Can Night defray
> The wrath of thundering *Jove* that rules both night and day?[47]

The noise of resistance, which is heard generally but indistinctly in allegory, bursts forth here in intelligible words, and they are words that remind us of Francesca da Rimini: "Here endlesse penaunce for one fault I pay." The effect Spenser achieves is momentarily to disrupt the order of a system that can only partly convert gods into signs and that can only partly conceal the violence with which it does so. Unlike allegorical interpretation, which can convert the gods peacefully, even routinely, allegory needs this resistance to function. Nor should we overlook the irony, one of the many that gather at the historical rift between Christianity and classical culture, whereby the name of an old god, "thundering *Jove*," is applied to the God who has banished the old gods to hell. To be sure, that the name *Jove* should be used by another damned god makes psychological sense; the poet is keeping decorum, as Milton does when he has the shepherds think of the incarnate Son as "Mighty Pan," Pan being not just one among the gods whom the Son is to drive into hell but the symbol of them all (*pan* in Greek means "all").[48] But this nec-

---

47 Ibid. 1.5.42.
48 John Milton, "Ode on the Morning of Christ's Nativity," l. 89 and note, in Carey, *Complete Shorter Poems*. Milton alludes to the famous story from Plutarch's treatise on the cessation of oracles—an event said to have occurred at the time of Christ—concerning the mysterious cry that the great Pan is dead. On the question whether Pan is to be inter-

essary observation hardly weakens the point—on the contrary, it lends further support to it—that allegory operates above, and draws its energy from, a region of dissimilitude, of otherness, from which order may be won only by forceful intervention.

The violent defeat of Prudentius's Worship of the Ancient Gods is a revelation of what underlies, at various depths, all allegorical expression. But the violence is not, as it is portrayed in the poem, a momentary event. It is a force that must be continuously exerted against continual (that is, repetitive) resistance, when the dead gods twitch. Yet the very resistance of the gods to their allegorization is exploited by the system of an allegory so that it can both develop in narrative time and evolve unexpected patterns of thought. For in the imaginary order that the allegory offers to our belief no thought is truly unexpected and no action really takes place. The order exists in eternity. As a result, the agents in the narrative of an actual allegorical work must draw what power of action they have from something that is below the threshold of what the imaginary order can acknowledge. Hence the very power of a narrative figure to act, a power that is the unsuppressed remnant of allegory's negative other, surrounds the figures in the narrative with a nimbus that seems to rise like a mist from the ground.

preted as Satan or Christ, see E.K.'s gloss to "May," line 54, *The Shepheardes Calendar*, in *The Yale Edition of the Shorter Poems of Edmund Spenser*, ed. William A. Oram et al. (New Haven: Yale University Press, 1989), pp. 99–100.

3

Irony, Allegory, and
Metaphysical Decay

Until Coleridge, the dominant conception of allegory was never far removed from the rhetorical definition standardized by Quintilian: "continued metaphor."[1] It is still a commonplace of handbooks and encyclopedias of literary terms. Quintilian says more about allegory than this, but for subsequent critical theory his presentation of irony as a species of allegory is especially important. Irony is inverted "other speaking": "On the other hand, that class [of allegorical tropes] in which opposites are shown is irony."[2] Because the two claims are incompatible (one cannot, by extending a metaphor, say the opposite of what one means), postclassical theory of allegory tends to leave

---

1 Quintilian, *Institutio oratoria* 8.6.44: "Allegory, which is translated in Latin by *inversio*, either presents one thing in words and another in meaning, or else something absolutely opposed to the meaning of the words. The first type is generally produced by a series of metaphors." Here and in what follows I give the Loeb translation of H. E. Butler. That the second type, which is "opposed to the meaning," is irony is made clear at 8.6.54. The standard discussion of irony and allegory for the Middle Ages is in Isidore of Seville, *Etymologiarum sive originum*, ed. W. M. Lindsay (Oxford: Clarendon Press, 1911), 1:37.22–26. He says that allegory is *alieniloquium*, "other speaking," and irony, as a species of allegory, is a kind of discourse that indicates an opposite meaning by its tone. The attribution of a voiced marker allows Isidore to distinguish irony from antiphrasis.

2 *Institutio oratoria* 8.6.54. A logical problem is raised at 8.6.58: allegory is not a genus because it retains an attribute, obscurity, that is proper to itself; allegory must therefore be a species alongside irony and not a class containing irony as one of its elements. I do not recall ever seeing it noted that the canonical definition of allegory as "continued metaphor," at 9.2.46, occurs as an aside in a discussion of irony.

irony off to one side. Quintilian elsewhere states that irony can manifest itself either in the realm of figures or in that of tropes, and that figurative irony can have nothing to do with tropes such as metaphor and its extended form, allegory. Even for him there are species of irony that appear to escape enclosure by allegory, although their escape is equivocal.

The first of these escapees "derives its name from negation" and is called *antiphrasis*, "opposite speaking."[3] Quintilian's uncertainty as to the inclusion of irony in allegory turns on whether antiphrasis, as absolute opposition, is a sport of irony or its radical essence. If antiphrasis is irony's essence, then all moods of irony, from affectionate teasing to *saeva indignatio*, must threaten the very existence of what allegory has to affirm: the logocentric coherence of its meanings, grounded in the material unity of its signs—in a word, polysemy. A polysemous sign can mean different things in different contexts because all such signs are supposed to belong to one truth toward which they collectively tend. Nothing in an allegory is absolutely opposed to anything else. Antiphrasis and polysemy are as incompatible as are the relations of the different to the same and the part to the whole. But they approach chaos, and rise out of it, along similar roads.

We might wish to know if they meet somewhere before the gates of this chaos—chaos, in Nietzschean terms, as that to which knowing as schematizing responds[4]—or if there is a barrier between them until they arrive, preventing them from forming an integral system. In either case we are concerned with the primal scene of their encounter on the brink of disorder, inasmuch as that scene is one in which a structure of some kind is imposed on wild juxtaposition, unrestrained analogy, violent struggle, and noise. The scene is not so much ordered itself, however, as it is made the preliminary condition for order, like a *chora*, the place in which forms are received, or an underlying substance, on which forms are impressed. But unlike these the scene is neither homogeneous nor metaphorically female. It is instead a scene of conflict between inimical formulations of chaos, each of which is constrained just enough to become engaged with the other. Total substitutability is constrained just

---

3 Ibid. 9.2.47. "There are, however, certain kinds of this figure [irony] which have no connexion with tropes. In the first place, there is the figure which derives its name from negation and is called by some *antiphrasis*."
4 Martin Heidegger, *Nietzsche*, ed. David Farrell Krell, trans. Joan Stambaugh, David Farrell Krell, and Frank A. Capuzzi (San Francisco: HarperCollins, 1991), 3:74 and 84. A definition of *chaos* similar to the more recent, informational concept, *noise*.

enough to become polysemy, and total noncoincidence is constrained just enough to become antiphrasis, such that the two form a net or a grid, each alternately passing under the other to assert itself as the more fundamental. Polysemy will try to make antiphrasis appear to be nothing more than a witty affirmation of the sameness that is hidden in difference. Antiphrasis will try to cut every synecdochical relation within polysemy, forcing elements that were once arranged hierarchically to stand apart as opposite terms. The tangled encounter of polysemy and antiphrasis may be represented by the much-allegorized, but originally ironic, myth of the adulterous Venus and Mars struggling in the net in which they have been caught, at once copulating and striving to break free.[5] The image may serve for the moment as an emblem of the turbulent substratum from which allegory raises its forms. Chief among these are the allegorized gods.

In attempting to penetrate the veil that is made by those forms one may use polysemy to interpret, as the conventions of allegory prompt one to do, supposing one will arrive in the full presence of meaning. Or one may ironize and demystify, using antiphrasis as a kind of abrasive to remove the allegorized gods, who have, as it were, congealed on the surface of chaos. Of course one cannot really *use* irony: it is not so much an implement as an ethical state. One can *be* ironic, like Socrates, or a little like him. But when irony is implemented by markers—changes of expression and tone, or the marginal notation *ironice*—it spoils. It might be asserted that the abrasive of irony, or one's own abrasively ironic state, is all that is left when the allegorized gods have been scraped down to noise. But one would first have to explore the possibility that a residue is left by this irony and that it is what one would least expect it to be: a historical event.

To speak of this event as a substance means that beneath the visible events of literary history there is a slower process (optimistically referred to as a tradition) for which I shall have to justify the term "metaphysical decay." For the moment this event can only be described as emerging from late ancient, syncretistic polytheism, articulating itself to the world as medieval polysemy, and concluding in Enlightenment psychologism, where allegory is a species of "wit," in Addison's (Lockean) sense of the word.[6] It might therefore be asked if the event, having gone through

5 Félix Buffière, *Les mythes d'Homère et la pensée grecque* (Paris: Belles Lettres, 1956), pp. 168–72.
6 Joseph Addison, *The Spectator*, ed. Donald F. Bond (Oxford: Clarendon Press, 1965), 1:263–64 (no. 62), citing Locke on the difference between judgment and wit. For an alle-

these phases, resolves itself in antiphrasis and then generates the symbol to compensate for the loss of numinous power conferred by the allegorized gods. Or is the symbol, like the chaste Ägytha's womb, all that is left of a body that has rotted away?[7]

We may begin to understand the ambiguity of the relationship of irony to allegory in ancient rhetoric by bringing to light a grammatical metaphor that organizes both from below. The deviation of allegory from its "proper" sense is comparable to the declension of nouns from the nominative or "upright" case. Allegory may be thought of as leaning away at various oblique angles from soldierly directness, where what is said and what is meant coincide. When the discourse bends around to the point where it can only turn upward again, it is no longer just deviating from but opposing uprightness. This is the position of irony, the tropological nadir. Anything posited here is posited as absolute negation.

The last statement belongs to (and itself possesses) Paul de Man, in his lecture "The Concept of Irony."[8] De Man is aware of the irony of this even as he warns us away from the thought that anyone, least of all the ironist, could have irony under control. The warning may itself be ironic (he warns of this too), at once affirming and negating the truth of the discourse in which it appears and for which it speaks. In de Man's account, however, it is precisely this excessiveness with regard to all systems (beginning with the one that posits a subject) which makes irony capable of generating any system that could possibly obtain among the less rigorously oppositional tropes; for irony is not a trope. We need not here go into the intricacies of de Man's argument, which involve an account of the genesis of synthetic and analytic determinations from oppositional positing and of the emergence of the entire system of tropes from that process. It is enough to say that the power of the argument lies in its inversion of the classical account, whereby tropology deviates from

---

gory by Addison of false, mixed, and true wit, see *Spectator*, no. 63. For allegory as "unsubstantial," and a "picture-language" that works according to "mechanical understanding," see Coleridge, *The Statesman's Manual*, in *Lay Sermons*, ed. R. J. White, vol. 6 in *The Collected Works of Samuel Taylor Coleridge* (London: Routledge and Kegan Paul, 1972), p. 30.
7   For Ägytha's womb, see Walter Benjamin, *The Origin of German Tragic Drama*, trans. John Osborne (London: Verso, 1985), p. 217. See also Nicholas Halmi, "An Anthropological Approach to the Romantic Symbol," *European Romantic Review* 4 (1993): 13–33.
8   Paul de Man, "The Concept of Irony," in *Aesthetic Ideology*, ed. Andrzej Warminski (forthcoming). See also Robert Moynihan's "Interview with Paul de Man," in *Yale Review* 73 (Summer 1984): 576–602.

upright, ego-centered, nominative, straightforward speaking. Speaking *against* now comes before, and enables, speaking *other.*

In the classical model of tropology as declension, it is possible to imagine getting back, by interpretive correction, to the upright position of an executive self, one that both intends a meaning, and deflects it tropologically, in a language it uses instrumentally. Irony overturns this account because it speaks not from the inclined position of a trope but from an opposed position, where the continuity of the circle is broken: "I" and "not I." Every ironic statement says both these things and says that it says them. (Samuel Beckett's play *Not I* is the purest expression of sustained dramatic irony.) Out of the rift opened by irony every possibility of figurative expression emerges.

In developing this argument de Man gives an account of how Friedrich Schlegel's theory of irony derives from Fichte's analysis of the subject, the "I," as the nondialectical positing of opposite terms. This radical element in Schlegel's theory aroused considerable irritation in some considerable figures, among them Hegel and Kierkegaard (that is not, as de Man says, "n'importe qui"). But the force of this radicalism does not derive merely from the problem of interpreting irony. It needs no Schlegel come back from the grave to tell us that a person, a voice, or a discourse can never again be reliably straightforward after once having been ironic. What Schlegel has come back to tell us—and it is a secret de Man claims (but with how much irony?) the entire academic discipline of *Germanistik* is devoted to hiding—is that irony is unlimited in its scope; everything we say, and perhaps everything we are, is but a temporary escape from its field, which opens beneath all possibilities of figurative language. Allegory is now a species of irony rather than the other way around. Irony devours its host from within.

An anxiety similar to that caused by Schlegel underlies the reluctance of postclassical literary theory to include, as Quintilian does, irony in allegory. Thus Puttenham, otherwise Quintilian's spaniel, departs from him here: "Allegoria is when we do speak in sense translative and wrested from the owne signification, *nevertheless not altogether contrary* but having much conveniencie with it" (my emphasis).[9] The reluctance to make irony a species of allegory clearly has much to do with irony's not requiring metaphor. But the deeper objection to including in allegory that

9   George Puttenham, *The Arte of English Poesie* (1589), ed. Gladys Doidge Willcock and Alice Walker (Cambridge: Cambridge University Press, 1936), 3:18.

which is "altogether contrary" to it is irony's resistance to interpretation. Objectively, there is nothing there to interpret. In the classical account of allegory the reader interprets by recognizing all points of correspondence in an overriding, objective "conveniencie," as when the state is recognized in the description of a ship heading into rough seas (Quintilian's example from Horace).[10] Postclassical theory of allegory likewise assumes that figurative obliquity is merely rhetorical and can at any moment be corrected. Thus Isidore of Seville defines *figure* as "a fault that occurs with reason."[11] But by Puttenham's time it was recognized that any effort to stabilize a theory of allegory that includes irony would be undermined by irony's corrosively oppositional power, a power that lies, as Kierkegaard says, in "infinite, absolute negativity."[12] Better to keep it outside.

The postclassical exclusion of irony from allegory made it possible to defer at some length the conceptualization of allegory as a mechanical exercise in wit. In other words, the practice of allegory from late antiquity to the Enlightenment was made possible by suppressing antiphrasis in favor of polysemy, drawing the grid inward so that it would look like a perspectival regress to an origin that remains out of sight. As a result, the temporality of reading was experienced in the subject as movement within what Coleridge, speaking of *The Faerie Queene*, calls "mental space."[13] But the resonance one hears as one moves in that continuum is given off not by polysemy alone but by polysemy in its struggle with antiphrasis, a struggle from which is produced a sense of the sacred within: "There are many mysteries contained in poetry," Sidney confides, "which of purpose were written darkly, lest by profane wits it should be abused."[14] It is hardly news that this assumption supports allegorical expression from

10   *Institutio oratoria* 8.6.44. See Eduard Fraenkel, *Horace* (Oxford: Clarendon Press, 1957), pp. 154–56.
11   Isidore of Seville, *Etymologiarum* 1.35.71; cited in A. J. Minnis and A. B. Scott, *Medieval Literary Theory and Criticism, c. 1100–c. 1375: The Commentary Tradition* (Oxford: Clarendon Press, 1988), p. 133.
12   Søren Kierkegaard, *The Concept of Irony, with Continual Reference to Socrates*, ed. and trans. Howard V. Hong and Edna H. Hong (Princeton: Princeton University Press, 1989), p. 26.
13   Coleridge, *Lectures, 1808–1819, on Literature*, ed. R. A. Foakes, vol. 5 (in two parts) of *The Collected Works of Samuel Taylor Coleridge* (Princeton: Princeton University Press, 1987), 2:409–10.
14   Philip Sidney, *The Defense of Poesie*, in *Miscellaneous Prose*, ed. Katharine Duncan-Jones and Jan van Dorsten (Oxford: Clarendon Press, 1973), p. 121.

late antiquity to the Enlightenment. The point is that the assumption of mystery is no less arbitrary than irony is in supposing there to be a subject thinking below (*hyponoia*) an impenetrable discourse. But the character of this imagined intelligence differs in each: in irony it is hostile but evasive, in allegory benign but reclusive. The intelligence behind ironic discourse splits into bafflingly opposite terms whenever we try to locate it, leaving behind the sense that we are being fixed in the gaze of an aggressively mobile attention. But the intelligence behind the veil of allegory is always withdrawing to more remote ground, leaving behind the sense that our aggressive attention has failed to grasp what is there.

Now these effects are opposite in character to what irony and allegory actually do. In the political realm it is irony that fails to wound, for it can be simply ignored, or taken literally, by those at whom it is directed, as the East German government, having declared its loss of confidence in the people, could ignore—or take literally—Brecht's suggestion that it dismiss the people and elect another.[15] Allegory, however, notwithstanding the contemplative air it assumes, is as aggressively seductive as propaganda, drawing its readers onward into deeper ideological commitments. It makes a show of including all dissent, all negation, in one hidden and ineffable truth. But the secret of those mysteries to which Sidney refers is that they descend into chaos, not into truth. The veiled threat of such chaos underlies and sustains allegorical expression throughout its history, creating the sense in each work of an immanent mind working within, of a luminousness in obscurity that Spenser, in the "Letter to Raleigh," calls "darke conceit." The history of allegory, from antiquity to the Enlightenment, is impelled by the suppression of irony and the haunting of noise.

The constitution of such a history is the main point of contact between allegory and psychoanalysis, which must likewise resort to "histories" made possible by the suppression of irony and the haunting of noise. Like Aristotelian matter, the unconscious, as pure potency, can never be seen in itself, though it is the place where the forms of consciousness, drawing a veil over what lies below, come into being. If allegorical interpretation makes a difference distinct from that made by psychoanalysis (and how distinct is a real question), it is like its modern successor in one important respect. Allegory breaks down the wall of division between

---

15 Bertolt Brecht, "Die Lösung" ("The Solution"), in *Gedichte 3*, ed. Elisabeth Hauptmann and Rosemarie Hill, vol. 10 of *Gesammelte Werke* (Frankfurt am Main: Suhrkamp, 1967), pp. 1009-10.

the mind of the reader and the mind that appears to think in the text as the two are engaged in a circuit. The other that thinks in the text must think through the reader that is thinking through it, just as the unconscious can make its thought known only in the consciousness by which it is probed. The concept of the unconscious, where, as Freud stressed, opposites are identities, is organized antiphrastically as a positive subject that is forever negating itself in vertiginous exchange with an other. It is always saying "I" and "Not I." By suppressing the absoluteness of that opposition psychoanalytic theory can develop a polysemous order among the most widely diverse elements to appear in the unconscious. Therein lies much of the drama, the astonishing revelation of the large in the small, that we experience when we read Freud.

I observed earlier that for allegory the ground on which heterogeneous elements are united is woven together as the grid of antiphrasis and polysemy, each being inimical to and bound up with the other. Allegory cannot emerge there without a logocentric regrounding by which polysemy is made the more fundamental. A historical indication that this has occurred is the postclassical exclusion of irony from allegory. The grid is drawn inward toward a center like the vanishing point in linear perspective—or, to use a modern cosmological term, the singularity. Considered formally, a singularity is an irrational point outside a system on which the possibility of ordered relations inside the system is based. Once that irrational ground is established, all relations can be understood as parts of a whole.

This whole will always, however, be liable to disruption by the antiphrastic dynamic it has tried to exclude and partly suppressed. But the underlying noise is interpreted, according to the conventions of the form, as the resonance of truth. Such is the interpretation of nature which Baudelaire invokes in "Correspondances" when he speaks of all things responding to one another remotely, like echoes that, when heard from a distance, become lost in one another, in an obscure and profound unity: "Comme de longs échos qui de loin se confondent / Dans une ténébreuse et profonde unité."[16] In a system of this kind every determination of meaning is rendered unstable by virtue of its almost limitless correspondences with other, potential determinations. These are limited only at the limit, by the arbitrary configuration of the system as a totality. The instability that antiphrasis introduces throughout cannot be

16 Charles Baudelaire, *The Flowers of Evil*, ed. and trans. James McGowan (New York: Oxford University Press, 1993), p. 18.

overcome by any operation that is logically secure—the system can never be made clean—but only by the continual interpretation of noise as the resonance of truth. Such an act of interpretation is what de Man, speaking of the genesis of the tropes, calls the performative. Interpretation performatively makes what it then claims to be its justifying ground, "une ténébreuse et profonde unité."

The claim that antiphrastic irony has the power to generate the tropes may seem unpersuasive, at least in the compressed form in which it is offered by de Man. We need some mechanism to get from the moment of contradiction to the tropological unfolding of determinative statements. I return to this point later on, which I raise here only to indicate that polysemy and antiphrasis establish incompatible but parallel relations with disorder, the one working by analogy, the other by absolute (that is, nondialectical) negation. If disorder is understood as unrestricted analogy (what I referred to earlier as "total substitutability"), anything can be made to mean anything else; such was the state of crisis reached by allegory, according to Benjamin, in the seventeenth century.[17] Polysemy, mobilizing a theory of correspondences, is the most direct means of production out of that state, as antiphrasis is the most direct means of egress from total noncoincidence. Antiphrasis imposes on disorder a rudimentary, nondialectical order of the different and the same: "I" and "Not I." Polysemy draws out of the fund of disorder arbitrary juxtapositions that look like the relations of parts to a whole. For the passersby of the Baudelaire sonnet, these relations evoke correspondences in a "forest" (a word intended to evoke its esoteric sense as substance, *silva*) of symbols that gaze back at one familiarly as if they had minds of their own: "L'homme y passe à travers des forêts de symboles / Qui l'observent avec des regards familiers." A multitude of dialectically negative associations ("Not I") is evolved for the purpose of extending the self through an alien text or, as in the Baudelaire sonnet, through an alien but textualized (and hence familiar) nature: I, but also my other, my id, which must ultimately lead back to me.

It is this circulation of the self through the nonself that generates the hidden thoughts, the "undermeanings," apparently concealed in an allegorical text. Polysemy is only a more hermeneutically active form of this primitive sense of the text as a subject. Instead of treating the "Not I" as an indeterminate void, polysemy finds in it another subject that can

17 Benjamin, *Origin of German Tragic Drama*, pp. 174–75, 189–90, and 231–32.

be engaged in a manner that progresses or ascends. In this way allegory generates intelligible statements out of disorder and acquires the mental characteristics of any system with multiple feedback loops. The longer a text understood to be polysemous is interpretively engaged, the more it will seem to have a mind of its own capable of explicating anything introduced into its structures (*exegesis* being always a function of *eisegesis*, or "input"). The text seems to contain under its surface not just a meaning but a reasoning power, a logos, which when carried to its limit is the logos that upholds the world.

The system in which polysemy establishes itself as more fundamental than antiphrasis was largely dispelled in the Enlightenment, with the result that allegory was pushed to its extremes in apocalyptic vision and satire. The entire intermediate realm of analogies and correspondences, the "forest" through which allegorical narratives pass, no longer existed. In its place was established an ideal of noiseless communication between minds that are perfectly detached from the channel between them. The more obvious historical consequences were that allegory lost much of its complexity and independence as a narrative form, that the theory of allegory was reoriented from the cosmic mysticism of the Renaissance to the classical model of angular speaking, and that the models of allegory that were thought to be most worthy of imitation were late antique descriptions of allegorical pictures, as in Lucian's "Calumny of Apelles" and the anonymous *Tablet of Cebes*. The absurdities remarked in Spenser by eighteenth-century critics would have been understood by him not as breaking the rules but as breaking through familiar patterns of thought to deeper and more difficult thought. So completely was this probing of noise rejected by Enlightenment theorists, who were under the influence of Lockean psychology, that the power of allegorical works to generate meaning from an underlying disorder was taken away. The disorder became nothing more than the proclivity of ideas to associate randomly and was regarded as absolute error. As interpretation was supplanted by judgment, polysemy was untangled and forced into two levels, the figurative and the figured, each coherent in itself and distinct from the other.

The thing that defers until the Enlightenment the reduction of allegory to a species of wit is designated by words such as *numinousness, resonance, mystery,* and *vision*. Although such terms are inadequate to what this thing is, they have a function to perform on its behalf, or rather on behalf of our enlightened understanding. As expressions of the promise that what lies beneath visible signs is something other than mere noise, they can be accommodated to the methods and aims of poetics. Although such an accommodation is indispensable to understanding how an allegory works, it can contribute little to what is undertaken here: a more radical questioning of what the essence, or ground, of the numinous is. Nor is the frame of cultural anthropology more useful than that of poetics. Both these technical discourses must exclude from the outset any questioning of what the numinous is. The numinous is simply denied—demystified—so that it may be reestablished as a conventional (poetics) or a cultural (anthropology) function: the singularity, or the totemic identity of a clan with its ancestral wolf. The ground of the numinous is at once historical, inasmuch as it changes, and metaphysical, inasmuch as it concerns what is not supposed to be subject to change: the divine. But it is just one event unfolding—and opening the time into which it unfolds—from antiquity to the Enlightenment. In it is imprinted the succession of events we call literary and cultural history.[18]

"Succession of events" is a drastic simplification. It may be more responsible to speak of locally autonomous arrays complicating and diversifying themselves over time: for example, the development of erotic allegorical poetry in France from Raoul de Houdenc to Jean de Meun or of typological iconography from the Abbey of Saint Denis to Chartres and Reims. But what all allegorical works in such arrays have in common is their rootedness in an event we participate in when we sense an immanent mind withholding something more. I said that this strange presence cannot be explained away as a technical requirement of the genre or as a cultural function. To account for it in such terms—to call it, for example, the singularity, or the logos of the culture of the sign—is to skip over the otherness of what one wants to explain in order to enlist it in the task of explaining. It is to bring the object around to our side for use, making it an implement in order to avoid contemplating its strangeness. We attend to something else, and when it too becomes strange we skip over that strangeness by bringing the new object (that which is "thrown against" consciousness) around. It is hard to do otherwise than to engage in this continual appropriation of the other to the self, enlisting it in the task of explaining a new other that will immediately rise into view; and the process can continue, having nothing within to resist it, until every-

18 See Paul de Man, "The Rhetoric of Temporality," in *Blindness and Insight: Essays in the Rhetoric of Contemporary Criticism*, 2d ed. (Minneapolis: University of Minnesota Press, 1983), p. 226.

thing has been taken into the subject that knows. This is the procedure of allegory itself in its striving to identify the subject, as a microcosm, with the objective world. But the otherness of everything that is known in this way has been skipped over at the moment of inclusion, so that the mystery of the world has been reproduced inside a self (the microcosm) that no longer knows how it differs from the world.

The only alternative to this voracious procedure of knowing is to let the thing stay where it is, in the strangeness that comes of its being an event that is opening its own time. This brings us to the main point of difference between irony and allegory. The event of withholding, of immanent mind, or, as I shall call it, of metaphysical decay, becomes the historical ground of allegorical expression in a way that cannot happen with irony because irony, as an ethical state, is never placed before the self as an other, ready to be left where it is or brought around for use as an implement. Having no history, irony is totally confined to the subject. What power does it then have?

Irony can disrupt anything, since there is nothing into which its disintegrative force cannot reach and nothing above which its scorn cannot rise. But it can do so only where everything it attacks is gathered before it in the realm of the subject. As Schlegel says in one of his literary aphorisms, even with the help of the most open explanation, irony remains a riddle to anyone who does not already inhabit it as an ethical state: "Wer sie nicht hat, dem bleibt sie auch nach dem offensten Geständnis ein Rätzel."[19] This is not altogether to its advantage. If irony seems impregnable in itself, it is helpless before brutal, deliberately uncomprehending power, "error, madness, and stupidity." As de Man says in "The Concept of Irony," what Schlegel is referring to in these words may be taken in the most extreme sense as the absolute disorder out of which world is raised by understanding: "Und ist sie selbst diese unendliche Welt nicht durch den Verstand aus der Unverständlichkeit oder dem Chaos gebildet?" [Is not this entire infinite world built out of nonunderstanding, out of chaos, by means of understanding?][20] The noise of the event must be skipped

19 Friedrich Schlegel, in *Charakteristiken und Kritiken 1 (1796–1801)*, vol. 2 of *Kritische Friedrich-Schlegel-Ausgabe*, ed. Hans Eichner (Munich: Schöningh, 1967), p. 160. See also Schlegel, *"Lucinda" and the Fragments*, trans. Peter Firchow (Minneapolis: University of Minnesota Press, 1971), p. 155.
20 Schlegel, *Characteristiken*, p. 370; trans. de Man, in "The Concept of Irony." See also Schlegel, *"Lucinde,"* p. 268. "Error, madness, and simpleminded stupidity" is de Man's rendering of a passage in Schlegel's *Gespräch über die Poesie*, in *Charakteristiken*, p. 319. Schlegel describes how the aesthetic system, woven together by strands of enthusiasm and

over by the understanding, which brings around to its side what it now understands instrumentally: "by means of understanding." One cannot, after all, understand the event in itself as the substance or ground of allegorical expression, for even these terms are implements. One has to leave it there in its uselessness and try to bear witness to what occurs on its scene.

De Man mobilizes these passages from Schlegel in his assault on the efforts of Schlegel's interpreters, including Kierkegaard, to understand the event as a substance, "to invoke history as hypostasis as a means of defense against this irony." In other words, he is criticizing any attempt to make the synecdochical order of narrative more fundamental than irony, such that history would underlie irony's disarticulating power. De Man is obviously right: there can be no objective defense against a weapon that is purely subjective. It is therefore strange that in the next sentence—the penultimate one of the essay—he says that "irony and history seem to be curiously linked to one another," when this linkage can be nothing more than the ability of the one to break any link in the other. Irony and history are curiously unlinked.

Allegory, however, unlike irony, is linked to history through its relation to metaphysical decay. Polysemy is the interpretive resonance of this decay, whereby the independence of metaphysical beings is broken down by their absorption into the universal order, or frame, of correspondences. This frame is not only evoked in the mind but activated in it by narrative. While individual elements of the narrative stimulate associations with their manifold correspondents outside it, the temporality of the narrative yields the frame up to the substance of history. What is already a decayed theology is thus exposed to further decay, until it is little more than a background for narratives of coming to be and passing away in human affairs. The decay is accelerated as allegory becomes increasingly subject to the logical weakness of universal analogy, to the point where anything can be a sign of anything else. Early modern realist fiction, the fiction of Thomas Nashe and especially of Thomas Deloney, emerges as a response to this threat, forcing polysemy into the distant background, where it is registered as a feeling for historical change against which the

---

irony, must allow its origin in contradiction to shine through at all points. For Freud's remark on the uninterpretable "navel" of an otherwise interpretable dream, "the spot where it reaches down into the unknown," see *The Interpretation of Dreams*, in *The Standard Edition of the Complete Psychological Works of Sigmund Freud*, ed. and trans. James Strachey (London: Hogarth Press, 1953-74), 5:525.

struggles of the individual are thrown into relief. The protagonist in such works is an economic individual, negotiating cleverly within a larger system, a social environment, rather than standing as a model of the world. When the protagonist is an economic agent we no longer feel, as we do in allegory, as if everything encountered in the narrative is inside him.

The passing away of allegory's claims to logical order calls forth some of Benjamin's most morbidly lyrical reflections on history and impels allegory to what he describes as its moment of dialectical transcendence and historical crisis.[21] What is coming to be in the midst of this passing away is not the symbol but the consciousness of history.

In the most critical stage of its alienation from nature, in the seventeenth century, allegory reduced everything in the material realm to a substance. In this way it augmented its power to lay hold of the temporal, objectifying its forms as belonging to history rather than to the realm of ideas. Although narratives such as Benjamin's, being polysemous in the extreme, will always be vulnerable to ironic disarticulation in the realm of the subject, no amount of irony can stop their blindly aggregative work in the realm of the object, where ideological delusion, madness, and stupidity ("Wer sie nicht hat . . .") reign. The basis of allegory in this realm has become a theory of history in which persons are reduced to an indifferent substance—the masses—in which abstractions (tendencies, classes, forces) inhere. And yet it is precisely this substance, as matter, that has become the referent of the system as a whole. As such, the substance that lies beneath allegorical works belongs originally above them, in the realm of metaphysics, of objects par excellence.

To be concerned with metaphysics in late antiquity is to be concerned with the gods, though in the quasi-philosophical light with which they were invested at a time when belief in them was in an advanced stage of decay. Moral, physical, and philosophical interpretation of the gods goes back at least to the sixth century B.C. But it is no accident that the gods could be involved in allegorical expression only in a culture that was linguistically alien to the culture in which they arose. The Homeric *theomachia*, or "battle of the gods," was allegorized from an early date but did not become a means to allegorical expression until Prudentius's *Psychomachia*. The gods were allegorized in Greek but became allegorical only in Latin.

When Aristotle divides theoretical knowledge into three kinds, physi-

---

21   Benjamin, *Origin of German Tragic Drama*, pp. 166 and 232.

cal, mathematical, and metaphysical, the word he uses for this last is "theological," the knowledge of things that have both independent being and freedom from change.[22] By late antiquity theology and metaphysics had become indistinguishable: people could interpret the gods and offer prayers to the "inconceivable idea" of the sun. This phrase is from Wallace Stevens's *Notes toward a Supreme Fiction,* the first section of which lucidly evokes the epistemological weather of late antiquity. It does this by showing metaphysical decay as an event:

> The death of one god is the death of all.
> Let purple Phoebus lie in umber harvest,
> Let Phoebus slumber and die in autumn umber,
>
> Phoebus is dead, ephebe. But Phoebus was
> A name for something that never could be named.
> There was a project for the sun and is.
>
> There is a project for the sun. The sun
> Must bear no name, gold-flourisher, but be
> In the difficulty of what it is to be.

It may be asked how this death is historically determined "to be" an event or, as Stevens calls it, a "project."[23]

Given its psychological structure, the event does not submit readily to an objective construction; we can know it only, as Vico would say, from the inside. Its truth depends not on its being an adequate reflection of something outside it but on its emergence, as a performative, from cultural work. In a more narrowly technical sense (as something one brings around in order to know something else) the event can be seen anthropologically as a process of displacement having a real influence on a world organized by patterns of cultural exchange.[24] In areas of social practice determined by this anthropological perspective—law, education, religious worship, and trade—the impact of the event may be even more evident than it is in the arts. Its manifestation in poetic

22 Aristotle, *Metaphysics* 1026a15 and 1064b3.
23 Wallace Stevens, *Notes toward a Supreme Fiction,* in *The Collected Poems of Wallace Stevens* (New York: Knopf, 1980), p. 381.
24 See Clifford Geertz, *The Interpretation of Cultures* (New York: Basic Books, 1973), pp. 142–69.

practice, however, is not just exemplary but constitutive of these other realms and demands to be spoken of first in imaginative terms. Only in this way can we witness what occurs on its scene without bringing it around to explain something else. The cause of the resonance in allegorical forms is metaphysical decay. It is this that gives a sort of galvanic liveliness to the personified virtues and vices, to the personified arts, and to the personified stages of love.[25] Metaphorical language derived from the body—survival, development, rebirth, transformation, decay—cannot be avoided when we are speaking of cultural change. The point is to avoid the premature reduction of such language to the narrower categories of social description, brilliantly evoked as they are by Coleridge.[26] It is therefore imperative for me to state that by "metaphysical decay" in late antiquity I do not mean the suppression of pagan forms of worship or the growing sense of the futility of classical idealism. Momentous as these events were, they followed from and were made possible by the event I am speaking of here: the rotting of the classical gods.

The fate of the classical gods was thus not so much that which Jean Seznec described as their "survival" in various alienated forms, such as Arab astronomy, as it was a moribund bearing up from below of visible cultural forms, even those with which the gods had nothing to do iconographically.[27] As they decomposed into their elements— cultic, etiological, theurgic, physiological, euhemeristic, iconographic, cosmic—the gods continued to give off from below, mixed with the smell of decay, an aroma of Olympian ozone that communicated danger. That is why, when their classical forms were literally raised up out of the earth, it could seem, in Pater's words, "as if an ancient plague-pit had been opened."[28] Boccaccio found the gods in much this condition when, as he says in the preface to his *Genealogy of the Ancient Gods*, he gathered them up like the scattered remains of a shipwreck. The decay of the classical

25 See Angus Fletcher, *Allegory: The Theory of a Symbolic Mode* (Ithaca: Cornell University Press, 1964), p. 41.

26 Coleridge, *Notebooks*, ed. Kathleen Coburn (New York: Pantheon, 1961), 2:3203.

27 Jean Seznec, *The Survival of the Pagan Gods: The Mythological Tradition and Its Place in Renaissance Humanism and Art*, trans. Barbara Sessions (1953; reprint, Princeton: Princeton University Press, 1972); and Benjamin, *Origin of German Tragic Drama*, p. 226.

28 Walter Pater, "Winckelmann," in *Selected Works*, ed. Richard Aldington (New York: Duell, Sloan & Pearce, 1948), p. 121. Gawin Douglas speaks of how his task of translating the *Aeneid* may be regarded as a dangerous opening of the grave of the classical gods. See *The Aeneid of Virgil, translated into Scottish Verse by Gawin Douglas, Bishop of Dunkeld* (1839; reprint, New York: AMS, 1971), 2:907, ll. 5-10.

gods was registered anthropologically in the process of symbolic muta-
tion by which a new, more authoritative structure of symbols emerged
to capture what was left of the old. America is haunted by names that
the aboriginal peoples have given its places, and the old names are preserved because they seem to have a numinous connection to what those
places are metaphysically: a vast cultural body, now in an advanced stage
of decay. I suggest that a similar but more extensive and layered process,
lacking the suddenness of conquest and genocide, took place in early
Christian Europe, and that its cultural effects were felt through a period
coextensive with the trajectory of allegory as the most authoritative literary form.

In a poetics of allegory, where these historical processes are contained
by a system, the decay of the classical gods is concealed in the numinous effects of the singularity, the vanishing point into which the grid of
antiphrasis and polysemy is drawn. As a fiction of the presence in which
polysemy is absolute, the singularity is at the opposite discursive extreme
from the abyss of antiphrasis, but it is no less chaotic and no less productive. Indeed, the way in which the singularity could be productive is
much clearer, at least on the level of poetics, because there is a positive
mechanism for it: interpretation. Interpretation imposes constraints on
disorder.

Although interpretation is in theory unlimited, it is typically guided in
allegorical works toward an apocalyptic conclusion. Vision moving inward toward the goal of total identification is at the opposite discursive
extreme to the antiphrastic structure of irony, where it seems as if language is being torn into fragments. These extremes are precisely marked
in Dante. Language descends into incoherence in the *Inferno* and falls
away into silence at the end of the *Paradiso*. The typical elements of an
allegorical work—personifications as agents in a landscape of significant
forms—unfold between these extremes, which are the radicals of polysemy and antiphrasis. This is the structure to which any poetics of allegory must address itself; and its radicals cannot be treated as aberrations
to be chastised as faults, as was done in the Enlightenment. For irony
itself is presented in allegory as if it were recuperable to a single intention, even in the dismembering, or sparagmatic rhetoric of Swift's *Tale of
a Tub*, which is always saying "I" and "Not I." But to appear to recuperate
irony in this way, including it in the polysemous work of the whole, is not
to dispel the abyss that it opens; it is to conceal such a prospect in a mys-

tical embrace that is no less chaotic than its opposite bodily expression, tearing apart. The singularity is a different interpretation of the chaos into which irony leads—a rhetorical spin given to antiphrasis to make it look like its opposite. This means that there is, after all, a mechanism within poetics for the generation of the tropes out of antiphrasis as well as out of polysemy. But the mechanism is simply an act of persuasion— the persuasive transference of nondialectical opposition into the logically alien field of the synecdochical, where elements belong to one another as parts of a whole. Just as metaphor may provoke one to assume a more primitive ground in synecdoche, such that lion and hero may be thought to be mystical parts of a whole, so antiphrasis may be assimilated by the logocentric imagination as a more radically articulated, more recondite expression of polysemy, as when, for example, Dionysius the Areopagite finds only the most monstrous forms suitable to represent God.[29]

When this assimilation of antiphrasis to polysemy is accomplished— or, rather, performed—the starkest contrasts can be mobilized in a narrative allegory, even a narrative such as Hegel's. The opposition of the one and the many is itself persuaded, so to speak, to generate a narrative out of one ironic moment and an order of symbols out of an undifferentiated chaos, a forest. As George Chapman puts it: "One no number is; but thence doth flow / The powerful race of number."[30] The singularity, like the assimilation of antiphrasis, is an act of persuasion in the sense de Man applies to Pascal (and with respect to the same mathematical question):

> The homogeneity of the universe is recovered, and the principal of infinitesimal symmetry is well established. But this has happened at a price: the coherence of the system is now seen to be entirely dependent on the introduction of an element—the zero and its equivalences in time and motion—that is entirely heterogeneous with regard to the system and is nowhere a part of it. The continuous universe held together by the double wings of the two infinites is interrupted, disrupted *at all points* by a principle of radical heterogeneity without which it cannot come into being.[31]

29 See René Rocques, "Tératologie et théologie chez Jean Scot Erigène," in *Mélanges offerts à M. D. Chenu*, ed. André Duval (Paris: Vrin, 1967), p. 429.
30 George Chapman, *Hero and Leander*, in *Marlowe's Poems*, ed. L. C. Martin (New York: Gordian, 1966), 5.339–40. See Millar MacLure, *George Chapman: A Critical Study* (Toronto: University of Toronto Press, 1966), p. 48.
31 Paul de Man, "Pascal's Allegory of Persuasion," in *Allegory and Representation*, ed. Stephen J. Greenblatt (Baltimore: Johns Hopkins University Press, 1981), p. 10.

These reflections on Pascal's *Reflections on Geometry* are hard to take out of their context, in which the linguistic equivalent of the arithmetical zero undermines all nominal definitions and the structures of homogeneity (what de Man calls "synecdochal totalizations") that arise from such definitions. The relevance here is confirmed by de Man in "The Concept of Irony," in which the linguistic equivalent of the zero is named and submitted, with inevitable irony, to nominal definition: "Irony is the permanent parabasis of the allegory of the tropes." Zero is no number, irony no trope.

It looks as if we shall have to go into de Man's allegory of the tropes after all. Earlier it was sufficient to characterize that allegory as an argument about the genesis of figurality from the positing of nondialectically opposite terms. In the language I have been applying to that argument here, the genesis of polysemy from antiphrasis is the suppression of the one by the other, of irony by allegory, so that what is thought to exist out of time is given a narrative form. This "allegory" (in de Man's sense of the word) is a more radical model of tropological development than the ancient model of tropology as grammatical declension, for it emerges from the failure of the latter to include antiphrasis. But to "go into" the genesis of figurality from the positing of opposite terms is to do more than to give to that process an allegorical form. It is to enter the scene of genesis oneself and to tackle an incoherence one had only witnessed before. Likewise, de Man's definition of irony, "permanent parabasis of the allegory of the tropes," involves more than the mere witnessing of logical disruption at all points in the tropological system. It implies direct interference, the ironic disruption of one's own act of telling how the tropes are turned out of the place of linguistic uprightness, the place, as Stevens puts it, "in the central of our being."[32] That is the sense in which irony and theory are, for de Man, one and the same.[33] The productive turning out, or evolution of the tropes is not a logical act available to understanding. It is a more radical performance achieved, as Schlegel says of the creation of the world, *by means* of understanding, where understanding is only one of the elements, though a crucial one, like a stage prop, that are necessary for completing the action in a larger, irrational scene.

32 Stevens, *Notes toward a Supreme Fiction*, preface, p. 380.
33 See Paul de Man, *Allegories of Reading: Figural Language in Rousseau, Nietzsche, Rilke, and Proust* (New Haven: Yale University Press, 1979), pp. 98–102.

The performance is, in a sense, a narrative one, which is why de Man calls it an allegory. But it is also a performance in the sense of a spectacle, one in which we are confronted by the peculiarly theatrical irony of being able to watch without the knowledge of those one is watching, like the Wolf Man observing his struggling parents. (They in turn, by their position, recreate the ironic structure of watching, for the father watches the mother without being seen.) But one surrenders that irony when one enters the scene to take part, for in the moment of entry the spectacle is transformed into a narrative, and antiphrastic opposition (pleasure and mutilation) is compelled to give way to a polysemous dialectic of the self. That dialectic takes the shape of a story of development from childhood, the history of an infantile neurosis, a medieval pilgrimage of the life of Man. It is the story, and a persuasive one, of the ego transmitting itself through the "Not I" of the id to anchor every deviation in its past in the uprightness to which it returns: the ego at home, in the nominative case.

If de Man's definition of irony as the "perpetual parabasis" of the genesis of the tropes cannot escape its own irony, the present attempt to look in on and bear witness to what allegory is in essence—violence emerging from noise—is no better off. Not only can the attempt not escape the antiphrastic dissonance it tries to drown out, but it must enter into what it represses. Such directness opposes itself to the dream of escape that sustains ironizing irony to any number of powers. The attempt to define allegory is left trying to hear itself above the noise it creates, which gets louder by the moment, as Freud stands where Quintilian stood and as the parents of the Wolf Man are transformed into Venus and Mars.

The scene wherein allegory is gathered before its emergence was disclosed earlier in the geometrical form of a grid where polysemy and antiphrasis alternately pass under each other and where the grid is drawn inward so as to appear to lead into a center. The invisible hand that draws the net in and then hoists it up is that of Hephaestus, the demiurgic *eiron* who has caught Venus and Mars in flagrante delicto. But in what position are they committing the crime? When the scene is contaminated by Freud's "primal scene," the opposite principles these gods represent, concord and discord, are juxtaposed to similarly opposite acts: the positing of the self by the copula ("I am") and the negation of the self by the spectacle of a copulation *a tergo* ("I" and "Not I"). In the former, the ego as father enters the other to return to itself, as in the classical model of declination from and return to the upright position. In the latter, the ego as mother never has to depart from itself to achieve its desire, but the desire is achieved at the price of castration.[34] The contradiction is identical in form to the genesis of the tropes out of what is in a state of "permanent parabasis" from them. But because the ironic subject does not depart from itself into the realm of the nonself, it never establishes limits that could give it any definite form. Irony is therefore unlimited in its scope but powerless before real power—that is, before those who are not just, as Schlegel says, unable to "have" irony but also determined not to hear it.

Allegory is not as impotent as irony, but neither is it so readily dissociated from the interests of power. On the contrary, its essence is violence emerging from chaos to impose schematic order on historical process, on the rotting of the classical gods. Beneath the conventional unity of its iconographic system, allegory struggles to bring forth from the union of Venus and Mars, even as they embrace in the grave, a world we can value and a narrative in which we can live. The child it hopes for is Harmony. Allegory is, at this level, the creative but also nauseating drive to force heterogeneities together, even as these struggle to break free of each other and die on their own. We can watch them as they accomplish what the Neoplatonists called the copulation of the world: subject and predicate, idea and substance, mind and nature, institution and body, ethos and history, promise and act, human and inhuman, doing it like wolves.

34   Freud, "The History of an Infantile Neurosis," in the *Standard Edition*, 17:34–37.

4

The Renaissance and
the Classical Gods

In recent years Renaissance studies has seen a turn toward politics that has been as dramatic an event as any in the field since its founding by Jakob Burckhardt. This is in a sense a return to Burckhardt, for whom the Renaissance was practically defined by the emergence of art as a political force in the early modern state. Such a state was conceived of as an object of planning and control or, in Burckhardt's formulation, as itself a work of art.[1]

The author of *The Civilization of the Renaissance in Italy* would have assented, therefore, to the inclination of late twentieth-century scholars to refer to the period as "early modern"; and he would have recognized as his own an inclination to regard the arts of the Renaissance as predecessors of the newspaper, the political cartoon, and of radio, television, and film. For Burckhardt saw that the theory of the arts in the Renaissance had developed a hedonistic, utopian drive, supplanting an earlier tendency to justify the arts as a means of spiritual transcendence. This submission of the arts to the goals of technology was perhaps most evident in architecture, which was centrally concerned to arrange the political space in the form of the ideal city. It was in the Renaissance that the arts began to effect a distinctively modern conjoining of political order to cultural

---

1 Jacob Burckhardt, *The Civilization of the Renaissance in Italy*, trans. S. G. C. Middlemore (New York: Modern Library, 1954), p. 3. See "Burckhardt's Renaissance," in William Kerrigan and Gordon Braden, *The Idea of the Renaissance* (Baltimore: Johns Hopkins University Press, 1989), pp. 3-35.

forms, with the aim of making pleasure and power, so far as is possible, one and the same: "Poesy," Francis Bacon remarked in his *Advancement of Learning*, "was ever thought to have some participation in divineness, because it doth raise and erect the mind, by submitting the shewes of things to the desires of the mind."[2] Whatever their origin, those desires were secular and teleological in nature. They were expressions of a comprehensive desire for an orderly world, a social cosmos, of which poetry and art could provide clear and distinct forms. Technology would then strive to fulfill the desire for which art had imagined a goal. The same utopian theme is sounded in Philip Sidney's "Defence of Poesie" and in Spenser's "Letter to Raleigh," where the imagination is an instrument for improving secular life, which is identified unambiguously with political life. The arts of the Renaissance thus had a new role to play in the emergence of the modern idea of community as a product of calculation and design and of the origin of such a community in the exertion of benevolent power. By and large, public discourse concerning the arts, especially when it is sharply divided along political lines, continues to move in this utopian-technological frame, without reference to the divine.

It may therefore seem otiose to concern ourselves now with the cultural role in the Renaissance, or in nascent modernity, of the classical gods, for their tenure was precarious and brief. By the eighteenth century the gods were objects of antiquarian research or, as in Hölderlin, powers that the poet says he may longer invoke. Are we not then in some danger, in reflecting on the significance of the gods in the Renaissance, of falling into the state of mind in which that "Renaissance"—and it is a name the period gave to itself—kept its face turned to the past, to the pure light of antiquity?[3] The gods cannot be termed "early modern"

---

2 *Of the Advancement of Learning*, in *The Works of Francis Bacon*, ed. James Spedding et al. (Boston: Brown & Taggard, 1864), 6:203.

3 See Erwin Panofsky, "Renaissance: Self-Description or Self-Deception?" in *Renaissance and Renascences in Western Art* (1960; reprint, New York: Harper & Row, 1972), pp. 1–41, and Eugenio Garin, "Interpretations of the Renaissance," in *Science and Civic Life in the Italian Renaissance*, trans. Peter Munz (Garden City, N.Y.: Doubleday, 1969), pp. 1–20. For representative scholarship on the Renaissance as the cradle of modernity, see Stephen Greenblatt, *Renaissance Self-Fashioning from More to Shakespeare* (Chicago: University of Chicago Press, 1980); Jonathan Goldberg, *James I and the Politics of Literature* (Baltimore: Johns Hopkins University Press, 1983); Annabel Patterson, *Censorship and Interpretation: The Conditions of Writing and Reading in Early Modern England* (Madison: University of Wisconsin Press, 1984); and Anthony Grafton and Lisa Jardine, *From Humanism to the Humanities: Education and Liberal Arts in Fifteenth- and Sixteenth-Century Europe* (Cam-

with the facility that economic, political, and social developments can. Why not forget them?

There are several answers to this question, not the least of which being that the gods will not allow us to forget them; they persist in high and low culture alike. But I propose a stronger case for their importance: that the prominence of the gods in the art of the Renaissance reflects their role in the conjoining of political authority to spiritually resonant cultural forms. It was around the revival of classical antiquity that the modern category of the aesthetic was formed; and it was in the more dangerously spiritual forces of antiquity, embodied in the gods, that the political force of the classical was revealed. In the relatively secularized culture of the Renaissance, the classical gods were politically sacred, conferring an aura of mysterious power on the symbols of the state, the most important of which was the body of the prince. The body, accordingly, was no longer the passive, material bearer of abstractions imprinted on it, as was the fate of Francesca da Rimini. Instead, the body was an agent surrounded by abstractions that were instruments extending its power; and the passive, material bearer on which these abstractions exerted the power of the prince was the body of the state. The abstractions were capable of standing on their own because they were embodied in the figures of the classical gods or because they had acquired a stature that was hardly distinct from the gods, as in Piero della Francesca's *Triumph of Federigo da Montefeltro* (see Figure 3). Moreover, in surrounding the body of the prince in this way the classical gods also conferred, as the symbols of the Christian religion could not, a certain capacity for restraint which was intimately involved with their beauty. While Christian images of the divine, when their meaning was contested, proved to be an incitement to open, unmediated, incremental violence, the classical gods were a source of legitimacy for the prince and of aesthetic pleasure for the subject.

The classical gods in the Renaissance thus mark the occasion of a new stage in the relations between allegory and violence, in which a mysterious power is bound to the body of the prince through the mediation of Olympian forms. We saw how in the Middle Ages allegory both depended on and gave expression to the concept of a transcendentally unified world, governed by the authority of abstract forms. In these circumstances allegory could mediate a universal but relatively subdued violence

bridge: Harvard University Press, 1986). For a discussion of period terms, see Heather Dubrow and Frances E. Dolan, in "Forum," *PMLA* 109 (October 1994): 1025–27.

3. Piero della Francesca. *Triumph of Federigo da Montefeltro.* Ca. 1465. Uffizi, Florence. Alinari/Art Resource, New York

directed at nature: everything in the world was a sign. In the Renaissance, however, allegory was used in the service of independent states that were more or less openly in competition with one another, each striving to be its own, allegorical cosmos. As a result, the Olympian order of the classical gods became the basis of what nearly amounted to a religion of power. What Hobbes observed of the ancients, that their religion was a "humane Politiques,"[4] is at least as true in his own time of the use of the iconography of the classical gods. The gods served as idols in the numerous competitive cults making up the Renaissance culture of power.

The qualification in the statement that the Olympian gods were the basis of what was *nearly* a religion of power is important. A religion is a

4   Thomas Hobbes, *Leviathan* (New York: Dutton, 1950), p. 91; cf. p. 96.

binding of the sacred to ritual practices wherein the members of a culture place ultimate hope. Notwithstanding the concerns that were occasionally raised on the subject, usually in Protestant polemics, there was in the Renaissance no genuine devotion in this sense to the gods of antiquity. They were deployed for ideological ends. But neither were the gods regarded with the archaeological detachment of the Enlightenment. They appear instead to have mediated the force of the sacred in the political realm while leaving much of that force in an unattached and exploitable state. The revival of the classical gods in Renaissance allegory was a fairly direct consequence of the emergence of the idea of the sovereign state, centered in the body of the prince, as a cosmos unto itself. That such a system was sustained by the threat of violence was concealed behind the aesthetic beauty of the allegorized classical gods, who were thus made to appear to be elements of an impregnable structure.

We should pause for a moment over the terms *violence, power,* and *the sacred,* which I use in the sense René Girard explored in *La violence et le sacré.* For Girard, the sacred is the power of reciprocal violence, tending to what we call, in the age of nuclear weapons, mutually assured destruction. In its pure state, unbound by religion, retributive, symmetrical violence reduces human society to chaos. In Euripides' *Bacchae* such violence is foreshadowed in the ironic speech and the contradictory nature of the god Dionysus, who causes Pentheus to see two suns in the sky—an image strangely prophetic of the logic of nuclear war.[5] For Girard, the destructive threat of reciprocal violence is the menace around which the ritual practices and, at a farther remove, the cultural products of every society turn.

In the Renaissance these distinct intensities of the sacred—the religious and the cultural—operated on different levels and at different scales. While the religious crisis of the Reformation and its violent aftermath were broad, European events, it was within the confines of individual states that the classical gods were deployed in the arts for the purpose of containing the sacred as power. By binding the forms of the classical gods to the symbols of the regime, and principally, as I said, to the body of the prince, the threat of violence could be held out from a commanding position, and in a form that was aesthetically pleasing. This holding of violence in aesthetic reserve, from which measured,

5 René Girard, *La violence et le sacré* (Paris: Grasset, 1972), pp. 299–303. Euripides, *Bacchae,* 2d ed. E. R. Dodds (Oxford: Clarendon Press, 1960), line 918.

theatrical demonstrations of force may be drawn, is power. Power remains power by restraining the violence that it threatens to use. What makes this restraint possible is legitimacy, a word that, like religion, is rooted metaphorically in the act of binding and, secondarily, in gathering. Through the legitimacy conferred on the prince and his state by the forms of the classical gods the potential for violence was gathered and bound in the service of power. In the turbulent politics of the Italian states, when political right could scarcely be distinguished from the power to kill, from what Machiavelli called *virtù*, the classical gods did not reappear by any spontaneous act of their own, by rebirth or survival. They were seized on and improvised with by those who had need of them most: the princes and their humanist servants. Skillfully deployed, the gods could confer on the prince an aura of inscrutable menace that was no small part of his *maiestas*, or "greatness," giving him—or, in the case of Elizabeth, her—the power of command.

The authoritative explanation in the Renaissance for the aura conferred by the classical gods was that they were symbols in an "ancient theology" that stretched back through Plato to such mythical figures as Orpheus, Hermes Trismegistus, and even, by oral tradition, to Moses. Through quasi-formalized institutions such as the Platonic Academy in Florence and, more generally, through the iconographic culture of the period, the classical gods were used to capture the power of the sacred while keeping it apart from the official religion, under the aegis of philosophy.[6] This process of mediating the sacred to the secular sphere accounts for the strange mixture of credulity and skepticism with which the classical gods were received. For the truth of the philosophical claims made on their behalf was of less importance than the purpose advanced under the disguise of those claims, which was to capture the potential

6 See James Hankins, "The Myth of the Platonic Academy in Florence," *Renaissance Quarterly* 44 (Autumn 1991): 429–75. A strong case for the political expediency of a mystical Plato under the autocratic Medici regime has been made by Eugenio Garin and others. This argument is rehearsed with some reservations in James Hankins's *Plato in the Italian Renaissance*, 2d ed. (Leiden: Brill, 1991), 1:15. But Hankins's own account of Ficino's teaching (1:28), which was aimed at a small, ruling elite, bears out Garin's view. For the contemporary concern that Plato was being made into a shadow religion, see 1:348. For the term *ancient theology*, see 2:460–64. See also Marsilio Ficino's *De amore* 4.2, *Commentaire sur le banquet de Platon*, ed. and trans. Raymond Marcel (Paris: Belles Lettres, 1956), p. 168, where the monstrousness of Aristophanes' tale is said to indicate that divine mysteries are hidden beneath the narrated events, as if under a veil.

for violence and to bind it to the interests of state power. It is reasonable to ask what changes in the political order made such a use of the gods possible.

A thorough exploration of this question, however, would lead back through Burckhardt to the sustained meditation on state power undertaken in the Renaissance itself by Guicciardini and Machiavelli in Italy and by Bacon and Hobbes in England. But the broad outlines of an answer are not hard to see. As the ideological hegemony of empire and papacy declined, and as the hollowness of feudal patterns of authority became increasingly apparent, new states, or, rather, new princes, required new means of asserting their legitimacy. Because power was personal, a matter of individual talent and fortune, it was fastened to the body of the prince, which was represented as endowed with an aura of majesty that would overspread his domains—and, if possible, those of his neighbors. The classical gods, by drawing the power of the sacred away from the framework of the Christian religion and attaching it to the body of the prince, provided the means to accomplish this end, lending divine authority to the idea of an expansionist state.

It is important that the body of the prince be stressed. As Burckhardt noted, the *state—lo stato*—referred literally to the prince and his dependents and only later acquired its more abstract, theoretical meaning.[7] Both senses of the word are apparent in Shakespeare, and Louis XIV's perhaps apocryphal remark "l'état c'est moi" would have recalled a literal sense of the term which was not yet entirely lost. The state was understood as a privileged body at a time of profound change in the conception of how bodies exist in the world, a change, let us say, from the body as analogue to the body as instrument.

In medieval thought the body was conceived of as a mixture of the four elements that make up the world.[8] As a microcosm, or an analogue of the world, the body coincides with an environment in which it does not have to struggle to survive. In these circumstances the highest aim of the intellect can be nothing other than the purely speculative one of

---

7   Burckhardt, *Civilization of the Renaissance in Italy*, p. 4 n. 2. and pp. 66–67.
8   See C. S. Lewis, *The Discarded Image: An Introduction to Medieval and Renaissance Literature* (Cambridge: Cambridge University Press, 1964), pp. 169–74, and the third book of Ficino's *Three Books of Life*, ed. and trans. Carol V. Kaske and John R. Clark (Binghamton, N.Y.: Center for Medieval and Early Renaissance Studies, 1989). For the survival and complication of such thought in Renaissance esotericism, see S. K. Heninger Jr., *Touches of Sweet Harmony: Pythagorean Cosmology and Renaissance Poetics* (San Marino, Calif.: Huntington Library, 1974), pp. 167–77, figs. 31–34 and 37.

realizing in knowledge what is already accomplished in being: the co-incidence of the self and the world. Such a body can have no interior that is truly apart from the world and can acknowledge no alien environment pressing upon it. The basis for the idea of the body as an analogue of the world was eclipsed by the rise of anatomical science, notably in the *De humani corporis fabrica* (1543) of Andreas Vesalius, which, as its title suggests, treats the human body as a machine. Published in the same year as Copernicus's *De revolutionibus orbium coelestium*, Vesalius's study of human anatomy was an event of even greater psychological importance. The illustrations alone, like Leonardo's before them, amount to nothing less than a corporeal apocalypse, revealing the interior of the body to be absolutely unique, and unlike anything outside it in the physical structure of the natural world. The body thus became a mechanical contrivance with which the self, retreating to a sanctuary that owes as much to stoicism as it does to Descartes, could exert power over an alien nature. This instrumental sense of the body is reflected in Bacon's revolutionary program for science, in which the purpose of intellectual inquiry is no longer speculative but practical: to extend the body's power over nature and to enlarge its capacity for pleasure. The body in the Renaissance acquires a clearly defined inside and outside, the one to be colonized by pleasure, the other by power.

The visual artists of the Renaissance developed a brilliant anatomical rhetoric to express this new sense of the body, redefining the environment as a field of heroic endeavor and unforeseen menace. Even the most classicizing examples of medieval art, such as Niccolò Pisano's muscular sculpture of Fortitude as Hercules, fail in this essential respect: to define the body as heroically overcoming the challenge of its environment, a challenge symbolized by other, threatening bodies. The classical body thus has its essential being not in any theory of ideal proportions but in struggle; and this is so even when that body is at rest, as in Michelangelo's "David." The invention of linear perspective in painting—drawing the lines, as it were, within which this new game was to be played—was a technically important but otherwise superficial manifestation of what bodily space had become. Michelangelo's famous cartoon of the Florentine soldiers surprised by the Pisans while bathing owed its sensational impact to its being a revelation of the body as a thing that has its essence in conflict. Moreover, even when bodies are entangled with one another in such conflict (as in the classical theme of the battle of the Lapiths and the centaurs), each one is isolated in its struggle to survive and prevail.

As the notion of the body as an analogue of the world was displaced by the idea of the body as isolated in struggle, the classical gods were drawn into ever closer proximity to the prince and were more nearly identified with him. Indeed princes were occasionally represented *as* gods, Elizabeth as Diana and Cynthia, Federigo Gonzaga as Jove, Andrea Doria as Neptune, and, of course, Louis XIV as Jove. The last designation would survive in the plumes of Napoleon's Imperial Guard and in the lightning bolts clasped by the American eagle, the bird of Jove.

Two monumental works in fresco, widely separated in time, show the change in the relative positions of the prince's body and the gods. The first work, the *Room of the Months*, in the Palazzo Schifanoia in Ferrara, is attributed to Francesco del Cossa and was completed in the second half of the fifteenth century. The walls of the room are divided into three distinct levels. On the highest level the gods are represented in a medieval, cosmographic order as the twelve astrological signs. On the middle level are subordinate astrological figures, the decans, who mediate the influence of the gods in the world. On the lowest level is the prince Borso d'Este, who is shown with his court in naturalistic settings, administering his state. In this work the prince is entirely separated from the gods, whose influence is real but invisible. The second work, completed about a century and a half later, is the series of planetary rooms in the Pitti palace in Florence, executed by Pietro da Cortona and assistants. There, the duke Cosimo de' Medici is represented naked and in close proximity to the gods, as when Pallas physically bears him away from the attractions of Venus (see Figure 4). The painting is accompanied, incidentally, by two texts, one inscribed beneath the picture, the other above it, but upside down. The text under the picture describes the literal action; and the text that can be read only when the picture is viewed upside down gives, in metaphorical language, the allegorical meaning of that action: "the root of virtue is bitter, but its fruit is sweet." In the fifteenth-century *Room of the Months* the prince is a figure in a cosmic hierarchy with which his own, well-ordered realm corresponds invisibly. In the seventeenth-century planetary rooms the prince is a body engaged in the struggle to rule and the gods are an extension of his power. (This struggle to rule, and the role of the gods in that struggle, are more evident still in the Room of Mars, with its panoramic battle and its aerial perspective, achievements that would be admired by Tiepolo.)

The claim I have been advancing concerning the political role of the classical gods may now be put into time. Over the course of the Re-

4. Pietro da Cortona. *Pallas Stripping Venus of Adolescence.* 1641–42. Pitti Palace, Florence. Alinari/Art Resource, New York

naissance the gods were transformed from elements of a cosmography in the service of truth to elements of a rhetoric in the service of power. As the use of the gods became more openly rhetorical, their capacity for evoking the sacred declined. And as this process advanced, the gods were more easily associated, as pure decoration, with Christian iconography. They thus lost their capacity for acting as a means of restraint, that is, as scapegoats drawing the political force of the sacred away from religion. What followed was a catastrophic fusion of politics and faith in the religious wars of the seventeenth century.

The effectiveness with which the classical gods were deployed for some time without occasioning an outbreak of violence on the scale of the seventeenth century was in large measure due to their incompatibility with the official religion. However assiduously pagan mythology was allegorized, it could not be reconciled with the official religion and incorporated in a cultural totality. Pagan mythology could not become what nature became in the medieval imagination: a homogeneous order of signs, written by the finger of God. It was therefore inevitable that voices skeptical of the wisdom of the ancients would be raised and, more important, that the skepticism of the ancients themselves should be heard once again. We thus find Bacon, in *The Advancement of Learning*, borrowing freely from Cicero to cast doubt on the notion that the classical poets intended some deeper meaning in their stories of the gods. But this skepticism was as fragile as the credulity that it attacked. The background of mystery repeatedly gave way before skepticism only to position itself at a greater remove. No sooner did Bacon observe that Homer and Hesiod could not have concealed philosophical meanings in the myths they deployed than he went on to speculate that the older, anonymous inventors of their myths may well have done so: that the truths hidden in Homer were there, but without Homer's knowledge. The passage in question holds, as it were in concentrate, the entire range of assertions it was possible to make at the time on the subject of classical myth:

> So in the fable that Achilles was brought up by Chiron the centaur, who was part a man and part a beast, expounded ingeniously but corruptly by Machiavel, that it belongeth to the education and discipline of princes to know as well how to play the part of the lion in violence, and the fox in guile, as of the man in virtue and justice. Nevertheless, in many the like encounters, I do rather think that the fable was first, and the exposition devised, than that the moral was first, and thereupon the fable framed. For I find it was an ancient vanity in Chrysippus, that troubled himself with great contention to fasten the assertions of the Stoics upon the fictions of the ancient poets; but yet that all the fables and fictions of the poets were but pleasure and not figure, I interpose no opinion. Surely of those poets which are now extant, even Homer himself (notwithstanding he was made a kind of scripture by the later schools of the Grecians), yet I should without any difficulty pronounce that his fables had no such inwardness in his own meaning. But what they might have upon a more original tradition, is not easy to affirm; for he was not the inventor of many of them.[9]

Although Bacon is eager to show that he is himself too shrewd to be taken in by the more extravagant claims of the allegorizers, he separates himself from a purely rhetorical deployment of myth exemplified,

9   Bacon, *Of the Advancement of Learning*, 6:205–6.

appropriately enough, by Machiavelli. For he supposes that whoever invented these myths, as opposed to the poets, such as Homer, who merely received them, must have had a revelation of "inwardness" for which the myth was the outer, protective shell. As he looks back in time, repeatedly discovering a more "original tradition," every demystification of myth occasions its remystification at a greater remove. For him, the aura of a myth is its distance in time. Bacon's predicament is expressed in an oscillation between skepticism and credulity in his view of the classical gods. Neither term is strong enough to obliterate the other or even to include that other in a more comprehensive assertion, such as that the mystery of the gods lies in their psychological truth. But it was precisely the impossibility of taking this step that left the gods in their curiously instrumental position as ideological forms. A Renaissance prince identifying himself with Jove wielding the thunderbolt or with Hercules slaying Cacus would have been perfectly aware that other princes, employing humanists who were using the same works of reference, were doing much the same thing. But this knowledge, which would naturally arouse skepticism about the objective truth of such claims, did not diminish significantly the psychological impact of identifying the prince with the classical gods. The conflict between incompatible claims unfolded in the new, ideological arena of the aesthetic, where the prince who could command the most stunning assertions of proximity to the classical gods (as Elizabeth did, through Greene, Shakespeare, Raleigh, and Spenser) would appear to have captured divine power. Not surprisingly, the competition among princes for the most accomplished artists was intense.

One might wish to let the matter stand there, to keep the irony to ourselves, so to speak, rather than to allow for the possibility of an irony in Bacon which is also a force in his political culture. I mean the irony by which one is aware of the convenience of what one decides to believe. In the Renaissance some degree of actual belief must have been necessary if the classical gods were to be deployed effectively around the body of the prince. But as the example of Roman emperor-worship may suggest, unwavering belief would have diminished the rhetorical flexibility of the gods. A degree of skepticism was necessary if the gods were to be deployed as instruments of ideological power. While the cosmic interpretation of the gods was sustained by polysemy, where multiple meanings participated in a unified whole, the political use of the gods was sustained by irony in its most radical form, antiphrasis. The gods were arbitrary forms to be deployed in any statement one chose to make; and the gods were magical talismans, surrounding the body of the prince with an aura of power drawn from remote and inscrutable sources.

This irony pervades Bacon's fascinating study of the gods in *Wisdom of the Ancients*, which appeared four years after *The Advancement of Learning*. Even as Bacon interprets the classical myths in an openly self-serving manner, he strongly affirms his belief in their having been mysteriously meant:

> I do certainly for my own part . . . incline to this opinion—that beneath no small number of the fables of the ancient poets there lay from the very beginning a mystery and an allegory. It may be that my reverence for the primitive time carries me too far, but the truth is that in some of these fables, as well as in the very frame and texture of the story as in the propriety of the names by which the persons that figure in it are distinguished, I find a conformity and connexion with the thing signified, so close and so evident, that one cannot help believing such a signification to have been designed and mediated from the first, and purposely shadowed out.[10]

This affirmation is accompanied, however, by the clearest assertion that the gods can be employed as a rhetoric in the service of power, so much so that the practice has been, as Bacon says, much abused in the past. What is less clear, if an original, mysterious meaning is always suppressed when the myth is deployed to some rhetorical end, is what would count for Bacon as a nonabusive deployment of myth:

> Not but that I know very well what pliant stuff fable is made of, how freely it will follow any way you please to draw it, and how easily with a little dexterity and discourse of wit meanings which it was never meant to bear may be plausibly put on it. Neither have I forgotten that there has been old abuse of the thing in practice; that many, wishing only to gain the sanction and reverence of antiquity for doctrines and inventions of their own, have tried to twist the fables of the poets into that sense; and that this is neither a modern vanity nor a rare one, but of old standing and frequent in use.[11]

10 Francis Bacon, *Of the Wisdom of the Ancients* (*De sapientia veterum*), in *Works*, 13:76–77.
11 Ibid., p. 76.

On the one hand, fables of the gods resonate with a truth that was already there when Homer received them; on the other hand, they are "pliant stuff" that is capable, like language itself, of being turned to any purpose whatever.

It would appear then that to use myth rhetorically one must somehow preserve in good order the belief that the meanings one imposes are already there; and one must preserve that belief in oneself, not just impose it on one's audience. Accordingly, after a show of skepticism that is genuine enough, Bacon assembles four quite traditional arguments in support of the proposition that ancient myths contain more ancient truths: the argument from correspondence, the argument from names, the argument from absurdity, and the argument from ancient theology. The first, cosmological argument I have already mentioned. The second, essentially stoic argument is obvious enough in names such as Metis (Counsel) and Pan (All). The hermeneutic argument, that is, the argument from absurdity, which was invented in late antiquity by the apologists for classical culture,[12] is entertainingly stated:

> Some of them are so absurd and stupid on the face of the narrative taken by itself, that they may be said to give notice from afar and cry out that there is a parable below. . . . What a fiction (for instance) is that of Jupiter and Metis! Jupiter took Metis to wife: as soon as he saw that she was with child he ate her up; whereupon he grew to be with child himself; and so brought forth out of his head Pallas in armour! Surely I think no man had ever a dream so monstrous and extravagant, and out of all natural ways of thinking.[13]

The argument from ancient theology was commonplace in the Renaissance, appearing in such readily accessible sources as the tenth book of Natalis Comes' *Mythologiae*. This, for Bacon, is the most important argument of all:

> Few of the fables were invented, as I take it, by those who recited and made them famous—Homer, Hesiod, and the rest. . . . It is easy to see that what all versions have in common came from ancient tradition . . . a

---

12 Plato, *Republic* 378d. See Jean Pépin, "L'absurdité, signe de l'allégorie," in *La Tradition de l'allégorie de Philon d'Alexandrie à Dante* (Paris: Études Augustiniennes, 1987), pp. 167–86.
13 Bacon, *Of the Wisdom of the Ancients*, p. 78.

circumstance that gives them in my eyes a much higher value: for so they must be regarded as neither being the inventions nor belonging to the age of the poets themselves, but as sacred relics and light airs breathing out of better times, that were caught from the traditions of more ancient nations and so received into the flutes and trumpets of the Greeks.[14]

As for the skeptical position he has articulated himself, Bacon mockingly concedes everything to it before exposing the irrelevance of that concession. It seems almost as if Bacon is talking himself out of the skepticism that he ridicules in others. Yet, on the other side, he knows that to revere the wisdom of the ancients too highly is, in a sense, to make it less wise; for it is to render that wisdom incapable of teaching, and even of finding, new truths:

> If anyone be determined to believe that the allegorical meaning of the fable was in no case original and genuine, but that always the fable was first and the allegory put in after, I will not press that point; but allowing him to enjoy that gravity of judgment (of the dull and leaden order though it be) which he affects, I will attack him, if indeed he be worth the pains, in another manner upon a fresh ground. Parables have been used in two ways and (which is strange) for contrary purposes. For they serve to disguise and veil the meaning, and they serve also to clear and throw light upon it. To avoid dispute then, let us give up the former of these uses. Let us suppose that these fables were things without any definite purpose, made only for pleasure. Still there remains the latter use. No force of wit can deprive us of that. Nor is there any man of ordinary learning that will object to the reception of it as a thing grave and sober, and free from all vanity; of prime use to the sciences, and sometimes indispensable: I mean the employment of parables as a method of teaching, whereby inventions that are new and abstruse and remote from vulgar opinions may find an easier passage to the understanding.[15]

---

14 Ibid., pp. 78–79.
15 Ibid., pp. 79–80; cf. p. 80: "In the old times, when the inventions and conclusions of human reason (even those that are now trite and vulgar) were as yet new and strange, the world was full of all kinds of fables and enigmas, and parables, and similitudes: and these were not used as a device for shadowing and concealing the meaning, but as a method of making it understood."

In moving from a position of credulity to one of resigned skepticism, Bacon arrives at a conception of ancient myth as an inherently noble instrument of teaching and of thought. But the indeterminacy remains at the core. Is it the wisdom of the ancients or of the moderns? Does the wisdom come early or late? Is the wisdom the inner cause of mythic forms or is it only imprinted on them? Faced with such questions, Bacon has only one recourse, a vertiginous irony that can adjust, as occasion demands, to contrary claims. It is a bet that he wins either way: as long as he remains committed to the project of interpreting the myths, he will be "throwing light either upon antiquity or upon nature itself." [16]

In the ensuing treatise, to which the passages I have quoted serve as preface, Bacon calls not infrequently on the resources of this irony. But he is able nevertheless to convey the impression of method by differentiating between theory and practice. When openly considering the question, Bacon states that the ancients were wise in their myths. But the actual interpretations he offers are so judiciously topical, or so brilliantly counterintuitive, or so forceful as propaganda for his revolutionary views of science that he seems almost Nietzschean in his exertions of the will-to-power over the matter of history. Even so (and in this he is perhaps also like Nietzsche), Bacon never unequivocally relinquishes the belief that an immemorial wisdom is present in the body of classical myth. In order to reach back into the material remains of the past and tear away fragments of myth, using these for his own rhetorical purposes, Bacon has to persuade himself that in doing so he is handing on the truth to the future.

"I shall be throwing light either upon antiquity or upon nature itself." For Bacon, myth is either wise in itself or the cause of wisdom in others, in those who look through it upon nature. As to the content of such wisdom, he cares little whether it belongs to philology or to philosophy. The point is to win. Bacon finesses the dilemma, rather than attempting to find out which of the alternatives is true, because his primary concern is to defeat his imaginary adversary, establishing himself as a unified, impregnable subject. Bacon's mind is like the classical body in Renaissance art, existing essentially in struggle. But the dilemma itself, which is in any case not one Bacon could have resolved, bears on the most fundamental change that occurred in allegorical expression in the period extending

16   Ibid., p. 80.

from the Renaissance to the Enlightenment, a change we have observed in the function of the gods in the *Room of the Months* and the *Planetary Rooms*. As the gods lost their numinous, astrological power and became rhetorical figures, they were freed from their metaphysical prison; thereafter they could be deployed in almost any position or circumstance that a writer or a painter chose.

This change was accompanied by a curious shift in the position of meaning with respect to allegorical forms. Earlier in the Renaissance, the meaning of an allegory was supposed to lie hidden in the interior of the work: the statue of the ugly Silenus in Erasmus's adage reveals, when opened, the image of a beautiful god.[17] But as we draw closer to the Enlightenment the meaning of an allegory was increasingly supposed to lie outside or beyond the allegorical signs, in the actual world. An allegory was expected to be organized internally as a logical system, indicating efficiently a meaning that is somewhere beyond it. As bodies in the Renaissance gained interiors and were surrounded by a more sharply externalized world, allegories lost their interiority and were expected to behave like machines. The place of mind was withdrawn from the text into the head.

In fact, the two views of the presence of meaning were never entirely separated; wherever one of them was given prominence, the other was suppressed. To read Spenser's *Faerie Queene* is to struggle through disorienting complexity to moments of vision that seem to lie deep within the text, near to its hidden center of meaning. Yet we also suppose as we read that the poem refers to something outside and beyond it, principally the Queen. This reference to the outside, however, is always being mediated through the ritual experience of deep interpretation, of unveiling mysteries. By the seventeenth century, in a neo-Spenserian allegory such as Phineas Fletcher's *Purple Island*, the mediating process of ritual reading has disappeared, leaving us to refer things in the text directly to things in the world. This development was an important one not least because as it advanced it made new and increasingly stringent demands on the author to maintain logical consistency among the terms of the narrative. One already senses in *The Purple Island*, as one does not in the episode of *The*

17   Erasmus, *Adages* 3.3.1, trans. R. A. B. Mynors, in *The Collected Works of Erasmus* (Toronto: University of Toronto Press, 1992), vol. 34, part 4, pp. 262–82. See also *De copia*, trans. Betty I. Knott, in *Works*, vol. 24, part 2, pp. 336 and 611, and Guy Demerson's excellent study, *La mythologie classique dans l'oeuvre lyrique de la "Pléiade"* (Geneva: Droz, 1972), p. 29 and n. 147.

Faerie Queene that inspired it, the absurdity of representing the body as an island, of describing the organs on the island in elaborate detail, with marginal notes from Vesalius, and of then having the island attacked by the vices, so that a psychomachy may follow. One senses the need for greater internal consistency in the design; and one senses that the poet has failed to provide it because he is still in the grip of an outdated assumption about meaning: that it should lie mysteriously inside the text.

In contrast to this ambiguity in the location of meaning, when we read an Enlightenment allegory such as Johnson's "Allegory of Criticism" in the third *Rambler*, our attention is directed consistently and continually outside the tale. There is no mystery. What pleasure we take in the work depends entirely on our noting with what wit the relations between the elements in Johnson's tale mimic the fate of good and bad books over time. The transition from the referential interiority of Renaissance allegory to its opposite in the Enlightenment was accompanied by a profound alteration of affect. Whereas in the Renaissance allegory presented itself as a mysterious, high-minded, quasi-prophetic form of expression, in the Enlightenment it was a medium for social satire and, in its more modest forms, for the instruction of youth. The two parts of Swift's *Tale of a Tub*, the satires on religion and learning, register this change brilliantly. In the satire on religion, with its fable of the coats, Swift's allegory meets the demands of Enlightenment allegory: consistency, perspicuity, and economy. In the satire on learning, which alludes to such things as a Pythagorean commentary on Tom Thumb, Swift parodies the outmoded but persistent belief that the most childish or grotesque fables have profound truths hidden within them. Bacon's position on the presence of meaning in myth is by no means as clear, or as narrow, as Swift's. But neither was Bacon willing to allow his integrity as a subject (as Swift was, spectacularly) to be broken up into separate voices by the autonomous action of language. Whether he is throwing light upon antiquity or upon nature, it is he and no other who is throwing the light. That is what counts.

It is instructive to compare Bacon in this respect with the most significant theorist of myth in the second half of the twentieth century, Claude Lévi-Strauss. In the introduction to his work on the subject, Lévi-Strauss famously remarked that myths think through us and without our knowledge.[18] To know that, of course, is to contradict what one knows, but the contradiction, placed at the outset, by no means vitiates the study on

18   Claude Lévi-Strauss, *Le cru et le cuit* (Paris: Plon, 1964), p. 20.

which Lévi-Strauss is at that moment embarking. Instead, by dividing the self into two parts, the contradiction enables the study to go forward, after relinquishing the heroic posture that had been struck by Bacon as a model of scientific integrity. The investigator divides himself into two subjects, the one being ignorantly thought through by myth while the other ironically observes that transaction. In effect, Lévi-Strauss is saying, "I see myth thinking through me, and through others, and only when I divide myself in this way do I know that that happens. What follows is to a certain degree spoken through me, by myth, as well as being spoken by me about myth. The mind cannot, in this area at least, be altogether independent of what it attends to. The point is for the investigation to go forward." The price of Bacon's more rigid integrity is paralysis. He cannot advance beyond the position marked by the dilemma he formulates so well. He can only strike a triumphant pose, having strangled in the air an imaginary skeptic who was really himself.

Scientific discourse was to advance beyond this position by reducing myth to a psychological phenomenon, as one of the more beautiful, if nugatory, products of the association of ideas. Because I find it hard to imagine that Bacon did not see this possibility, I am inclined to think he rejected it deliberately. On this subject at least he had more in common with the classical skeptics, with, for example, Cotta in Cicero's treatise on the nature of the gods, than he did with the scientists who took him to be their prophet. Where the scientist works to some extent by trial and error, creating hypotheses and designing experiments to confirm or refute them, the skeptic is concerned never to make a false move, immovableness itself being for him an impregnable intellectual stance from which every opponent may be strangled and cast to the ground. That is why Bacon mistakenly supposed that an investigator had to proceed inductively, believing nothing in advance, when in fact experiment is the means by which deductions are confirmed or refuted, upheld or cast down. Such a practice must have seemed undignified to Bacon, who was more concerned with his own skeptical integrity, with not being deceived, than he was with advancing knowledge. Yet this very stubbornness perhaps made him a better example to those who could submit themselves to the humiliations, as well as to the discipline, of science. Bacon's integrity is, in its own way, as admirable as Lévi-Strauss's dexterity.

As the sense of mystery evoked by the classical gods declined in the Renaissance so too did the impulse to be skeptical about them as symbols belonging to an ancient theology. Skepticism needs opponents to cast down. It might be supposed, therefore, that skepticism, together with the rise of scientific philology, was the cause of this decline, rather than the decline itself being the occasion for skepticism. But it looks as if the expulsion of the sacred from classical myth had more to do with the increasing violence of religious controversy, against which skepticism was, as always, powerless. Graver minds, being duller than Bacon's, were more impressed by matters of doctrine and faith than by the strange, logical knots one may invent while contemplating the beauty of classical myth. It was not scholarship, skepticism, or enlightenment that drove out the classical gods but fanaticism. In his elegy on Donne, Thomas Carew credits that poet with having purged the muses' garden of such "Pedantique weedes" as Ovidian goddesses and gods. But what is most significant in the passage is the poet's raising the specter of idolatry. The "Libertines in Poetrie" will, he says,

> repeale the goodly exil'd traine
> Of gods and goddesses, which in thy just raigne
> Were banish'd nobler Poems; now, with these
> The silenc'd tales o'th'Metamorphoses
> Shall stuffe their lines, and swell the windy Page,
> Till Verse refin'd by thee, in this last Age
> Turne ballad rime, Or those old Idolls bee
> Ador'd againe, with new apostasie.[19]

These lines proclaim the same zealous spirit found in Milton's reference to those Christian ceremonial practices he condemned as "the new vomited Paganisme of sensuall Idolatry."[20] Classical myth lost its power to enchant when a stronger enchantment took hold.

As religious war began to be supplanted by conflict between sovereign states, and the discourse of faith by a rhetoric of grand strategy, the classical gods reappeared as the accoutrements of power. Two great works at the height of the baroque, on the threshold of the Enlightenment, exemplify this trend. Interestingly enough, they were both criticized in Enlightenment discussions of allegory for placing mortals and gods on the

---

19 Thomas Carew, "An Elegie upon the Death of the Deane of Pauls, Dr. John Donne," l. 25 and ll. 63–70, in *Poems*, ed. Rhodes Dunlap (Oxford: Clarendon Press, 1949), pp. 72 and 73.
20 John Milton, "Of Reformation," in *Complete Prose Works*, ed. Don M. Wolfe (New Haven: Yale University Press, 1953), 1:520.

same ontological level. And they both served as encyclopedic resources for the political cartoonists of the eighteenth and nineteenth centuries. I refer to Rubens's great cycle of paintings, now in the Louvre, on the life of Marie de' Medici, and Charles le Brun's cycle of paintings, executed at Versailles, to glorify Louis XIV.[21] The most impressive scene in the latter cycle, *The Crossing of the Rhine*, depicts the king as Jove wielding the thunderbolt, driving the Chariot of Victory. He is attended by Fame, Providence, and Strength, this last in the classical person of Hercules; and a river god, representing the Rhine, is aghast. Thus far, we are in the world of Renaissance allegory, with the classical gods conferring on the body of the prince an aura of power, of a violence that is effortlessly held in reserve or, as here, released in one effortless, astonishing act. The work differs from Renaissance allegory—for example, from Piero della Francesca's *Triumph of Federigo da Montefeltro*—in representing a single, military action with the topicality of an event in the news: Louis XIV's invasion of the Low Countries. And it is precisely in this topicality that the work anticipates the mass-produced political cartoons of the eighteenth and nineteenth centuries. The element of surprise is achieved because the chariot is preceded by Fraud, who has just been cast away. Meanwhile the figure of Lady Spain, masked because she was at the time an ally of France, vainly attempts to stop the chariot from passing into the Low Countries. As the chariot speeds by her, Spain is represented a second time, now to one side, removing her mask with one hand and grasping at the harness with the other, openly opposing the attack. In the path of the chariot stand the comically astounded cities of the Low Countries, each one holding a key inscribed with its name, eager to surrender it to the conqueror.

Le Brun's painting shows Renaissance allegory at the point of transition to political cartoon, when the gods, no longer cosmological powers, were hardly required even as rhetorical figures lending majesty to the person of the ruler. Although Louis is represented as Jove, we hardly think of that god when we see him, for to be what he is, is enough.

21   "The Crossing of the Rhine" is reproduced in Walter Vitzthum, *Charles le Brun e sua scuola a Versailles* (Milan: Fabbri-Skirra, n.d.), pp. 28–29. For the seminal remarks of the Abbé Dubos on this work, see *Réflexions critiques sur la poésie et sur la peinture*, 7th ed. (Paris, 1770), 1:208–9. The first edition appeared anonymously in 1719. For Rubens, see 1:198 and 212, a criticism followed closely by Joseph Spence in *Polymetis; or, An Enquiry concerning the Agreement between the Works of the Roman Poets and the Remains of the Ancient Artists* (London, 1748), p. 117, and applied to Spenser on pp. 300–306. See also Jacob Burckhardt, *Reflections on Rubens*, ed. H. Gerson, trans. Mary Hottinger (London: Phaidon, 1950), p. 117.

5

The Self in
Enlightenment Allegory

The critical discussion of allegory as a distinct genre, rather than as a rhetorical figure, began in the Enlightenment. The leading theorist was the Abbé Dubos, whose demand for coherence on the literal plane was readily accommodated to the Lockean tenor of eighteenth-century English criticism.[1] That an allegory should be constructed with the rigor of a geometric demonstration is a claim that would have been all but unintelligible in the Renaissance, for it presupposes that the reader is a detached subject capable of judging the work as an object. Allegory had become an experience of the subject confined to the self, rather than an experience in the subject extended through a narrative. This is a significant change. When we read *The Faerie Queene*, we enter into the labyrinthine world of the poem, accepting its inconsistencies as expressions of the mysteries of nature and grace. We are not considering an object but entering on a quest; and a quest demands readiness to adjust unselfconsciously to the flow of events. We move

[1] See Jean Baptiste Dubos, *Réflexions critiques sur la poésie et sur la peinture*, 7th ed. (Paris, 1770), 1:190-230. The first edition was published anonymously in 1719 and translated into English by Thomas Nugent in 1748. The influence of Dubos's criticism of Rubens's allegory can be seen in Henry Home, Lord Kames, *Elements of Criticism*, 7th ed. (Edinburgh, 1788), 2:293-94, and in Joseph Spence, *Polymetis; or, An Enquiry concerning the Agreement between the Works of the Roman Poets and the Remains of the Ancient Artists* (London, 1747), pp. 296-98. For earlier, rhetorical theories of allegory, see Heinrich F. Plett, "Konzepte des Allegorischen in der englischen Renaissance," in *Formen und Funktionen der Allegorie, Symposion Wolfenbüttel 1978*, ed. Walter Haug (Stuttgart: Metzler, 1979), pp. 310-35.

freely between the literal tale and its several intensities of meaning without much concern to keep these distinct by calling them "levels." The mind that is involved in this process (as I mentioned in Chapter 2) cannot be located at any fixed point; it is distributed around the circuit of interpretive play, taking its color from the thought in the text, as an insect turns green on its leaf. Spenserian allegory is more a means to an end, a heuristic instrument for exciting the mind to activity, than it is an end in itself. This is what Spenser means in the "Letter to Raleigh" when he says that the "generall end" of his book is "to fashion a gentleman or noble person in vertuous and gentle discipline." By drawing the reader into its system, the poem "fashions" an intellectual habit.

In the Enlightenment, however, an allegory was an aesthetic end in itself, an artifact to be considered by the mind from a distance and appreciated for its simplicity and propriety. Absurdities were plucked out of Dryden—it was said to be easier to imagine mice bilking a coachman, and then supping at the Devil, than to suppose a Hind entertaining a Panther at a hermit's cell—and Spenser was chastised for allowing the teeth to bow to the soul.[2] In the interminable discussions of Milton's Sin and Death the main point at issue was the same: the inadvisability of permitting the narrative to take on a life of its own. As Johnson cautioned, "Allegorical persons . . . may produce effects, but cannot conduct actions. . . . Discord may raise a mutiny, but Discord cannot conduct a march, nor besiege a town."[3] But when Discord besieges a town, or becomes otherwise involved in more complicated actions—as Ate, or Discord, does in *The Faerie Queene*—the narrative becomes the generative source of the meaning, rather than the other way around. Meaning is complicated be-

2 For the standard of simplicity and propriety, see Joseph Spence, "The Defects of Our Modern Poets, in Their Allegories: Instanced from Spenser's *Faerie Queene*," in *Polymetis*, pp. 302–8. For the attack on Dryden, which was moved by the spirit of party, see the preface to Matthew Prior and Charles Montagu's *The Hind and the Panther Transvers'd to the Story of the Country Mouse and the City Mouse* (London, 1687), sig. A3r-v. For criticisms of such things as the teeth bowing to the soul, see Thomas Warton, *Observations on the "Fairy Queen" of Spenser*, 2d ed. (New York: Garland, 1970), 2:95–96.

3 Samuel Johnson, *Life of Pope*, in *Lives of the English Poets*, ed. G. B. Hill (Oxford: Clarendon Press, 1905), 3:233; for the application of this principle to Milton, see 1:185. See Steven Knapp, "Milton's Allegory of Sin and Death in Eighteenth-Century Criticism," in *Personification and the Sublime: Milton to Coleridge* (Cambridge: Harvard University Press, 1985), pp. 51–65, and Fredric V. Bogel, *The Dream of My Brother: An Essay on Johnson's Authority* (Victoria, B.C.: University of Victoria English Literary Studies, 1990), pp. 49–55. For various essays on allegory in the period, see Kevin L. Cope, ed., *Enlightening Allegory: Theory, Practice, and Contexts of Allegory in the Late Seventeenth and Eighteenth Centuries* (New York: AMS Press, 1993).

yond anything planned in advance. This effect, which Spenser exploits, is precisely what Enlightenment allegory is concerned to avoid.

One could cite as causes for this change the influence of neoclassicism generally, the exaggerated prestige given to such late ancient models of allegory as *The Tablet of Cebes* and Apuleius's fable of Cupid and Psyche, and the misapplication of the rhetorical standard of consistency in metaphor to the construction of entire narratives. But these factors are held in the frame of a larger event: the emergence of a thinking subject that stands apart from experience and is fearful of being confused or deceived, above all of being dispersed into what it considers. In Chapter 4 we observed in Francis Bacon this new sense of the self as an impregnable skeptic. Just as mental experience, separated from the external world, had to impose consistency on its own processes, so the literal level of an allegory was expected to be coherent in itself and clearly distinct from its meaning. No dog was to snap at its shadow and lose its troop of horse. These new strictures were particularly harmful to narrative. Romance, judged to be "gothic" by the standards of a more civilized age, was displaced by personification as the basis of allegorical expression[4]; and without the variety, even the disorder of romance, allegories became intellectually sterile. I suggested that these developments were brought about by a new sense of the self as an enclosed subject that is wholly distinct, indeed isolated, from the external world. As that world was situated unambiguously outside the mind, so the meaning of an allegory was to be situated unambiguously outside the work; and consistency was to be maintained within. Hence the more outlandish concoctions of baroque iconography were regarded in the Enlightenment as evidence not of profundity but of mental disorder.

Whatever we think of these changes, the better examples of allegory in the Enlightenment were openly artificial, lucidly if somewhat airlessly didactic, and effective as satire. These qualities are shown in an anthology from the period, revealingly titled *Allegories and Visions for the Entertainment and Instruction of Younger Minds.* Among its thirty-eight pieces the collection contains a translation of *The Tablet of Cebes,* Addi-

---

4 For ridicule of the "improper and unnatural allegories" of the emblematists, especially the influential Cesare Ripa, see Spence, *Polymetis*, p. 294. For gothic and romance, see Patricia Parker, *Inescapable Romance: Studies in the Poetics of a Mode* (Princeton: Princeton University Press, 1979), p. 161, and Maureen Quilligan, *The Language of Allegory: Defining the Genre* (Ithaca: Cornell University Press, 1979), p. 281.

son's "Vision of Mirza," William Shenstone's poetic version of the ancient allegory "The Choice of Hercules," and six of Johnson's allegories from *The Rambler*, including "The Vision of Theodore," which Johnson is reported—and this, if true, would be strange—to have called his best work.[5] That allegory was no longer mythopoeic and visionary but didactic and argumentative is apparent in the very titles of many eighteenth-century examples. Enthusiasm is not fired at the prospect of reading J. T. Desaguliers's *Newtonian System of the World, the Best Model of Government* or James Beattie's *Castle of Scepticism*, although the inquiring reader of Beattie will be rewarded with a puppet, represent'ng Hume's *Treatise of Human Nature*, that jumps down its own throat.[6] A work of more scope, written in Spenserian stanzas, is James Thomson's *Castle of Indolence*, from which Coleridge extracted an Aeolian harp. But in the end banality is restored: Indolence is undone by the Knight of Arts and Industry, leaving the enchanter's followers to be tortured by Beggary and Scorn.[7]

As for Blake, Swift, and Pope, these great writers move out to the extremes of satire and vision, rejecting the intellectual foundations on which the new theory of allegory rested: that the external world is matter in motion, and that the experience of the mind is, in Locke's words, "not much unlike a Closet wholly shut from light, with only some little openings left, to let in external visible Resemblances, or *Ideas* of things without."[8] The vast, intermediate realm of hierarchy, analogy, and correspondence, stretching between nihilistic satire and apocalyptic vision, was reduced to the status of an illusion. Addison associates that realm with narrative romance: "Our Souls are at present delightfully lost and bewildered in a pleasing Delusion, and we walk about like the Enchanted Hero of a Romance, who sees beautiful Castles, Woods and Meadows . . . but upon the finishing of some secret Spell, the fantastick Scene breaks

5   *Allegories and Visions for the Entertainment and Instruction of Younger Minds*, 2d ed. (London, 1773). The running title inside the volume is "Allegories for Young Ladies."
6   J. T. Desaguliers, *The Newtonian System of the World, the Best Model of Government: An Allegorical Poem* (Westminster, 1728). For James Beattie, see Ernest Campbell Mossner, "Beattie's 'The Castle of Scepticism': An Unpublished Allegory Against Hume, Voltaire, and Hobbes," *Texas Studies in English* 27 (1948): 108–45.
7   *The Castle of Indolence*, canto 2, stanza 77, in James Thomson, *Liberty, The Castle of Indolence, and Other Poems*, ed. James Sambrook (Oxford: Clarendon Press, 1986), p. 222.
8   John Locke, *An Essay Concerning Human Understanding*, ed. Peter H. Nidditch (Oxford: Clarendon Press, 1975), 2.11.17 (p. 163). For the camera obscura, see Marjorie Hope Nicolson, *Newton Demands the Muse: Newton's "Opticks" and the Eighteenth-Century Poets* (Princeton: Princeton University Press, 1946), pp. 78–81.

up, and the disconsolate Knight finds himself on a barren Heath, or in a solitary Desert."[9] One can only admire this articulation of Locke to romance, for it really does tell us something about Locke. But to conceive of experience itself in such terms, as an illusion created by the mechanics of mind, is to confine life to what Blake, in *Europe*, called "an allegorical abode where existence hath never come." One lives in a world fashioned, as Blake says in *Jerusalem*, on "the Loom of Locke whose Woof rages dire / Washd by the Water-wheels of Newton."[10] In a universe driven by Newton's laws, mental life—and, we may add, narrative freedom—is reduced to an isolated, mechanical effect of those laws. At the center of that effect is the subject, the inner self that one supposes to be separate from what it perceives, as Addison supposes his disconsolate knight to be ontologically distinct from what he surveys. As Locke himself says, "It requires Art and Pains to set [the Understanding] at a distance, and make it its own Object."[11] When we set the understanding at a distance, however, it becomes a fixed image, an idea, generated by the very process we want to observe. What sort of self is woven on the loom of Locke?

One of its most succinct descriptions, fished from the jargon of the mechanical psychology, is given by Berkeley's materialist, Hylas:

> It is supposed that the soul makes her residence in some part of the brain, from which the nerves take their rise, and are thence extended to all parts of the body: and that outward objects by the different impressions they make on the organs of sense, communicate certain vibrative motions to the nerves; and these being filled with spirit, propagate them to the brain or seat of the soul, which according to the various impressions or traces thereby made in the brain, is variously affected with ideas.[12]

9 Joseph Addison, *The Spectator*, ed. Donald F. Bond (Oxford: Clarendon Press, 1965), 3:546–47 (no. 413).
10 William Blake, *Europe*, plate 8, in *William Blake's Writings*, ed. G. E. Bentley Jr. (Oxford: Clarendon Press, 1978), 1:228 and *Jerusalem*, plate 15, in *William Blake's Writings*, 1:445. See Northrop Frye, "The Case Against Locke," in *Fearful Symmetry: A Study of William Blake* (Princeton: Princeton University Press, 1947), pp. 3–29.
11 Locke, *Essay*, 1.1.1 (p. 43).
12 *Three Dialogues between Hylas and Philonous*, in vol. 2 of *The Works of George Berkeley, Bishop of Cloyne*, ed. A. A. Luce and T. E. Jessop (London: Thomas Nelson, 1949), pp. 208–9.

A moment's reflection will reveal that the problem with this model does not lie merely in the transformation of "vibrative motions" into "ideas." The problem is that the very concept of an idea, whether it is located above the heavens or in the brain, necessarily includes an apprehending subject. (The word *object* suggests a thing that is "thrown against" consciousness.) An idea is not an object alone but a relation between subject and object. If, therefore, an idea is forced inside its perceiving subject—like the puppet that jumps down its own throat—that idea will reconstitute itself as a relation by projecting a new subject inside the old one, thus opening an infinite regression of the self into the self.

Logically speaking, this means only that the fantasy of a self inside the self must be rejected as absurd, having been reduced to a paradox similar to that of the Third Man, which we examined in Chapter 1.[13] But we are speaking of the imaginative, not the logical, consequences of an infinite regression. Just as ancient idealism responded to the paradox of the Third Man by generating personifications, so Enlightenment psychology generated personifications at the boundary between the self and the world.[14] Abstract universals such as Justice, which were thought to appear at the end of a chain of causes that began in sensation, tether the self to the external world and keep it from falling back into itself. The happy extroversion of the Enlightenment subject is driven by a horror of the chaos within.

In his *Observations*, the authoritative amplification of Lockean psychology, David Hartley intended to establish an inner complement to Newton's mechanics.[15] Newton's laws, having proven themselves internally consistent, experimentally predictive, and applicable to the real world, were the standard for intellectual endeavor. If similar laws could be elicited from the association of ideas, a new order of correspondences between the inner and the outer worlds would emerge, replacing the older, Neoplatonic analogy of microcosm and macrocosm. In this new

13 See A. D. Nuttall, "The Sealing of the Doors," in *A Common Sky: Philosophy and the Literary Imagination* (Berkeley and Los Angeles: University of California Press, 1974), pp. 13-44.
14 For an analysis of Lockean psychology as allegory reduced to the margin between consciousness and the organs of perception, see Vera Veronica Kelly, "Embodied and Inane: Literature on the Perceptual Threshold, 1689-1743" (Ph.D. diss., Cornell University, 1987).
15 David Hartley, *Observations on the Frame of the Human Body and Mind, and Their Mutual Connexions and Influences* (London, 1749), 1:5; for allegory, see 1:214.

order the human mind—frequently personified by the figure of Newton himself[16]—is placed at the center of experience, voyaging through seas of thought, alone. But this loneliness is not just a consequence of genius. It is common to us all. In "the mind's Presence-room," as Locke calls it, only ideas can be "perceived by the Understanding," not the things to which they refer. The absence of a direct relationship between ideas and the world raises a compensatory demand for rigorous consistency among the ideas. Locke says of the edifice of his own thoughts, "If mine prove a Castle in the Air, I shall endeavour it shall be all of a piece, and hang together."[17]

Because allegory endures the same isolation from what it refers to, it must submit itself to the same discipline. Critics in the eighteenth century may seem pedantic in their haste to impose on allegorical expression standards of consistency belonging more properly to the conduct of metaphor. But the relation of an allegory to its referent was no longer one of participation, in which signs are invested with numinous power. The relation was instead one of formal correspondence, in which the allegory and its referent are separate but parallel in structure. No image that is inconsistent with the literal fable—or the "representative subject," to use the terminology of Henry Home, Lord Kames—is to be introduced into that representation, however strikingly it may bear on our understanding of the "principal subject."[18]

Allegory was therefore submitted to *method*, that discipline of inquiry denoting the correct means of transit from one stage of thought to another. In an earlier, cosmographic view of the world, the knowledge mediated by allegory was sustained by magical correspondences between apparently unrelated things, between planets, constellations, animals, plants, and the passions. Unlikely juxtapositions were regarded not as violations of propriety but as revelations of secret affinities and channels in the natural world.[19] When, however, meaning was no longer supposed to lie inside the image, or to flow through invisible channels between corresponding things, the only relation that an allegory could bear to

16 For the theme of Newton's mind in verse of the period, see Bonamy Dobrée, *English Literature in the Early Eighteenth Century, 1700–1740* (Oxford: Clarendon Press, 1959), pp. 500–501.
17 Locke, *Essay*, 2.3.1 (p. 121), and 1.4.25 (pp. 102–3).
18 Kames, *Elements of Criticism*, 2:294, cf. 2:278 for the pleasure of perceiving the relation "because it is our own work."
19 The notion of a "perpetual Thread of Analogy" running through nature survives in Hartley; see *Observations*, 2:294–97.

the truth was in the resemblance of one whole to another. An allegory had to hang together.

In the system of knowledge that existed before the Enlightenment—or, to be a little more cautious, in the imaginative appropriation of that system by allegory—even the truths of mathematics were subject to resonance and play. In Alan of Lille's *Anticlaudianus* the maiden Arithmetic, as part of the vehicle in which Phronesis (Wisdom) makes her journey to heaven, wears a dress that displays the cosmic power of number. Number binds nature together; and the first number, the One, begets the other numbers from itself. Even the simplest operation of arithmetic, therefore, can be apprehended only in part, for it contains something progressive within it that tends toward absolute knowledge.[20] In Descartes's *Discourse on the Method*, by contrast, every moment of knowledge is complete in itself. It is also, like the skeptical Bacon, immobile:

> Having but one truth to discover in respect of each matter, whoever succeeds in finding it knows in its regard as much as can be known. It is the same as with the child, for instance, who has been instructed in Arithmetic and has made an addition according to the rule prescribed: he may be sure of having found as regards the sum of figures given to him all that the human mind can know. For, in conclusion, the Method which teaches us to follow the true order, and to enumerate exactly every term in the matter under investigation, contains everything which gives certainty in the rules of arithmetic.[21]

The point to the claim that the child can know as much as the scholar about an arithmetical sum is to eliminate any residual presence of meaning beneath what is known distinctly and clearly. The old principle of analogy is equated with obscurity; and the slightest obscurity leads to error, rendering every subsequent step useless.

The Neoplatonic doctrine of the presence of the whole of the cosmos in each of its parts was revived in the romantic doctrine of the symbol. It was, moreover, through a notion of *method*, etymologically interpreted as a "path" or "means of transit," that Coleridge made that doctrine look

20　Alan of Lille, *Anticlaudianus*, ed. R. Bossuat (Paris: Vrin, 1955), 3.303-12. Cf. S. T. Coleridge, *Philosophical Lectures*, ed. Kathleen Coburn (London: Pilot Press, 1949), pp. 107-8: "In each number there was an integral or individual that still contained in its nature something progressive, that went beyond it."
21　*Discourse on the Method*, vol. 1 of *The Philosophical Works of Descartes*, trans. Elizabeth S. Haldane and G. R. T. Ross (1931; reprint, New York: Dover, 1955), p. 94.

modern. Whereas in Descartes method is a discipline imposed on oneself so that one will reject the illusion of connectedness between superficially similar things, in Coleridge method becomes a means of accepting that connectedness as an index of truth. He characterizes the new science of chemistry as "poetry substantiated" because it deals with secret affinities in nature. These had been apprehended hitherto only by the poets, as when, in *Paradise Lost*, Sin says that she feels herself drawn to the earth by "some connatural force / Powerful at greatest distance to unite / With secret amity things of like kind."[22] Coleridge's notion of the symbol is, like his notion of chemistry, essentially Neoplatonic. The symbol is the visible part of an ontological connection in a hierarchy of being, one in which all such connections are made by "connatural force."

At moments when Coleridge is speaking out of his deepest convictions, his thoughts tend toward Neoplatonic rather than Christian structures, ultimately toward an image of the individual as "a syllepsis, a compendium of Nature—the Microcosm": "In Man the centripetal and individualizing tendency of all Nature is itself concentred and individualized—he is a Revelation of Nature! Henceforward, he is referred to himself, delivered up to his own charge; and he who stands the most on himself, and stands the firmest, is the truest, because the most individual, Man."[23] The natural world, by the law of polarity, fashions this individual man even as it is informed by him, so that what he knows and what he is are the same. Because the world acts on him wholly and at once he does not disappear into himself, like the Enlightenment subject. He seems in more danger of the opposite loss, of flowing out of himself into the world and becoming indistinguishable from it, of failing, as Coleridge says, to stand firm.[24] Coleridge's claustrophobic reaction to mechanical psychology provoked him to adopt a theory of the symbol which would be explicitly defined by its opposition to allegory and which

22   Samuel Taylor Coleridge, *Treatise on Method*, in *Shorter Works and Fragments*, ed. H. J. Jackson and J. R. de J. Jackson, vol. 11 of *The Collected Works of Samuel Taylor Coleridge* (Princeton: Princeton University Press, 1995), p. 649. See also *The Friend*, ed. Barbara Rooke, vol. 4 (in 2 parts) of *Collected Works*, 1:471. For the words of Sin, see *Paradise Lost*, ed. Alastair Fowler (London: Longman, 1971), 10.246–49. See also M. H. Abrams, *The Correspondent Breeze: Essays on English Romanticism* (New York: Norton, 1984), pp. 211–12.
23   Samuel Taylor Coleridge, *Theory of Life*, in *Shorter Works and Fragments*, pp. 550–51. Cf. Pico della Mirandola, 2d proem to *Heptaplus*, in *De hominis dignitate, Heptaplus, De ente et uno e scritti vari*, ed. and trans. E. Garin (Florence: Vallecchi, 1942), p. 188. See Nicholas Halmi, "How Christian is the Coleridgean Symbol?" *The Wordsworth Circle* 26.1 (1995): 26–30.
24   *Collected Letters of Samuel Taylor Coleridge*, ed. Earl Leslie Griggs (Oxford: Clarendon Press, 1956), 2:867.

would allow him, in classic, Neoplatonic fashion, to escape from the enclosure of the self and be at one with the world.[25] This process has little to do with literary theory, in which the opposition of symbol to allegory makes little sense; but it has its basis in something of more importance than a simple mistake.

The influence of stoicism, on Wordsworth especially, can be discerned in the notion of a universal spirit, an intellectual breeze, leavening the material world. That doctrine was most familiar to Wordsworth and his readers from the speech of Anchises in the sixth book of the *Aeneid*, where the stoic ideal of the self appears to generate its reflection in nature.[26] On the other side, the materialist and mechanical philosophy that the romantics opposed, the philosophy inherited from Bacon, Newton, Locke, and Hartley, is essentially Epicurean. It sees nature as matter moved by mechanical laws; it analyzes wholes into parts, ultimately into atoms; it proclaims the irrelevance of gods; and, like its several modern versions, it regards happiness as the goal of life and the ultimate aim of science. Bacon, who could follow this reasoning to its conclusion, saw that the final stage of scientific progress along these lines would be concerned not with making nature more pleasing in itself but with expanding the body's capacity for pleasure.

This hedonistic, utopian enterprise of the Enlightenment is vividly expressed in the allegories of Erasmus Darwin (the grandfather of Charles), *The Botanic Garden* and *The Temple of Nature*. Both works are extravagant encyclopedic fantasies accompanied by scientific notes. The title of *The Botanic Garden* is somewhat misleading. Its first part, "The Economy of Vegetation," concerns the structure of the cosmos as a whole, which is described from the original explosion of light into being. Darwin is occasionally sublime, but his heart is not in it, and his typical mood is that of a genial entertainer who does not himself believe in what he is setting before us: "Lo here a Camera Obscura is presented to thy view, in which are lights and shades dancing on a whited canvass, and magnified into apparent life! — if thou art perfectly a leisure for such trivial amusement, walk in, and view the wonders of my Inchanted Garden."[27] Darwin's aim, however, is not entirely hedonistic: "The general

25 S. T. Coleridge, *Lectures, 1808–1819, On Literature*, ed. R. A. Foakes, vol. 5 (in 2 parts) of *The Collected Works of Samuel Taylor Coleridge* (Princeton: Princeton University Press, 1987), 1:101.
26 Virgil, *Aeneid* 6.724–27.
27 Erasmus Darwin, *The Botanic Garden: A Poem in Two Parts . . . Containing the Economy of Vegetation [and] the Loves of the Plants. With Philosophical Notes* (London, 1791), 2:vii–viii.

design of the following sheets is to inlist Imagination under the banner of Science; and to lead her votaries from the looser analogies, which dress out the image of poetry, to the stricter ones which form the ratiocination of philosophy."[28]

Among these "looser analogies" are the classical gods and, following Pope's example, the Rosicrucian spirits of the elements. The gnomes, or spirits of the earth, for example, tend to the rotting of vegetable matter so that the underlying life may be raised up again in new forms. Darwin's phrase for that life indicates why Coleridge read him:

> Gnomes! with nice eye the slow solution watch,
> With fostering hand the parting atoms catch,
> Join in new forms, combine with life and sense,
> And guide and guard the transmigrating Ens.

In the verses that follow we see the state to which classical myth has declined:

> So when on Lebanon's sequester'd height
> The fair Adonis left the realm of light,
> Bow'd his bright locks, and, fated from his birth
> To change eternal, mingled with the earth.[29]

Darwin is not saying that the truth on this subject must be something like this—like the death of Adonis or the work of the gnomes. He is saying that the truth is nothing like these things at all, but that in the present state of knowledge such fantasies must be put in its place. In what amounts to a reassuring allegory of knowledge, Darwin's elaborate notes, ranging chaotically from the theory of magnetism to classical vases and tadpoles, present an external world to which the mind has no access. But like Locke's beneficent deity, who ensures the general correspondence of our ideas to the world, Darwin's reader may move freely between the verse and its commentary, judging the accuracy with which the one corresponds to the other. Such reading can be, even at length, highly enjoyable. If its effect is anodyne, it is no less so than the blandly eudemonic assurance we are given in Wordsworth's *Excursion:*

28 Ibid., 1:v.
29 Ibid., 1:106–8; canto 2, ll. 581–88.

How exquisitely the individual Mind
(And the progressive powers perhaps no less
Of the whole Species) to the external World
Is fitted: —and how exquisitely, too—
Theme this but little heard of among men—
The external World is fitted to the Mind.

Blake's retort is as predictable as it is just: "You shall not bring me down to believe such fitting and fitted."[30]

Darwin's scientific interests, modern as they are, do not separate him from more traditional allegorical works. On the contrary, he is very much a part of a tradition in which the world is reorganized as an order of signs, even if that order has been withdrawn from the world into the head. The forcing together of heterogeneous subject matter in verse and prose indicates that the genre of the poems is Menippean satire, and the encyclopedic range of Darwin's interests, expressed in a tone of somewhat daft festiveness, makes him the Martianus Capella of the Enlightenment. C. S. Lewis memorably observed of Martianus that "this universe, which has produced the bee-orchid and the giraffe, has produced nothing stranger."[31] Perhaps not, but Darwin is almost as strange. He was also, like Martianus, popular among the learned for reasons that are hard to understand now, but that have something to do with allaying anxieties raised by the vast extent of human knowledge. Darwin's works were read with attention by Coleridge and Wordsworth, however much they despised him. And it is probably Darwin whom Coleridge has principally in view in the *Biographia Literaria* when he condemns the poetic consequences of the mechanical psychology of Hartley.[32]

We may pause for a moment to reflect on the symbolic purpose of notes accompanying a poetic text. In the Renaissance they conferred on a poem the dignity of a classical work and enhanced the sense of mystery

30 Wordsworth, 1814 preface to *The Excursion*, ll. 63–68, in *The Poetical Works of William Wordsworth*, eds. E. De Selincourt and Helen Darbyshire (Oxford: Clarendon Press, 1949), 5:5. Bentley, *William Blake's Writings*, 2:1508.
31 C. S. Lewis, *The Allegory of Love: A Study in Medieval Tradition* (Oxford: Oxford University Press, 1938), p. 78.
32 Coleridge in his youth fell under Darwin's spell, describing him as "the first literary character in Europe." See *Letters*, 1:305. See also Desmond King-Hele, *Doctor of Revolution: The Life and Genius of Erasmus Darwin* (London: Faber, 1977), pp. 259–61, and John Livingston Lowes, *The Road to Xanadu: A Study in the Ways of the Imagination* (Boston: Houghton Mifflin, 1927), pp. 99 and 189.

in the poem itself. Poetry stood between the plain language of marginal commentary and the ineffable truths that were adumbrated in the poem, such that clearness and proximity to truth were inversely proportional. By Darwin's time the hierarchy of discourses was turned on its head. Poetry became an illustrative but "trivial amusement" derived from a truth that more properly exists in the notes, just as ideas are derived from impressions of sense. Already in the seventeenth century there are examples of annotation, such as Abraham Cowley's notes to his *Davideis*, where the commentary is presented in the confident tone of a scholar in command of his facts while the poem stands as a conjectural hypothesis, or an illustrative fantasy, based on those facts. Truth had begun to migrate from its earlier place in the hieratic language of the poem into the commentary surrounding the text.

The most striking example of this reversal of authority occurs in a seventeenth-century work that almost certainly influenced Darwin, and which I had occasion to mention in Chapter 4: Phineas Fletcher's *Purple Island*. This neo-Spenserian allegorical poem, though hardly more than a literary curiosity now, must have seemed toward the end of the eighteenth century to represent the only hope for poetry in the future. Poetry would ally itself with the heroic achievements of science, imposing an imaginative, even visionary order on those achievements. How else were the poets to rival the ancients and, more to the point, Milton, except by taking up the challenge of a world that had been radically transformed by the new science? Even Coleridge stated that in the twenty years it would take him to compose an epic poem he would have to master mathematics, mechanics, hydrostatics, optics, astronomy, botany, metallurgy, fossilism, chemistry, geology, anatomy, and medicine, turning only then to the human mind, as revealed in voyages, travels, and histories.[33] Considered in this light, Fletcher's poem, which Darwin could have read in the new edition of 1784,[34] must have seemed a revelation, a clue from the past to how modern poets might get out from under the burden of that past.

I mentioned in Chapter 4 the enormous psychological impact of the science of anatomy, which was an apocalypse, an unveiling of the body as a structure that is altogether distinct from the structure of the world.

33 Coleridge, *Letters*, 1:320-21. W. Jackson Bate, *The Burden of the Past and the English Poet* (Cambridge: Harvard University Press, 1970), p. 109.
34 James Venable Logan, *The Poetry and Aesthetics of Erasmus Darwin* (Princeton: Princeton University Press, 1936), pp. 132-33.

The resulting eclipse of the microcosm-macrocosm analogy occasioned the best-known part of Fletcher's poem: the sequence of four cantos in which the interior of the body is described in anatomical detail, with technical notes supplied in the margins. Perhaps, we may imagine him thinking, it is possible to recuperate the analogy between the body and the world, starting with an intermediate, geographical structure: an island. The zany logic of the choice results in passages that are not unentertaining. Here, for example, is Fletcher's account of the bowels, followed by his didactic notes:

> Such would the state of this whole Island be
> If those pipes windings (passage quick delaying)
> Should not refrain too much edacitie,
> With longer stay fierce appetite allaying.
> These pipes are seven-fold longer than the Isle,
> Yet all are folded in a little pile,
> Whereof three noble are, and thinne, three thick, and vile.

It is approved that the entrails dried, and blown, are seven times longer then the body: they are all one entire body, yet their differing substance hath distinguished them into the thinne, and thick: the thinne have the more noble office. The first is straight without any winding that the chyle might not return and most narrow, that it might not finde too hasty a passage. It takes in a little passage from the gall, which there purges his choler, to provoke the entrails (when they are slow) to cast out the excrements. This is called the Duodenum (or twelve finger) from his length.[35]

We see in a passage such as this one how the verse has been demoted to the status of an ornament, lending sparkle to the truth as we know it in prose. Much as Darwin was indebted to Fletcher's example, there is an important difference between the two poets. As we read Fletcher, we suppose that we are witnessing something real, the actual anatomy of a body, each organ being removed in its turn and set out for inspection in the margins. The poem does not raise phenomenological doubt. Darwin, however, being immersed in the mechanical psychology, makes us feel as if we are inside the camera obscura of the mind, observing the

35 Phineas Fletcher, *The Purple Island*, in vol. 1 of Giles and Phineas Fletcher, *Poetical Works*, ed. Frederick S. Boas, 2 vols. (1909; reprint, Cambridge: Cambridge University Press, 1970), canto 2. stanza 39.

processes by which the understanding represents to itself the mystery of the external world.

Both models carry with them assumptions about the place of the body and the mind in the world. In the older, cosmographic tradition of the *Timaeus* the macrocosm is spherical because there is nothing outside it. It has no need for limbs or for what Bernardus Silvestris called the "all-making hand."[36] The Enlightenment concept of mind likewise reproduces the self inside the self, although it is now the inner self that has no need of limbs; the inner self simply perceives. But the outer self, the body, is also curiously inactive, avoiding any direct, workmanlike engagement with the world in favor of a series of perceptual mediations. This is apparent in Darwin's account of the hand. The hand is not a productive organ, as it is for Bernardus Silvestris' microcosmic man, but a receptive one:

> The hand, first gift of Heaven! to man belongs;
> Untipt with claws the circling fingers close,
> With rival points the bending thumbs oppose,
> Trace the nice lines of Form with sense refined,
> And clear ideas charm the thinking mind.

From these clear ideas an internal allegory is erected which is not unlike those of the medieval Platonists, who described the creation of the world from inchoate matter and the progress of wisdom through the celestial spheres. But Darwin's allegory, instead of ranging through the cosmos, unfolds in the head.

Coleridge and Darwin faced in contrasting but related ways the challenge of Enlightenment epistemology. Both saw how that theory of knowledge turned the mind into a prison cut off from the external world; both saw that as long as the poet was confined to that prison poetry could lay no claim on the truth; and both called the poetry made in that prison, under those conditions, allegory. But whereas Coleridge devoted himself to recovering the ancient, vatic authority of the poet, Darwin accepted the conditions to which poetry had been reduced by Enlightenment science. Both choices could be expressed in narrower, political programs, as Coleridge did in *The Statesman's Manual*, grounding Tory ideology in the hierarchical concept of the symbol.

36 Bernardus Silvestris, *Cosmographia*, ed. Peter Dronke (Leiden: Brill, 1978), 14.182.

Darwin's political vision was broader and, as an enthusiastic promoter of technological progress within a Whig interpretation of history, he had the future on his side. This visionary enthusiasm may remind us, in the late twentieth century, of the unalloyed optimism with which the celebrators of technological revolution imagine the future. There is little point in questioning the value, or deploring the effects, of the inventions themselves. (One is reminded of Heidegger's quixotic jeremiad on the typewriter.) But there is some point in observing how the inventions become an occasion for celebrating the innocence of human desire. Desire is good. This impulsive judgment informs everything in Darwin; and it is a judgment that was in large measure responsible for his amazing popularity, turning all eyes away from the darkness inside. For Darwin the faith in material improvement through technology—early on in *The Botanic Garden* we meet an aircraft powered by steam—becomes an excuse for refusing to look into the self. For desire seems innocent only so long as the eye is turned outward to the objects that desire selects, and with which it conceals its true nature.

Such extroversion allows one to suppose that all human problems derive either from the resistance of external nature, which must therefore be conquered, or from the dead hand of the past, which must be struggled against—and if necessary purged—until the will-to-improvement frees us from history. The utopian drive of technology encourages us to think in terms of a series of practical problems to be solved, desire being nothing other than the innocent appropriation of the objects it envisions. There is, it is supposed, nothing perverse in desire. But the end of desire, the absolute appropriation of the external world (and, as we shall see, of other bodies), is not a utopia in which humans would live in harmony with one another and rule over nature. The vision of utopia is a vision only of the most comprehensive object with which desire turns our attention away from its goal: the infinite extension of the subject, which can occur only by enclosing all other subjects. That goal can be imagined only as a single person—traditionally a man—who devours the world. Darwin, in a moment of striking disclosure, brings such a subject before us:

> Immortal Guide! O, now with accents kind
> Give to my ear the progress of the Mind.
> How loves, and tastes, and sympathies commence
> From evanescent notices of sense?
> How from the yielding touch and rolling eyes

The piles immense of human science rise?—
With mind gigantic steps the puny Elf,
And weighs and measures all things but himself![37]

The last two words acknowledge a crucial and, in a sense, world-destroying limitation in the field of self-knowledge, for the cosmos that Darwin evokes with encyclopedic thoroughness depends entirely on the subjectivity of this gigantic mind. Yet by the strange economy of loss which is constitutive of the Enlightenment experience of the sublime, this incapacity in the subject is turned to account, giving the passage its powerful aesthetic charge. We see here how that peculiarly Enlightenment experience, the sublime, has its origin in the decay of allegory, of confidence in the power of reason to grasp the totality of the cosmos in an arrangement of visual forms.[38] In the Kantian sublime it is the incapacity of reason to grasp the external world that turns reason inward, to a recognition of its own power. But in this passage from Darwin the power of reason to grasp the external world is left intact while everything that belongs to the self that is not reason—principally, human desire—remains in obscurity. What specific desire, or what fear, nourished by the power of reason, drives that "puny elf" to encompass the world with its mind? To answer this question we must consider Darwin's homunculus more closely.

Looking inward, Darwin sees a self that is moving in two directions at once, its body diminishing as its reason expands. The self represented by this body, as was noted earlier, is the Enlightenment version of the paradox of the Third Man, the perceiving self inside the self, which must contain a third self inside it, and so on. The aesthetic charge of the passage draws its power from the relief with which the poet turns outward, away from the horror of the logical chaos within. The subject is rescued from the abyss within and reappears at the boundaries of the universe, resolving the contradiction that had existed as long as there was anything outside itself. In terms of the symbolism of the body, the chaos that is left behind is an excremental horror. As the universe is encompassed

37 Erasmus Darwin, *The Temple of Nature; or, the Origin of Society. A Poem, with Philo-sophical Notes* (London, 1803), 3.41–48.
38 N. A. Halmi, "From Hierarchy to Opposition: Allegory and the Sublime," *Comparative Literature* 44 (Fall 1992): 337–60. See Samuel H. Monk, *The Sublime: A Study of Critical Theories in XVIII-Century England* (1935; reprint, Ann Arbor: University of Michigan Press, 1960), and Neil Hertz, *The End of the Line: Essays on Psychoanalysis and the Sublime* (New York: Columbia University Press, 1985).

and digested by the mind, the body to which the mind is attached moves forward in time, leaving the "piles immense" of science behind it. The past is that portion of the material world which humanity has already encompassed and to which it pays no attention as it advances. So long as humanity looks forward along the trajectory of progress it is oblivious of its own waste and can regard the external world as nothing other than that which it has yet to draw into itself. The answer to the question, What desire drives man to encompass the world? is an unacceptable one: it is the desire for absolute, annihilating power. That this image of the universe in the form of a body can still seem to us a desirable conclusion to history indicates the extent to which we remain under its spell. But two poets of surprisingly kindred sensibility, Pope and Baudelaire, imagined this conclusion in less flattering terms. Pope's goddess Dulness and Baudelaire's *Ennui* both annihilate their worlds in a yawn.[39]

Their mythological prototype is the god Saturn, who devours his sons, the ages of the world, and who represents the madness of allelophagic desire (see Figure 5). The idea of "man" encompassing the cosmos relies on the simple fact of there being only one man. But the insurmountable obstacle to the fulfillment of that desire is not the resistance of the material world. It is, as we observed, the existence of other bodies that also desire to encompass the world. Darwin stands at the beginning of the optimistic, Enlightenment project of conquering the world with reason, a project that depends, as we saw, on turning outward, away from the darkness within, and away from the fear of that darkness's logical form: the infinite regression of the self into the self. We see such an act of terrifying introversion in Conrad's *Heart of Darkness*, where the Enlightenment subject is realized in the figure of Kurtz, who is the god Saturn, incarnate as an agent of colonial power. In attempting to master the chaos of the external world, Kurtz re-encounters that disorder in himself, as an unappeasable hunger, the curse of Erysichthon.[40] Like Darwin's homun-

39   Alexander Pope, *The Dunciad*, 4.629-56, in *The Twickenham Edition of the Works of Alexander Pope*, vol. 5, *The Dunciad*, ed. James Sutherland, 2d ed. (New Haven: Yale University Press, 1953). Cf. Charles, Baudelaire's "Au lecteur," in *The Flowers of Evil*, ed. and trans. James McGowan (New York: Oxford University Press, 1993), p. 7 and p. 351n. For a view of Pope's Dulness as a "secret sharer" in the poet, see Fredric V. Bogel, "Dulness Unbound: Rhetoric and Pope's *Dunciad*," *PMLA* 97 (October 1982): 854.
40   Ovid, *Metamorphoses* 8. 738-878. Having destroyed a forest and cut down a great oak sacred to Ceres, Erysichthon is cursed by the goddess with unappeasable hunger, becoming ever more empty by eating (*inanis edendo*) until he is driven (like Beattie's puppet) to devour himself.

5. Francisco de Goya. *Saturn*. 1819–23. Prado, Madrid. Giraudon/Art Resource, New York

culus Kurtz is physically diminished as something inside him expands. But it is his desire, not his mind, that expands. His desire reveals itself in the yawning abyss of a mouth that opens, Conrad says, "as though he had wanted to swallow all the air, all the earth, all the men before him."[41]

At the conclusion of Chapter 4 I mentioned a work in the visual arts, Charles le Brun's *Crossing the Rhine*, as the final example of how the classical gods in the Renaissance surrounded the body of the prince with an aura of power. Near the midpoint of the eighteenth century we encounter an allegorical work in which the aura of power has become the light of reason, symbolized by the sun god Apollo (see Figure 6). I refer to Tiepolo's *Allegory of the Continents*, which was executed on the barrel vault over the monumental staircase of the prince-bishop's palace in Würzburg. Reason, rather than glory, has become the means for extending the power of the body. But this power of reason is at the same time, as with the mind of Darwin's homunculus, curiously detached from the body; it is a universal force enclosing the world.

The Allegory of the Continents stands in a tradition of civic allegorical painting which begins in the fourteenth century, in the town hall of Siena and the Spanish Chapel in Florence, and which reaches Tiepolo through the great baroque masters of the seventeenth century. It is a tradition in which the contexts of power are widened from the scale of the city to that of the nation state, and from thence to the global theater of European colonialism, when the personal power of the prince is no longer the visible center of that power. The final stage of this development may be seen in the early twentieth century, in the *Colonial Allegories* decorating the walls of the Musée des colonies in Paris (now the Museum of African and Oceanic Art), in which the continents are engaged in a happy exchange of raw materials for European cultural forms.[42] The building is now the home of artworks that came out of Conrad's dark places of the earth to inspire the central movement of twentieth-century European art.

Of the formal aspects of Tiepolo's work the most important is its achievement of a fully panoramic spectacle, representing the continents—Europe, Asia, Africa, and America—as continuous in space on the surface of the globe. The other formal aspect I would note is that

41 Joseph Conrad, *Heart of Darkness* (Harmondsworth: Penguin, 1973), pp. 85–86.
42 Catherine Bouché, "Allégories coloniales," *L'Objet d'art* (April 1988): 88–97.

6. Giambattista Tiepolo. *Apollo*. Detail of ceiling above staircase of Residenz, Würzburg. 1753. Bildarchiv Foto Marburg/Art Resource, New York

7. Giambattista Tiepolo. Detail of staircase, Residenz, Würzburg. 1753. Bildarchiv Foto Marburg/Art Resource, New York

there is no position from which the entire work is visible at once. It must be experienced in time, like an allegory, and the architecture of the staircase causes that experience to unfold in a manner that is richly suggestive, creating a labyrinth of meanings.[43] As one approaches the staircase the personification of America, representing the primitive stage of human civilization, rises into view while Apollo, with the help of the Hours, prepares the chariot of the sun (see Figure 7). By the time one reaches the landing Asia and Africa can just be seen over the balustrade

43 Svetlana Alpers and Michael Baxandall, *Tiepolo and the Pictorial Intelligence* (New Haven: Yale University Press, 1994), p. 115.

encircling the staircase above. There is a dramatic moment when one turns on the landing and Europe appears, with the god Mercury high above, pointing along the line of the vault to Apollo, who is bringing the light of reason to the uncivilized parts of the world.[44]

One can spend days moving about under this work, discovering a seemingly inexhaustible array of meanings in the relationships between the work's various parts; and these meanings are all placed by the mind in a synchronic structure. Although one is moving through a temporal labyrinth, one is always aware of the whole; and that difference is continually marked by an interpretive tension between perception and reason. By that tension the viewer becomes aware of a narrative of the rise of civilization from its crude beginnings in primitive rites to its apogee in Enlightenment Europe. Everything is brilliantly lit, including the suggestion of cannibalism in those primitive rites. Among the variety of raw materials that are to be exchanged for European cultural forms we see, to one side of the personification of Africa, an ivory tusk. This is the only premonition of Conrad's revelation of Enlightenment as having at its basis an unappeasable, allelophagic desire.

But perhaps it is not the only premonition. For beyond the magnificent personification of Africa we may discern her avatar in Conrad. This woman is also, when we first see her, the dark continent's "tenebrous and passionate soul":

> She carried her head high; her hair was done in the shape of a helmet; she had brass leggings to the knees, brass wire gauntlets to the elbow, a crimson spot on her tawny cheek, innumerable necklaces of glass beads on her neck; bizarre things, charms, gifts of witch-men, that hung about her, glittered and trembled at every step. She must have had the value of several elephant tusks upon her. She was savage and superb, wild-eyed and magnificent; there was something ominous and stately in her deliberate progress. And in the hush that had fallen suddenly upon the whole sorrowful land, the immense wilderness, the colossal body of the fecund and mysterious life seemed to look at her, pensive, as though it had been looking at the image of its own tenebrous and passionate soul.[45]

44 The addition of a portrait medallion of the prince-bishop made it necessary to transpose Mercury and Apollo, Apollo having been originally placed over Europe. See Frank Büttner, *Giovanni Battista Tiepolo: Die Fresken in der Residenz zu Würzburg* (Würzburg: Popp, 1980), p. 107, and Massimo Gemin and Filippo Pedrocco, *Giambattista Tiepolo: i dipinti, opera completa* (Venice: Arsenale, 1993), pp. 152–61.
45 Conrad, *Heart of Darkness*, p. 89.

Complete in her symbolic accoutrements, to the value of several elephant tusks, and depriving Europeans of that many piano keys and billiard balls, she is a revelation of how allegory imprints meaning on the body of difference. She is Conrad's Francesca da Rimini, committed to the circle of Hell reserved for those who prefer wasteful self-assertion to reasonable economic exchange. Conrad's narrator has an unusual capacity for observing, with magnificent irony, how the chaos of life escapes such imprinting. The economic aside in this passage prepares us for what is to come: the disconcerting revelation that this woman is familiar, troubled, theatrical, uncertain, and human, that she too has a story.

6

Allegory and Politics

During the crisis of 59 B.C., before his flight from Italy and the destruction of his house on the Palatine, Cicero wrote to Atticus: "Of the political situation I shall say little. I am terrified by now for fear the very paper may betray us. So henceforward, if I have occasion to write to you at any length, I shall obscure my meanings with allegories."[1] There were in antiquity two distinct notions of allegory that would be fused in the Middle Ages and have seldom been kept apart since, one having its origin in rhetoric, the technical analysis of figures of speech, the other in hermeneutics, the discovery of metaphysical and spiritual programs in tales. Allegory is sometimes narrowly conceived of as continued metaphor and is sometimes so broadly conceived of as to be indistinguishable from myth, "a false tale forming an image of truth."[2]

What does the word mean to Cicero here? Although he speaks in the plural of "allegories" and, later, of having to devise simple code terms,

---

1 ἀλληγορίαις *obscurabo. Cicero's Letters to Atticus*, ed. and trans. D. R. Shackleton Bailey, 7 vols. (Cambridge: Cambridge University Press, 1965), 1:252, letter 40. In the previous letter (1:252), Cicero speaks of writing "in enigmas"; and he uses the more cryptic Greek term there as he does when he uses *allegory* here: *cetera erunt* ἐν αἰνιγμοῖς [the rest shall be in veiled language].

2 For the rhetorical definition, see Quintilian, *Institutio oratoria* 9.2.46, and Cicero, *Orator* 2.7.94. For myth defined as "a false discourse forming an image [*eikonizon*] of truth," see Aelius Theon, *Progymnasmata*, in *Rhetores Graeci*, ed. Christian Walz (Stuttgart, 1832), 1:172. See also Roger Hinks, *Myth and Allegory in Ancient Art* (London: Warburg Institute, 1939), p. 3, and Patricia Matsen and Phillip Rollinson, *Classical Theories of Allegory and Christian Culture* (Pittsburgh: Duquesne University Press, 1981), pp. 143-47.

his purpose is far from rhetorical. And although he is proposing a comprehensive strategy of mystification, he is preoccupied not with remote truths but with dangerously immediate facts. Cicero's allegory will concern itself with matters pertaining to the clearing—the agora or forum— where, under other circumstances, open political speaking can occur. For the ancients the *agora* is at once a model of the state and an analogy of the *chora* in which forms are imprinted. But this underlying substance is composed of the bodies inhabiting the state, which are subject to various competing political forms. That *allegory* refers to political discourse is suggested to the ancients by its rootedness in the verbs *agoreuo* ("to speak publically, to harangue") and *ageiro* ("to gather"). Allegory speaks in the agora, the gathering place, but in an "other" way, mysteriously, disclosing a secret to the initiated while keeping away the profane.

Although the importance of political speaking to an understanding of allegory was recognized some time ago by Michael Murrin, the relation between allegory and politics has been little explored since.[3] Yet from Dante to Shelley allegorical poets advanced the most sweepingly authoritative political claims. They did so, however, through secrecy and ritual (to take both senses of the word *mystery*), rather than through open deliberation and reasoned debate.[4] The mystery, however, is not about meaning. Meaning in political allegory comes forward to entangle itself in the veil, leaving behind something more profoundly obscured. We may turn again to Cicero's letter to see what this is. Intending to frustrate any effort to trace his words to their source, Cicero says that when he writes allegorically he will not use his personal seal and will dictate to a different hand.[5] Cicero is concealing his body.

The concept of the body is the ground from which any fundamental thinking about human aggregation (thinking, for example, about human rights) must be derived. To say this is to invert the classical standard, according to which political order derives from abstract principles, to which bodies are supposed to conform.[6] Such idealism is not, as has been

3 Michael Murrin, *The Veil of Allegory: Some Notes toward a Theory of Allegorical Rhetoric in the Renaissance* (Chicago: University of Chicago Press, 1969), p. 2. But see Maureen Quilligan, *The Allegory of Female Authority: Christine de Pizan's "Cité des dames"* (Ithaca: Cornell University Press, 1991), pp. 212–18.
4 For the two senses of *mystery*, see Edgar Wind, *Pagan Mysteries in the Renaissance* (New Haven: Yale University Press, 1958), p. 13 n. 1.
5 For the hand and the early modern subject, see Jonathan Goldberg, *Writing Matter: From the Hands of the English Renaissance* (Stanford: Stanford University Press, 1990).
6 Pierre Manent, *An Intellectual History of Liberalism*, trans. Rebecca Balinski (Princeton: Princeton University Press, 1994), pp. 25–26; and Manent, "The Modern State," trans.

supposed, inherently elitist. In archaic thought the rights of common people were supported, and entrenched aristocratic power opposed, by appeals to Justice; before whom all men, regardless of their ancestry and possessions, were equal. But such abstractions had their beginning, if not in the body, then in more radical principles that do. Two such principles are especially important and will inform the discussion to follow: the *agora*, or political space, where bodies are gathered together, and the *voice*, which issues from the interior of the body into the political space.

The agora is not just a physical clearing. It is an order that is sustained by contrary forces, the one tending to the aggregation of all bodies in one ("e pluribus unum"), the other to the separation of bodies by speech. The very concept of the body as something that has a private interior and a public exterior is created by the voice. It is the voice that gives the body an inner sanctum where deliberation can occur and whence speech can issue; one thinks of the Homeric "wall of the teeth" and the Old English "word hoard." But this voice, considered as a political concept, must be understood as a functioning element in a conceptual order, not as the mere sounding of words. One can have a voice in sign language or in writing, as with Cicero's hand, and one can be voiceless while making articulate sound. When the mute boy in Brecht's *Mother Courage* beats the drum while rifles are trained on him, knowing he will be shot if he continues, he is manifesting the political voice at its eloquent extreme. But he is also revealing that he has an interior, a place of reflection and heroic resolve. Without voice the body is meat.

As a gathering of bodies with interiors the agora is a corporeal manifold, a space containing spaces that are nevertheless external to it. Only when voice is denied them do bodies in the agora lose this interiority, becoming an indifferent substance ready to be imprinted by ideology. In the human swastikas of the Third Reich and in the May Day parades representing (to use Milan Kundera's phrase) the Grand March of History,[7] bodies in the political space were incorporated into hieroglyphic writing and no longer had voices, however much noise they may have made with their mouths (see Figure 8). The most impressive vision of such a transformation is in the circle of Mars in Dante's *Paradiso*. We see a cross that

Balinsky, in *New French Thought: Political Philosophy*, ed. Mark Lilla (Princeton: Princeton University Press, 1994), pp. 128-30.

7 Milan Kundera, *The Unbearable Lightness of Being*, trans. Michael Henry Heim (New York: Harper & Row, 1984), p. 257. Cf. Mona Ozouf, *Festivals of the French Revolution*, trans. Alan Sheridan (Cambridge: Harvard University Press, 1988), p. 12.

8. Max Beckmann. *Birds' Hell* (*Die Hölle der Vögel*). 1938. Courtesy of Richard L. Feigen, New York

is composed of bodies suspended in light, like motes in a sunbeam, while the cross as a whole flashes forth the body of Christ.[8] This image captures the two phases in which the agora is transformed into a place without freedom: that in which bodies compose a symbol of the collective, such

8 Dante, *Paradiso* 14.103–17. For the theory of the state as an incorporate body, see the classic work by Ernst H. Kantorowicz, *The King's Two Bodies: A Study in Mediaeval Political Theology* (Princeton: Princeton University Press, 1957), pp. 471–72. Kantorowicz's emphasis on continuity obscures the difference between a medieval, eschatological image, to be fulfilled at the end of time, and the more violent language of the Tudor jurists (pp. 7–23), which is to be fulfilled in the world. For the latter, see Edward Forset's *Comparative Discourse of the Bodies Natural and Politique*, in *The Frame of Order: An Outline of Elizabethan Belief Taken from Treatises of the Late Sixteenth Century*, ed. James Winny (London: George Allen & Unwin, 1957), pp. 89–103. See also David Lee Miller, *The Poem's Two Bodies: The Poetics of the 1590 "Faerie Queene"* (Princeton: Princeton University Press, 1988), p. 68.

as the fasces, and that in which bodies enter into one body, as when Mussolini was represented as containing all the citizens of the Italian state.[9]

Now this image of one body incorporating others is the goal, so to speak, of allegorical expression, its anagogical fulfillment, as we see in Spenser's "Letter to Raleigh," where the twelve knights of the twelve projected books represent the virtues contained in the person of Arthur. Spenser's principal model for this structure is the prose allegory that Torquato Tasso added to his epic poem, *Gerusalemme Liberata*, in which the entire Christian army is interpreted as a single body representing "all the actions of the political man." The various, individual, romantic adventures in the poem are gathered together when the army is united to resume the assault on the city, which, according to Tasso, represents "civil felicity." [10]

It is interesting to observe how Tasso lost touch with his own interior as he allegorized his epic, intending to make the poem morally innocuous and structurally sound. By his own report he began allegorizing the *Gerusalemme Liberata* in a more or less cynical spirit, to avoid trouble with the Inquisition. But as he proceeded with the work he became astonished at how well all the parts of his allegorical scheme fit together, at how closely each detail conformed to the narrative and at how well the result supported his theoretical design. These correspondences led Tasso to suppose that he had worked out the allegory before beginning the poem—and then forgot having done so.[11] The moment in which Tasso records his perplexity on this matter strikes me as eerily prescient of the

9   The poster, by Xanti Schawinsky, is titled "1934-XII"; see Jeffrey T. Schnapp, *Staging Fascism: "18 BL" and the Theater of Masses for Masses* (Stanford: Stanford University Press, 1996), fig. 59.

10   Torquato Tasso, "Allegoria del poema," in *Gierusalemme Liberata* (Ferrara, 1581), sig. CC3r. See also Simone Fornari's allegorical commentary on the *Orlando Furioso*, in which pagan and Christian knights are allegorized as the faculties of their respective commanders.

11   For Tasso's accommodating his poem to "the strictness of the times," see *Le lettere di Torquato Tasso*, ed. Cesare Guasti (Naples, 1857), vol. 1, no. 79, p. 192. For his surprise at the coherence of his allegorization, see no. 76, p. 185. See also Angelo Solerti, *Vita di Torquato Tasso* (Turin, 1895), 1:233–34; William J. Kennedy, "The Problem of Allegory in Tasso's *Gerusalemme Liberata*," *Italian Quarterly* 60 (1973): 45–47; Michael Murrin, *The Allegorical Epic: Essays in Its Rise and Decline* (Chicago: University of Chicago Press, 1980), pp. 87–127; and Mindele Anne Treip, *Allegorical Poetics and the Epic: The Renaissance Tradition to "Paradise Lost"* (Lexington: University of Kentucky Press, 1994), pp. 65–67. Of related interest is David Quint's "Political Allegory in the *Gerusalemme Liberata*," in *Epic and Empire: Politics and Generic Form from Virgil to Milton* (Princeton: Princeton University Press, 1993), pp. 213–47.

mental illness that would overtake him at last, causing him to request that he be tortured by the Inquisition in order to root out the heresies he believed to be hidden inside him.[12] It is as if, meditating on the collective body of the Church Militant and identifying himself with it, Tasso came to regard as subversive the mere existence in himself of an interior apart from the whole. The discharge of interiority accomplished by torture bears more than an accidental resemblance to the process of allegorical interpretation.

The scene of political interpretation, unfolding within what Elaine Scarry has called "the structure of torture,"[13] is observed with great acuity in Solzhenitsyn's account of the behavior of orthodox communists when processed by the "organs," as they were called, of the Soviet prison system. Having been tortured and given false confessions to sign, these orthodox communists were returned to the crowded holding cells, where they huddled together in groups of their own, regarding the others as enemies in the war against counterrevolution. As soldiers in this war they agreed among themselves to sign their confessions and, as a matter of course, to add false accusations of others, in order to show their support of "Soviet interrogation."[14] It was not just their misfortune to be tortured: it was their duty to endure it and to extend it to others. Their reading of the state as a body and of themselves as organs in its service is essentially an allegorical one. The episode reveals the conjunction of allegory and politics at its authoritarian extreme; but we shall see that this extreme stands on a continuum with its opposite, when Cicero uses allegory to conceal his body.

The two best-known images of the state as a body are the fable of Menenius Agrippa, in Livy, and the frontispiece to Hobbes's *Leviathan* (see Figure 9). The latter reveals, in a visual pun, the ambiguous fate of bodies in the agora when voice is denied them.[15] One at first sees many

---

12 Solerti, *Vita di Torquato Tasso*, 1:258–60; cf. 1:210.
13 Elaine Scarry, *The Body in Pain: The Making and Unmaking of the World* (New York: Oxford University Press, 1985), p. 27.
14 Aleksandr I. Solzhenitsyn, *The Gulag Archipelago, 1918–1956: An Experiment in Literary Investigation*, trans. Thomas P. Whitney (New York: Harper & Row, 1973), pp. 69–70. See also Robert Conquest, *The Great Terror: A Reassessment* (New York: Oxford University Press, 1990), p. 266.
15 See Richard Helgerson, *Forms of Nationhood: The Elizabethan Writing of England* (Chicago: University of Chicago Press, 1992), p. 294, commenting on Hobbes's definition, in *Leviathan*, ed. A. R. Waller (Cambridge: Cambridge University Press, 1935), p. 119, of the

9. Detail from title page to Thomas Hobbes's *Leviathan*. 1651. Courtesy of the Division of Rare and Manuscript Collections, Cornell University Library

bodies contained in the body of the monarch; but the contained bodies are also represented as if standing in a clearing, an *agora*, where they listen to what is dictated to them. The image records, even as it distorts, the opposition of forces out of which the political space is composed: the gathering of bodies through mutual need into one body and the separation of bodies by the voice. But the separation is a collective illusion. In the Hobbesian political order subjects have contractually surrendered the power of the voice as a political force in return for protection from the war of all against all. The one absolute right left to the subject is the

---

commonwealth as "one person, of whose acts a great multitude by mutual covenants one with another have made themselves every one the author."

defense of the body, since it was for the preservation of the body that the contract was entered into in the first place. But in surrendering the voice the subject loses the very body, as a private interior, the act of surrender was supposed to preserve. The subjects inside Leviathan do not have interiors because the monarch, whose political body contains their political bodies, speaks for them all. They cannot even scream, if the scream is understood, as it is in Picasso's *Guernica*, as the final political act of the voice. They can at most whisper among themselves, in response to what is dictated to them, "I hear, therefore he is, and therefore we are."

In the fable from Livy incorporation and separation, which are represented simultaneously by Hobbes, are placed in a temporal development from the latter to the former. The fable is related by Menenius Agrippa, who is quieting a rebellion of the plebs. He tells of a time when the separate parts of the body lived together in a looser, more politically contentious form of association than they did after they agreed to form an organic whole. It was in this earlier state that they resolved to banish the stomach from their commonwealth; for the stomach contributes nothing to the general good, even as it receives benefits from all the other parts. When, however, they discovered the folly of their decision, they incorporated themselves as an organic whole, allowing the stomach to benefit from the labor of all in return for the nourishment the stomach furnishes them. The moral of the tale is of course carefully explained at the end. By comparing the anger of the plebeians against the patricians to the internal, parliamentary dissension of the bodily members ("intestina corporis seditio"), Menenius persuades the plebeians to abandon their cause.[16] The tale suggests that development to political maturity in a state proceeds from contention in the open space of the forum to harmony in the enclosure of a body. Subjects are either organs of the state or materials to be processed by organs.

By separating bodies as integral, independent beings-at-risk, the voice keeps the agora open and the individual body enclosed in itself, capable of withholding or of proffering its voice. The freedom to withhold or to proffer the voice is the basis of the concept of liberty. In Shakespeare's "Rape of Lucrece" we are told (in another tale from Livy) how Brutus

---

16 Livy, *Ab urbe condita libri* 2.32.9–12. The tale is retold at the beginning of Shakespeare's *Coriolanus*, but note Coriolanus's later reference, at 1.1.222, to the plebs as "fragments." Milton satirizes such reasoning in "Of Reformation," in *Complete Prose Works*, ed. Don M. Wolfe (New Haven: Yale University Press, 1953), 1:583–84, where the isolated member is "a huge and monstrous Wen."

has for years acted the simpleton, a political mute, in order to conceal his resolve to overthrow the Tarquin kings. At the opportune moment, when the Roman nobles are gathered around the body, he enters the realm of political speech, interpreting Lucrece's violation and her death in an unexpected manner. The outrage is not a matter of personal betrayal or of the breaking of the sacred bond between a guest and a host. It is a sign of oppression in the political order, demanding a political response: the overthrow of the Tarquin kings.[17] A poem that is ostensibly concerned with the violation of the sanctuary of the feminine body is translated into a political register where what is violated is the sanctuary of the masculine mind, the home of liberty. That the mind, like the interior of the body, is its own place, to be disclosed or concealed by the voice, is a belief that is fundamental to the formation of political agency; and it is the secrecy of Brutus's mind which ensures his success when he declares his intention in speech. The destruction of the sanctuary of the mind is the true object of torture, which reduces the voice, the index of the mind, to a scream.[18] But if the scream is the object of torture it is also the last moment when the political voice issues from a bodily interior, as when an eviscerated horse reveals in its screaming that it has not yet been reduced to the status of meat. The scream is the artifact of torture, but it is also, in Milton's terrific phrase, the last cry of an expiring liberty.

The reduction of the body to meat entails more than turning it into an indifferent substance capable of receiving the stamp of utopian forms. For as the frontispiece to *Leviathan* suggests, the ultimate danger of the political relation is that of being devoured, a fate symbolically ample enough to include the reduction of bodies to soap or to ash and the cathartic excretion of bodies through ethnic cleansing. This danger is set to work ironically in Swift's "Modest Proposal" and allegorically in a French political cartoon in which the beast of aristocracy is shown engulfing the people (see Figure 10). The image is particularly forceful, more forceful even than Hobbes's, because it reduces the confrontation of bodies to the most radical terms, where two bodies confront each other and one is engulfed. The threat of being devoured is the ultimate expression of political danger. It underlies the allegorical confrontation of microcosm and macrocosm, as it does the imposition of form on indifferent sub-

17 "The Rape of Lucrece," ll. 1814–15, in *The Riverside Shakespeare*, ed. G. Blakemore Evans (Boston: Houghton Mifflin, 1974).
18 "The answer, whatever its content, is a scream." Scarry, *Body in Pain*, p. 46; see also p. 49.

Un Monstre a trois têtes designant les trois Etats de l'Aristocratie s'occupe a devorer le reste du Cadavre du peuple qu'il a englouti impitoyablement dans ses entrailles carnivores. Il est precedé du Fanatisme aux Queues de Dragon et qui est vettu d'un Froc Monacal, il porte a Califourchon sur son dos l'Hypocrisie pressante un Serpent qui distile son Poison Aristocratique.

10. Anonymous. *Un monstre à trois têtes.* 1790s. Courtesy of the Division of Rare and Manuscript Collections, Cornell University Library, French Revolution Collection

stance. Because the danger is symmetrical—each body threatens every other—it may be termed "mutual devouring," *allelophagy. Allelophagy* is the political expression of the confrontation, implied in the word *allegory,* of opposite others.

The image of two bodies with two empty stomachs, each intending to fill itself with the other, betrays a precarious logic not unlike that of the snake swallowing itself by the tail. Yet the very rigor of the opposition gives rise to the structure of balanced antagonisms that constitutes political order, just as the hierarchy of forms in allegory is generated from antiphrasis. At a higher level in the structure of political order we may find, for example, a constitutional separation of powers, wherein each branch of government strives for an absoluteness that would be disastrous for all. (The struggle between political parties affords material for reflection along the same lines.) Although such structures arise from the inarticulate horror of mutual devouring, they are composed by acts of the voice, linguistic gestures that are immediately tied to the body and that entail the acceptance of risk. A signature on a public document such as the Declaration of Independence lends the voice of the signatory to the words on the page and puts his body at risk. The voice, issuing from a body, is the logos that calls forth political order from the chaos of allelophagic desire.

There is, therefore, no safety in the voice. Because the body is liable to retributive violence—and hence to the terror to which Cicero refers— political speaking is always a speaking *at risk*. I shall have more to say later on about care, the dialectical complement of risk, care of other bodies as well as one's own: "But where danger threatens / That which rescues also grows." [19] For the present I note only that the concept of risk is the leading edge of a more familiar truth: that the locatability of the body in the agora implies a position on the issues—in the crudest terms a position on the left or the right. We acknowledge this when we ask where a speaker is coming from. Political discourse is speaking with the body at risk and with something to be cared for at stake.

We may now consider how allegory disposes itself with respect to such discourse. In general, allegory cares without risk. Unlike irony, which is typically subversive, allegory interprets any existing regime not as what it actually is—a political entity created through struggle—but as the natural expression of universal order. Being the closest of the artistic forms to mere propaganda, allegories are, in Angus Fletcher's words, "mirrors of ideologies." [20] Even so, allegories do not just reflect ideological structures; they engage us in the practice of ritual interpretation by which those structures are reproduced in bodies and reexpressed through the voice. As a substitute for genuine political speaking, allegory elicits the ritual repetition of an ideologically significant world.

Ritual is a bodily expression of the hope that behind the threat that we pose to one another lies the truth of our belonging to one spiritual project. But the specifically political expectation of a happy union of many bodies in one conceals the scandal that at once makes culture possible and undermines the authority on which culture stands. The scandal

---

19 "Wo aber Gefahr ist, wächst / Das Rettende auch." Friedrich Hölderlin, "Patmos," in *Poems and Fragments*, ed. and trans. Michael Hamburger (Cambridge: Cambridge University Press, 1980), p. 462.
20 Angus Fletcher, *Allegory: The Theory of a Symbolic Mode* (Ithaca: Cornell University Press, 1964), p. 368.

is that our bodies live by incorporating other bodies, taking real and intense pleasure in every stage of the act, from the hunt to excretion; and the pleasure consists in this symbolic anthropophagy being, in Elias Canetti's words, "the central, if most hidden, process of power." The structure of imagery in any complex allegory such as *The Faerie Queene* has its roots in this desire to incorporate everything outside the self. But if the anagogical truth about bodies is that each one desires to incorporate all others, the process of sharing in cultural forms is a means of at once satisfying and deflecting that desire. Ritual interpretation of an allegorical work is the sharing of a meal in which the participants are separated in time as well as in space. The interpreters sit down to their work with a seriousness in the taking of pleasure that is not unlike Canetti's account of the shared meal: "The bond between the eaters is strongest when it is *one* animal they partake of. . . . But the touch of solemnity in their attitude cannot be explained by this alone; their mutual esteem also means that they will not eat each other. . . . They respect themselves for this, and respect their companions for an abstemiousness equal to their own."[21] These participants are, in the language of Greek ritual, *homotrapezoi*, "at the same table," prohibited from offering violence to one another. As the social aim of ritual sharing is not nourishment but communion, so the social aim of interpretation is not the acquisition of hidden knowledge but uncritical participation in an ideological order. We become Christian imperialists when we read the *Commedia* and Christian moralists when we read *The Faerie Queene*. But it is only by submitting to this process that we learn from these poems, or from moments inside them, how to do something else.

Human existence, as it is contemplated in allegory, is enclosed within a metaphysical order in which we are, to use a Neoplatonic phrase, children of the cosmos, children who in their infancy can only repeat what has been said to them first through symbols, which are the voice of the world. Hence it is by a kind of ventriloquism that the allegorist "throws" his voice so that it seems to descend into the political space from on high.[22] Truth tells us to be truthful and Justice demands we be just. Con-

---

21 Elias Canetti, *Crowds and Power*, trans. Carol Stewart (New York: Viking, 1962), pp. 210 and 220–21.
22 For a logos that "throws" its voice, see David Dawson, *Allegorical Readers and Cultural Revision in Ancient Alexandria* (Berkeley and Los Angeles: University of California Press, 1992), p. 184.

sidered politically, allegory is an apotropaic deflection of the voice from the body, freeing the poet from risk.

Such a conclusion may be hard to accept, especially for readers of Dante, whose voice is profoundly his own and whose body is so much on view in the *Commedia* that it casts a shadow, to the astonishment of the dead. His very name is registered "by necessity" at the critical moment of the poem, when Beatrice calls him.[23] So forthright is Dante in representing himself that scholars feel obliged to distinguish between the poet and his self-representation, referring to the latter as "the pilgrim." On the face of it, the *Commedia* would appear to be anything but an apotropaic deflection of the voice from the body of the poet, freeing him of responsibility. To this objection I can only repeat that the *Commedia* does not simply coincide with its genre; nor does any prime example of a genre simply coincide with its laws. The term *genre* can at most indicate a set of normative rules that may be opposed from within. In the *Commedia* that opposition may be heard, for example, in the *sound* of the poem, in the acoustic density of its multitudinous voices, which undermine its allegorical tendency to give prominence to visual forms. When I remember those voices it seems as if the visionary symbol to which the *Commedia* rises, the great rose with the saints enfolded in its petals, has been transformed into one of De Quincey's auditory hallucinations: "The sea appeared paved with innumerable faces, upturned to the heavens: faces, imploring, wrathful, despairing, surged upwards by thousands, by myriads, by generations, by centuries: — my agitation was infinite, — my mind tossed — and surged with the ocean."[24]

The commitment of allegory to transforming the agora into a *chora*, a scene of imprinting, is explored with great subtlety in Machiavelli's *Prince*. The transformation of the political space is accomplished by concealing the body of the prince, so that it cannot be imprinted, and by making other bodies the basis of signs. It seems at first as if simple violence is sufficient to reduce the political space to a substance, Fortune being, as Machiavelli says, a woman who must be beaten, and who responds only to insolent and audacious commands. Cesare Borgia is admired for showing "tanta ferocia et tanta virtù" and Hannibal is praised

23 Dante, *Purgatorio* 30.62–63: "quando mi volsi al suon del nome mio, / che di necessità qui si registra."
24 Thomas De Quincey, *Confessions of an English Opium Eater,* ed. Alethea Hayter (Harmondsworth: Penguin, 1973), p. 108. See Dante, *Paradiso* 30.124–26.

for his greatest virtue, inhuman cruelty.[25] Yet when Machiavelli served as the Florentine ambassador to Cesare Borgia what impressed him most was not the duke's brutality but his secrecy, a mysteriousness of which brutality is only the outward, allegorical sign. Indeed, it is Cesare Borgia's father, the notorious Pope Alexander VI, who receives the highest praise in *The Prince*, for he "never did anything else, never had another thought, except to deceive men, and he always found fresh material to work on."[26]

"Fresh material" is Robert M. Adams's rendering of the more technical term "subietto," or subject, a phrase implying that bodies in the agora are femininized, like Lady Fortune, by the power of this deceit. Indeed, there is a suggestion in Machiavelli, one that is perhaps not altogether absent from Livy, that the male bodies of his subjects are sodomized by the prince, violated at the opposite end to the voice. This power is conceivable, however, only as a function of the mystery in which the prince's power is cloaked. The prince who can make one woman of many men, naming the woman Fortune and calling her his "state," invades every man's body unseen, as pure terror, while himself remaining invulnerable to attack from behind.

The argument of the eighteenth chapter of *The Prince* unfolds with a typical, Machiavellian performance of orderly subdivision. One may fight, we are told, lawfully or lawlessly; the first is proper to men, the second to beasts; but because the first often fails, the second must be used. Accordingly, the prince must know how to act both like a man and like a beast, as the ancients allegorically taught in the figure of the centaur Chiron. Yet because men, being evil, resemble beasts more than not, it is the bestial character (shortly to be subdivided in turn) that the prince should assume, merely disguising himself as the man he should be. Machiavelli then says—in a passage so famous we are apt not to read it with the care it deserves—that two beasts afford the prince examples of how he should act: the lion and the fox. The prince needs the qualities of the fox to recognize traps and the power of the lion to terrify wolves.

We are thus left with the impression, a false one, that the prince must alternate according to need between the character of a lion and that of a fox; for there are, we are told, infinite modern examples of the prince's

---

25 For Fortune, see Niccolò Machiavelli, *"Il Principe" e "Discorsi,"* vol. 1 of *Opere*, ed. Sergio Bertelli (Milan: Feltrini, 1960), p. 101; trans. Robert M. Adams under the title *The Prince* (New York: Norton, 1977), p. 72. For Cesare Borgia's ferocity and Hannibal's inhuman cruelty see *Principe*, pp. 39 and 71; *Prince*, pp. 23 and 48.
26 *Principe*, p. 73; *Prince*, p. 50.

acts being those of the lion. But Machiavelli cannot help attributing even these leonine acts to an abiding and fundamental intent to deceive. His prince is always a fox in the skin of a lion, but a fox that can do more than recognize traps. The many see what you appear to be, Machiavelli says, addressing the prince, while only a few will know you "by touch," and these few will be cowed by the opinion of the many and by the majesty of the state. While few know the prince's body "by touch," he can touch other bodies at will, like the fox that gnawed the Spartan youth's entrails. Machiavelli, who upon the fall of the Florentine Republic was tortured, knew this invisible and intimate touch. It taught him how all bodies in the agora are at the mercy of a violence that can spring to life anywhere at any moment, converting them at will into allegorical signs (see Figure 11). In the Machiavellian state, bodies that have not yet been tortured, or that are not at that moment being tortured, are only enjoying a reprieve from the truth of their political being. To be a subject is to be vulnerable at every moment to an inscrutable violence on which the power of the state depends utterly.

The revelation of this truth occurs in a flash: "Spenti, adunque, questi capiti . . . aveva il duca gittato assai buoni fondamenti alla potenza sua" [These leaders being killed . . . the duke had laid foundations adequate to his power].[27] The ablative syntax — "*spenti*, adunque, questi capiti" — advances by cutting away obstacles and moving them off to the side, where they are left to lie as emblems of a violence that has already passed, moving invisibly.

How to establish such an emblem in the political space is the lesson of the tale recounted in the seventh chapter of *The Prince*, in which Remirro de Orco, a man known for his cruelty and efficiency, is appointed by Cesare Borgia to pacify the Romagna. The task complete, the duke resolves to ingratiate himself with the populace without lowering the level of terror established. He therefore has Remirro placed one morning in the square of Cesena "in two pieces," with a piece of wood and a bloody knife to one side. This is a complex emblem; but its general meaning is clear. The episode concludes, in Adams's translation: "The ferocity of this scene ["la ferocità del quale spettaculo"] left the people at once stunned and satisfied."[28]

27 *Principe*, p. 36; *Prince*, p. 21.
28 *Principe*, p. 37; *Prince*, p. 22. The body was visited by the citizens throughout the day, as Machiavelli reports in his diplomatic correspondence, on December 26, 1502. See *Legazioni, commissarie, scritti di governo*, ed. Fredi Chiapelli (Bari: Laterza, 1973), 2:365.

11. Max Beckmann. *Departure.* 1932–33. Oil on canvas. The Museum of Modern Art, New York, Given anonymously (by exchange)

We notice that it is the ferocity of the *spectacle*, not the original *act*, that stuns the people, and that no verb for *cutting* is used. The true act is one of *placing*, of *thesis* or proposition, and an indirect placing at that, a counterpart to allegorical ventriloquism: "lo fece mettere" [he had him placed]. What is taught by this rhetorical slaughter is that the interior of any body in the political space can at any time be opened and exposed by the prince. The meaning of Cesare Borgia's emblem is that the body of the subject is indifferent substance, a piece of wood, "un pezzo di legno," which has no more interior than meat.

The bloody knife is harder to read. It appears to have been chosen to represent the violent act without being the actual instrument of the act: one does not chop a body in half with a knife. The point of this substitution appears to be that the actual instrument has been left out of sight so that the viewers will wonder about it, just as Machiavelli leaves his readers to wonder just how that body was cut, lengthwise or across, at the waist or at the neck. By separating the sign (knife) from the act (cutting in two), Cesare Borgia confers on that knife the power to indicate the future as well as the past, signifying what may be done to any body at any moment. In such a state, as was the case under Stalin, any death, however natural, may be attributed to this invisible hand.[29] Cicero himself became such an emblem at last, when his severed hands and head were found on the *rostra*, the platform on which orators stood in the forum. Under extreme political conditions, killing becomes allegorical.

A somewhat different emblem of extreme political conditions is set forth in Yeats's poem "Leda and the Swan," in which Leda's feminine body comes to represent the bodies of men in the agora, feminized in their subjection to Jove:

> A sudden blow: the great wings beating still
> Above the staggering girl, her thighs caressed
> By the dark webs, her nape caught in his bill,
> He holds her helpless breast upon his breast.
>
> How can those terrified vague fingers push
> The feathered glory from her loosening thighs?
> And how can body, laid in that white rush,
> But feel the strange heart beating where it lies?
>
> A shudder in the loins engenders there
> The broken wall, the burning roof and tower
> And Agamemnon dead.
>
>   Being so caught up,
> So mastered by the brute blood of the air,
> Did she put on his knowledge with his power
> Before the indifferent beak could let her drop?[30]

We should note at the outset that Leda's assailant is invisible to her. Nor can she clearly discern at each moment where her own body ends and

29 Conversation with Mikhail Ryklen, Cornell Society for the Humanities, Fall, 1992. See Robert Conquest, *The Great Terror*, p. 169.
30 *The Collected Poems of W.B. Yeats*, 2d ed., ed. Richard J. Finneran (New York: Simon and Schuster, 1996), pp. 214–15.

the body of the other, the intruder, begins, the two being entangled in a single act of power. She feels the webs against her thighs, the imperious hold on her neck, the vague resistance in her own fingers, her dissolution into indifferent "body," the thrust of the intrusive, "feathered glory," the white rush, the strange heart, the shudder. In keeping with traditional iconography, if not with the behavior of swans, Yeats initially indicates a frontal position. But it soon becomes reasonably apparent, Leda's "nape" being caught in Jove's bill, that Jove has taken the girl from behind, as he did Ganymede on the only other occasion when he wooed in the form of a bird. That position suggests, as in Machiavelli, the omnipotence and invisibility of an absolute power that attacks from above and behind. Only at the end of the poem is the possibility raised of a knowledge around which Leda might recompose herself and interpret the force that has seized her. But the possibility is left in the uncertain form of a question because Leda's experience is no longer her own. At the critical moment, the "shudder" is made the subject of a sentence the object of which is not in Leda's body but in history: "A shudder in the loins engenders there / The broken wall, the burning roof and tower." Being transformed into the body of fate, Leda is subdued even more thoroughly than she was when reduced to indifferent substance, to "body." Yeats's emblem of abjection differs from Machiavelli's, however, in introducing at its conclusion the possibility of a reversal: "Did she put on his knowledge with his power?" The possibility is raised of Leda's acquiring the knowledge to turn the power that seized her back on its source. The swan appears to know this and is eager (note the word *could*) to be rid of this dangerous girl: "before the indifferent beak could let her drop."

Leda thus represents more than Remirro de Orca does; for her body does not represent that of a typical subject but the fate of a historical epoch, of which the poem is the primal scene, and her rape is the origin of political struggle. We see this in Yeats's account of the climate of ideas in which the poem was formed:

I thought "After the individualist, demagogic movement, founded by Hobbes and popularised by the Encyclopaedists and the French Revolution, we have a soil so exhausted that it cannot grow that crop again for centuries." Then I thought "Nothing is now possible but some movement or birth from above, preceded by some violent annunciation." My fancy began to play with Leda and the Swan for a metaphor and I began this poem; but as I wrote, bird and lady took such possession of the scene that all politics went out of it.[31]

The nonsense about exhausted soil went out, together with the authoritarian allegiances Yeats harbored at the time. But the politics, understood as the pure forms of human struggle, went deeper in, giving the poem the mysteriousness that tightens its grip on the mind. Some of these nuances may appear to be lost if we say that Jove is an absolute ruler, wielding invisible power, and that Leda is the collective body of subjects, in whom the power of the prince engenders a new age of history. But whenever a mystery seems to be dispelled in a poem by Yeats a new mystery emerges, casting its aura back on the old one. There is, for example, the mystery of Leda's gender, which is allegorically feminine but politically male; and, as always in Yeats, there is the mystery of knowledge and power.

"Did she put on his knowledge with his power?" It is unclear whether the question asks if Leda acquires knowledge in addition to the power that engenders history inside her or whether it asks if she acquires knowledge and power together. While Yeats appears consciously to have intended the former, raising the age-old question of the incompatibility of knowledge and power, we may wonder what it means for Leda to acquire a power that has imposed itself on her, unless she also acquires the means, knowledge, for wielding that power. The more forceful interpretation of the question is this: Did Leda seize both the power, and the knowledge to use it, before Jove let her drop? In this form the question is about something much more important than the state of Leda's consciousness. It is merely sentimental to ask whether she had any idea of the mighty events that would follow from the shudder in her loins, treasuring these things in her heart. Of more force is the question whether Leda, having acquired knowledge and power from Jove, will herself become an agent in history. A poem that was conceived as an authoritarian fantasy concludes in a prophecy of revolution.

As for Leda's gender, we have seen that it is politically male, for her femaleness represents the subject position of males in the political space. But the mystery lies deeper than that because the poet is involved in it personally. He is imaginatively assuming the position of Leda, as Freud's

31   Quoted in Norman A. Jeffares, *A Commentary on the Collected Poems of W. B. Yeats* (London: Macmillan, 1968), p. 296. See also Yeats, *A Vision* (New York: Macmillan, 1966), pp. 67 and 267-69.

Wolf Man imagines himself in his mother's position.[32] The analogy is useful only if we do not fail to note the principal differences between the two scenes. Freud's psychoanalytic primal scene leads to debility, even to pathology, and to a futile search by the patient for sexual gratification. Yeats's political primal scene gives him poetic strength and in some sense fulfills his desire for political power. The humiliation is strangely liberating for the poet, in marked contrast to the fate of the Wolf Man, because the poet can tolerate the anxiety of abjection and can translate masochistic gratification into knowledge and power. He can also transfer personal anxiety into the arena of collective risk, where the anxiety is exploited to confront authentically historical decisions. We may therefore answer the final question of the poem in the affirmative, to the extent that it is Yeats himself who has knowledge of the violent annunciation to come and is confessing how he got it: by being sodomized by a god. Having been in the poetic state of inspiration that Plato called *enthousiasmos*, "the presence of a god within,"[33] the poet has acquired knowledge and power by taking the god into himself. By making this confession Yeats frees himself of moral responsibility for what the poem foretells: an age of war and of naked, glorious, unrestrained power, in which he has already taken delight. Yeats divides himself in order to identify himself with both sides in the struggle the poem foretells. The poet's body is hidden in Leda's, and the swan is his alienated voice.

We move toward this concern when we recognize a perhaps inadvertent political lesson of "Leda and the Swan": that secrecy in the agora progresses from tactical to tyrannical invisibility, from Cicero's prudential encodings to the quasi-fascist symbology of Yeats's *Vision*. Nor is there anything internal to the logic of secrecy that diminishes the terror of which Cicero speaks, even as one terrorizes others. A committee for state security, terrorizing millions, can regard itself as a clandestine cell in a dangerous political environment. On the path leading from the avoidance of bodily harm to the use of other bodies as substance, prudence insensibly shades into oppression: Cicero and Cesare Borgia are both engaged in concealing the origin of the signs that they make. Secrecy in the agora entails more than the concealing of the bodily ori-

---

32 Sigmund Freud, "The History of an Infantile Neurosis," in *The Standard Edition of the Complete Psychological Works of Sigmund Freud*, ed. and trans. James Strachey (London: Hogarth Press, 1953-74), 17:37.
33 Plato, *Apology* 22b–c; *Ion* 536c. See *A Vision*, p. 8, for Yeats's account of the inspiration for the vast historical scheme described in the fifth book of *A Vision*.

gin of one's voice. It entails the throwing of one's voice so that it will descend from above, categorically, into the political space, just as the forms descend into the world.

To surrender to the dictates of such a voice, to obey its commands, is to enjoy the power to hurt without personal risk and to care without personal cost. We have seen in the twentieth century the astonishing capacity of the electronically amplied voice to transform individuals into one mass. It may at first sound glib to assert that the swan in Yeats's poem is the voice on the radio, that Leda is the ear of the crowd, and that that ear is the transferred site of the anus, through which Jovian power enters the body. But the poem is highly evocative of supine, political crowds, which were being created by the radio and the loudspeaker on a scale never before seen. In the crowd, concern for one's own body becomes concern for the well-being of a collective, metaphorical body, which is penetrated and enlivened by the voice from above. But concern for the well-being and health of the crowd never passes through a stage in which the integrity of other bodies is acknowledged; indeed it relies on the violent abolition of such integrity which Canetti referred to as the "discharge." The moment of discharge creates in the members of a crowd an "immense feeling of relief" which is derived from the loss of one's physical boundaries.[34] The discharge has a sexual aspect and affords the relief that Yeats confesses to experiencing as Leda. The care that the crowd has for itself has two important features: it overleaps any care for the other and is experienced as the absence of risk, risk being the dialectical complement of genuine care. You can never care without risk. In politics, risk is brought into play by the voice issuing from a locatable and integral body.

The term *care* has an inevitable Heideggerian resonance, which it will be well to confront directly, since Heidegger's discourse is one of the closest we have had in the twentieth century to what allegory supplied to an earlier age: a discourse of secrecy that elicits a ritual response. When Heidegger finds, beneath the Aristotelian conception of truth as correctness of assertion, a more fundamental understanding of truth as *aletheia*, dis-closure or unveiling, he is exposing something prior to Platonic idealism and to metaphysics as such.[35] But he is also reviving the

34 Canetti, *Crowds and Power*, p. 18.
35 Martin Heidegger, *Being and Time*, trans. John Macquarrie and Edward Robinson (San Francisco: Harper & Row, 1962), p. 257. See also Heidegger, *Basic Questions of Philoso-*

mystical experience of truth as unveiling which was essential to the ideology of Neoplatonism and which was recreated in allegorical literature and art. Nor is this affinity with allegory a casual one; it is a consequence of Heidegger's early inclination in *Being and Time* to give a totalizing function to the concept of care. This totalizing of care led to Heidegger's disastrously collectivist reading of Nietzsche's injunction to live dangerously and to his consequent embrace of fascism.

Care (*Sorge*) functions in Heidegger's argument in *Being and Time* as a means of avoiding traditional interpretations of human being (*Dasein*), which he believed were based on prior and inadequate ontological assumptions. Care, in the double sense of purposeful exertion and watchful concern, is, to put it in Heideggerian terms, Dasein's pre-ontological interpretation of itself. This primordial status is illustrated in a fable from Hyginus, which Heidegger quotes at some length. Care was once crossing a river when she saw some clay, which she molded into the shape of a human body. Having persuaded Jove to give the body a spirit, she was about to name it after herself when Jove demanded that it be given his name instead. At that moment the earth, Tellus, demanded the same honor, because she had supplied the body with its substance. Saturn (whose iconographic significance as Time Heidegger does not fail to invoke) was appointed judge of the case. The judgment of Saturn was as follows. Although Jove shall in time have the spirit of this creature and Tellus its body, "Let Care, who first fashioned this creature, possess it as long as it lives" [Cura eum quia prima finxit, teneat quamdiu vixerit]. In the double meaning of "care," Heidegger concludes, "what we have in view is a *single* basic state [of] twofold . . . thrown projection."[36]

Now if the concept of "thrownness" is to have any meaning it cannot be included in and determined by care. For one element of the twofold structure of care—purposeful exertion, or risk—is originally outside the circle of primitive care. Every purposeful act is a thrown one, a disruption of the primitive care of the self which is concerned above all to maintain equilibrium. Only by opposing each other can purposeful exertion and watchful concern bring each other to maturity, raising the immediate, bodily experience of the subject to the level of political con-

---

phy: Selected "Problems" of "Logic," trans. Richard Rojcewicz and André Schuwer (Bloomington: Indiana University Press, 1994), pp. 64–65 and 186, where allegory is said to be the preëminent means of encountering *aletheia*.

36   Heidegger, *Being and Time*, pp. 241–43.

cern. Heidegger mistakes primitive care, self-preservation, for a "pre-ontological" state.

The consequences of this mistake—and it is the mistake of allegory too—are extreme. For to exclude risk from the start is to leave oneself open to being seized on by risk at a later, historical phase of development, and in precisely the manner Yeats was seized in "Leda and the Swan." Openness to a seizure of this kind is promoted in Heidegger's inaugural address as rector to the University of Freiburg; it is more evident still in texts following the address, such as the call to the students to support the Führer as the embodiment of the nation. Nor did Heidegger simply call for a "yes." In what amounted to an allegory of the doctrine of *Gleichschaltung*, the enforced "coordination" of all areas of German life with Nazi ideology, Heidegger made the students march in formation to the polling station so that they could take their courageous decision *en bloc*.[37] In his address, risk appears as a world of extreme danger won for a racial collective, a *Volk*, which will stand firm in the storm of uncertainty.[38] Risk is to be accepted en masse.

Collective risk, however, is a delusion. Nations do not risk. Only a subject, being conscious of its agency and of its vulnerability, can risk. Nations with imaginary bodies take imaginary risks, for which embodied individuals actually pay. Collective risk is always someone else's risk, its excitement proceeding from the mental picture of *others* falling under fire as one courageously thrusts oneself forward—a picture evoked in the Nazi anthem, the Horst-Wessel song, which was sung at Heidegger's inauguration. The courage one feels as one commits oneself to history, advancing, as Heidegger put it, into the "outermost positions . . . exposed to the danger of the world's constant uncertainty,"[39] is in truth

37   Karl Löwith, *My Life in Germany before and after 1933*, trans. Elizabeth King (Urbana: University of Illinois Press, 1994), pp. 39–40. See Löwith's discussion of "Heidegger's translation of 'One's Ownmost Individual *Dasein*' into the 'German *Dasein*,'" pp. 34–44, in which the call to live dangerously is in reality a command to conform. For Heidegger's militarization of the university, his martial posturing, and the attitude toward him of colleagues who were veterans of World War I, see Hugo Ott, *Martin Heidegger: A Political Life* (New York: HarperCollins, 1993), pp. 152–54.

38   Martin Heidegger, "The Self-Assertion of the German University," trans. William S. Lewis, in *The Heidegger Controversy: A Critical Reader*, ed. Richard Wolin, 2d ed. (Cambridge: MIT Press, 1993), pp. 33 and 39; *Die Selbstbehauptung der Deutschen Universität* (Frankfurt am Main: Klostermann, 1990), pp. 14 and 19. For the Nazi term *Volksgemeinschaft*, see "Self-Assertion," p. 35n.

39   Heidegger, "Self-Assertion," p. 34, and *Die Selbstbehauptung*, p. 14. See Ott, *Martin Heidegger*, p. 148.

the placing of other bodies in peril instead of one's own. Risk is solitary and is not arrived at belatedly through history. As Hegel said, "The individual who has not risked his life may well be recognized as a *person*, but he has not attained to the truth of this recognition as an independent self-consciousness." [40] But only when risk is engaged by its opposite, care, does it lead to this recognized truth. Risk without care is predation; care without risk is sloth. Lacking the principle of risk at its foundation, Heidegger's thought was powerless to develop internally a criticism of its own fascination with the other as Jovian power. As he said in 1966, in the *Der Spiegel* interview, "only a god can save us." [41] This is another god in a swan.

A discussion of allegory and politics may conclude with an allegorical trope of its own, so long as we know where the voice behind the allegory comes from, and so long as no metaphysical claim is implied with regard to its figures. The allegory I propose is an argument, not a revelation of truth. Although what I say is, I believe, true of the political space as a whole, I am not speaking down to that space but from a position (admittedly, a fairly safe one) within it. Broadly speaking, it is a position that places before the demands of one's ethnicity, religion, culture, or nation a concern for the integrity and autonomy of bodies and for the authority of the voice—a concern, that is, for human rights. The integrity and autonomy of bodies imply the right to a self apart from politics and the right to a political voice.

In the ancient allegory of Hercules at the crossroads, Virtue and Pleasure stand before Hercules, each urging him to accompany her and to abandon the other. [42] Let us call these figures Risk and Care. Each of them addresses the embodied political subject, who stands in the position of Hercules and who would attain (to resume Hegel's phrase) the truth of independent self-consciousness. Care urges the body to seek

40   G. W. F. Hegel, *Phenomenology of Spirit*, trans. A. V. Miller (Oxford: Oxford University Press, 1977), p. 114. Hegel, however, opposes *fear* to risk and regards fear as being likewise productive of a self-consciousness, that of stoicism.
41   Martin Heidegger, " 'Only a God Can Save Us': *Der Spiegel*'s Interview with Martin Heidegger," in *The Heidegger Controversy: A Critical Reader*, ed. Richard Wolin, 2d ed. (Cambridge: MIT Press, 1993), pp. 91–116. See Luc Ferry and Alain Renaut, *Heidegger and Modernity*, trans. Franklin Philip (Chicago: University of Chicago Press, 1990), pp. 68 and 90.
42   The allegory, attributed to Prodicus of Ceos, is reported by Xenophon in *Memorabilia* 2.1.21.

comfort in itself, and Risk urges the body to dominate all other bodies. Both see the body as infinite, either in gratification or power. For Care, all things exist, as for the infant, to gratify the body. For Risk, all things exist to be opposed by the body and mastered. These impulses oppose each other in a struggle wherein Risk forces Care to go outside itself and Care forces Risk to acknowledge other bodies as independent of it. As a result of this struggle the political subject learns to care for the bodily integrity of other political subjects almost as much as it cares for its own.

The conflict between Risk and Care, unlike the allegory of Hercules at the crossroads, cannot be resolved by simply choosing between alternatives, one of them unattractive but good, the other attractive but bad. Risk and Care must struggle with each other inside the individual who advances along the road of political concern. When primitive Care is overcome by primitive Risk, it is forced to a higher level of commitment, where Care becomes the expression of a principle: concern for the integrity of bodies. And when primitive Risk is overcome by this Care, it too is raised to a higher plane, where it becomes readiness to accept danger on behalf of Care's principled concern. For Risk recognizes, as Care alone cannot, that the body can be subjected to a political fate, the fate of Hobbes's citizens, worse than a death suffered by resisting that fate. And Care recognizes, as Risk alone cannot, that a state in which bodies are reduced to a substance is one in which even the monarch who reduces them is deprived of humanity. Risk is thus included in Care and Care is safeguarded by the acceptance of Risk.

Genuine political discourse emerges when Risk, turning toward Care, discovers the one thing in its opposite on which it can lay hold: the voice. The voice is the logos mediating between Care and Risk, between the privacy of the body, out of which it proceeds, and the public space in which it is heard. In speaking from the body the voice risks, and in speaking for the body it cares. We do not, therefore, arrive at political maturity under the guidance of a Hegelian Spirit that is more cunning than we are, or by any allegorical voice that would speak down to bodies and arrange them as signs. We arrive at political maturity through a series of free choices in which the struggle between primitive risk and primitive care is directed creatively. One risks out of care for others and one cares for what is worthy of risk.

A modern instance comes to mind of an event in the agora that may be set against the example of allegorical concealment with which I began, Cicero's letter to Atticus. When the Tienanmen Square protest was crushed, the doctors who were shot while treating the wounded were at once showing total concern for the body and putting it at ultimate risk. They were not unaware of the difference between care of their own bodies and care of their patients. But they took the risk of canceling that difference.

7

Allegory and History

More than once in these pages I have spoken of the history of allegory in terms that imply a trajectory, if not a development, from late antiquity to the Enlightenment. In that span of time there emerged in the literary and visual arts a class of works that present themselves as secondary to a primary meaning, offering instructions for their interpretation. Owing to the ideological coherence of the medieval culture of the sign (and what was left of it in the Renaissance), the instructions could be highly allusive, calling to mind familiar iconographical norms and interpretive contexts. These were, speaking generally, the iconographical norms of allegorized, classical myth and the interpretive contexts of biblical exegesis. Commentaries, handbooks, dictionaries and encyclopedias of various kinds, and public monuments—notably the cathedrals and, in the Renaissance, the town halls and palaces—made those contexts, which accumulated over centuries, ideologically and materially present.

It is then partly by their belonging to a culture of the sign that we are able to discern among allegories a relatedness that falls into the province of history. Allegories are historical, it would seem, inasmuch as they share specifiable conditions and contexts. In later works of an allegorical kind, in the poems of Baudelaire, for example, with their numerous personifications and their satanic hermeticism, we encounter an aura of mystery which was no longer sustained by the culture: on the contrary. Baudelaire's evocation of nature as a forest of symbols belongs to an age when the dominant analogue of nature is the machine. In English poetry William Blake, whose private system of symbols appears to mean the most when it means nearly nothing (as in "The Mental Traveller"), is an extreme instance of this compensatory response to the loss of a numinous world. The work of compensation begins as early as the sixteenth century, in mannerist allegorical painting, for example, and in works such as George Chapman's *Shadow of Night*, the obscurity of which is more than a little voulu.

The collapsing of numinous contexts into numinous works reached its terminus, when the process reversed itself, with the advent of the theory of the symbol. As the movement of collapse continued inside the work it reached the point where the mystery of the world appeared to be concentrated in a single object, in a bird, a blue flower, a river, a mountain, a star. No effectual distinction was made between this object and its representation, between existence in the work and in the world. The symbol thus held the place that was once held, in allegory, by the singularity: "Only one symbol exists," Yeats says, "though the reflecting mirrors make many appear and all different."[1] As this remark suggests, the immanence of the world in the literary symbol becomes indistinguishable from an immanence that is longed for (and therefore discovered) in nature. The genesis of the symbol unfolded in three stages: (1) the collapse of numinous contexts into the mysterious work; (2) the theoretical reduction, inside the work, of general mystery into the particular symbol; and (3) the expansion of the symbol into nature, which is reanimated by mystery (now referred to as imagination) and reoccupied as an order of signs. The reversal of direction in the intermediate stage was made possible by the belief that the symbol is an identity of meaning and being, that it is, as Coleridge said, "consubstantial" with the truth it conveys.[2] The marked differences between the principal theorists of

---

1   W. B. Yeats, *A Vision* (New York: Macmillan, 1966), p. 240.
2   Samuel Taylor Coleridge, *The Statesman's Manual*, in *Lay Sermons*, ed. R. J. White, vol. 6 in *The Collected Works of Samuel Taylor Coleridge* (London: Routledge and Kegan Paul, 1972), p. 29. See Nicholas Halmi, "An Anthropological Approach to the Romantic Symbol," *European Romantic Review* 4 (1993): 15–16. For Goethe's theory of the symbol as the mystical *Urpflanze*, the ur-plant, an essential, objective presence in nature which mediates between the general and the particular, and the opposition of this theory to Schiller's idealistic sense of the symbol as a "Konstruktion des Ichs," a thing built up in the ego and unifying nature there, see Bengt Algot Sørensen, "Die 'zarte Differenz': Symbol und Allegorie in der ästhetischen Diskussion zwischen Schiller und Goethe," in *Formen und Funktionen der Allegorie, Symposion Wolfenbüttel 1978*, ed. Walter Haug (Stuttgart: Metzler, 1979), p. 634.

the symbol—from Goethe, Creuzer, and Schelling to Coleridge, Carlyle, and Yeats—indicate how powerful was the attraction exerted by this inexistent object of romantic attention.

The emergence of the theory of the symbol was one consequence of the breakdown of allegory as a historically articulated form. Another, larger but less evident consequence was the emergence of literary history. The practice of literary history begins when the history of allegory ends.

From its beginning, literary history continued, in a nonmetaphysical frame, the allegorical labor of gathering the remains of the past into an intelligible structure.[3] For the allegorist that structure was intended to stand as a timeless order, in imitation of the heavens, for to be intelligible was precisely to do that: to imitate the order of the heavens. For the literary historian, however, the structure into which past works were arranged was to be intelligible according to a different epistemological standard, one that lent itself to the narrative form of tradition: the demonstrable sequence of causes. Because the narrative sequence of causes was not, like the allegorical structure of signs, secured by the power of transcendental reference, the literary-historical narrative required a basis for permanence amid change that would be latent in the tradition itself. Such a foundation was supplied by the concept of culture, of a collective subjectivity that can contemplate itself in the things it has made. In its broadest form (one that still holds considerable sway in the late twentieth century), the subject that knows itself in the contemplation of what it has made is the mind of an entire civilization: "The mind of Europe," T. S. Eliot wrote, "is a mind which changes, and . . . this change is a development which abandons nothing *en route*, which does not superannuate Shakespeare, or Homer, or the rock drawing of the Magdalenian draughtsmen."[4] Whether this mind directs the work of literary-historical transmission within a particular language and nation, from Chaucer to Eliot, or across languages and nations, from the Ganges to the Hudson, its relation to historical objects is the same as the symbol's to the

3 Thomas Warton's pathbreaking *History of English Poetry* has its origin in his earlier study of Spenser, in the chapter concerned with the history of allegorical expression. See Thomas Warton, "Of Spenser's Allegorical Character," in *Observations on the "Fairy Queen" of Spenser* (New York: Garland, 1970), 2:87-113, esp. 102, and *History of English Poetry from the Twelfth to the Close of the Sixteenth Century* (London, 1871), 4:161-212. See René Wellek, *The Rise of English Literary History* (Chapel Hill: University of North Carolina Press, 1941), p. 121.
4 T. S. Eliot, "Tradition and the Individual Talent," in *Selected Essays* (London: Faber and Faber, 1980), p. 16.

objects in nature: that of a consciousness reinvested in things. This consciousness is the psychic remainder of the logos of allegory, of what had once been a mysterious intelligence circulating through all the contexts of meaning, referring them back to their origin in the Word.

By the twentieth century the deepest motives of allegorical expression—to transform time into consciousness and space into body—had been taken up into literary theory. Literary theory inherited these motives because of its critical engagement with the relics of allegory, that is, with literary history on the one hand and with the theory of the symbol (more broadly, romanticism) on the other. There were two signal moments in this development, one occurring near the beginning of the century, the second about fifty years later.

The first, which I have already had occasion to quote from, is Eliot's influential essay "Tradition and the Individual Talent" (1919), which halts, as he says, "at the frontier of metaphysics or mysticism," where literary history has been gathered up into the thought of one mind; and it is a mind in which temporal contingency no longer exists (to be conscious is not to be in time). The poet's mind participates in this larger mind to the extent that it is free of emotion.[5] The mirror in which the mind of Europe contemplates itself is composed of what Eliot refers to as "existing monuments"; but what the mind sees in that mirror is no longer the absolute truth, to which allegory aspires, but a culture's unique, and hence relative, values. In this substitution of the values of a particular culture for absolute truth we see the prospect of the end of literary history. I mean the end of the pursuit, carried out in a nonmetaphysical frame, of a secretly metaphysical desire: to turn the ruins of time into the thoughts of one mind.

As for the monuments in which this mind becomes aware of itself, they compose an "ideal order" that is borne up on a continuum of transmitting hands. Into this order new creative work is merely introduced, as in a drawing-room:

> The existing monuments form an ideal order among themselves, which is modified by the introduction of the new (the really new) work of art among them. The existing order is complete before the new work arrives; for order to persist after the supervention of novelty, the *whole* existing

5 Ibid., p. 21.

order must be, if ever so slightly, altered; and so the relations, proportions, values of each work of art toward the whole are readjusted; and this is conformity between the old and the new.[6]

Eliot's essay establishes a principle of permanence within change by means of an interesting amalgam reminiscent of the theory of the symbol. To the relatively new concept of culture he joins the newer, biological concept of morphological homeostasis, where the slightest variation in any part of an organism is accommodated by variations in all other parts.[7] This organic principle governs the relations between the monuments, causing them to stand as the material substratum, the body, of the mind of Europe. Eliot's "frontier of metaphysics" is the theoretical limit of the practice of literary history, where the assumptions underlying that practice begin to emerge into view.

Turning back from that limit, literary history in the twentieth century has devoted itself to research within a paradigm in which a consciousness is quietly supposed for the culture and a canon of works is quietly supposed as its body. Toward the end of the century those sustaining assumptions have been partly exposed and made the subject of investigation themselves.[8] This has occurred largely because of the emergence of alternative traditions and the valuation of diversity as a cultural ideal. But the question whether the historical consciousness of Europe is a nightmare from which we are trying to wake or a fragile possession we are trying to preserve and transmit is somewhat passé. The theory of the symbol and the practice of literary history, the latter understood as a general program of cultural self-recognition, have disappeared into the practice we refer to simply as "theory," which is perhaps not without its own, culturally specific assumptions, unclear as those assumptions may be. In any case, such theory appears to share with its antecedents an inability to come to terms with what Eliot calls talent.

The brilliance of Eliot's image of the monuments as a homeostatic order lies in its restriction of talent, creative work—or, as I call it,

6 Ibid., p. 15.
7 For morphological homeostasis, see Thomas Richards, *The Imperial Archive: Knowledge and the Fantasy of Empire* (London: Verso, 1993), p. 57, and Morris Berman, *The Reenchantment of the World* (Ithaca: Cornell University Press, 1981), p. 200, citing William Bateson: "No variation, however small, can occur in any part without . . . variation occurring in correlation to it in all other parts."
8 See John Guillory, *Cultural Capital: The Problem of Literary Canon Formation* (Chicago: University of Chicago Press, 1993).

poiesis, "making"—to the role of an intruder in the work of transmission; novelty supervenes. Eliot saw that if talent were permitted to work from within the process of change, it would reverse the direction of cultural time, producing a view of the artist that is different from the essentially custodial one that he wished to promote. The artist would stand revealed as a contrary force with respect to tradition, as one who reaches back into the material remains of the past in order to tear them into usable fragments. Eliot conceals the nature of talent behind the attractively chilling idea of possession—possession not by the muse but by ghosts. For Eliot, it is naive to suppose that the artist is simply preoccupied with excellent things made in the past and aspires to emulate those achievements. Emulation is for Eliot merely a preparatory stage. The artist is creative to the extent that he or she is spiritually possessed by the artists of the past; and this fact allows the dead artists to continue to create, so to speak, forward in time. Notwithstanding his opinion that art never improves, Eliot manages to reverse the true direction of creative work so that it will appear to go forward in step with the progress of mind. A poet, Eliot says, is most "individual" where "dead poets, his ancestors, assert their immortality most vigorously." In the final sentence of the essay Eliot says that the poet understands "what is to be done" when he is conscious "not of what is dead, but of what is already living."[9] The curious force of "already" is meant to administer a shock. Having emptied himself of personality the poet discovers that the ancestors whom he had expected to exhume and devour are already inside him, moving his tongue and his hands—as if he, being dead, were their mask. This is not allegory but something inherited from it, in which the "individual talent" is the persona through which a tradition continues to speak.

The second of the two moments in which literary theory inherits the motives of allegory is also the final event in the history of the romantic concept of the symbol. I refer to Northrop Frye's *Anatomy of Criticism* (1957), in particular to the essay on the theory of symbols, culminating in the section "Anagogic Phase: Symbol as Monad." Here too the dead rise up to enter into the living. But the body they inhabit is not, as in Eliot, that of the individual talent, the poet as allegorical persona. It is instead the apocalyptic body of Man enclosing the cosmos.

9 Eliot, "Tradition," pp. 4 and 22.

The essay begins with a definition that is intended to warn us that no romantic woolly-mindedness will be tolerated here: a symbol is "any unit of any literary structure that can be isolated for critical attention."[10] By the fourth, or anagogic, phase of the symbol, however, Frye's enthusiasm outdoes even Coleridge's vision of man as a syllepsis of nature. In what is intended to be an inclusive answer to Eliot's exclusive mind of Europe—and a resolution of the noisy contention of traditions and cultures to which literary history inevitably leads—Frye tells us that all symbols point to an image of humanity as one man containing the cosmos:

> When we pass into anagogy, nature becomes, not the container, but the thing contained, and the archetypal universal symbols, the city, the garden, the quest, the marriage, are no longer the desirable forms that man constructs inside nature, but are themselves the forms of nature. Nature is now inside the mind of an infinite man who builds his cities out of the Milky Way. This is not reality, but it is the conceivable or imaginative limit of desire, which is infinite, eternal, and hence apocalyptic. By an apocalypse I mean primarily the imaginative conception of the whole of nature as the content of an infinite and eternal living body which, if not human, is closer to being human than to being inanimate. "The desire of man being infinite," said Blake, "the possession is infinite and himself infinite."[11]

The symbols are no longer offered as simple identities of meaning and being. They are "the goals of human work," resolving themselves into a unity that holds the place that was previously held, in allegory, by the singularity: "Anagogically, then, the symbol is a monad, all symbols being united in a single infinite and eternal verbal symbol which is, as *dianoia*, the Logos, and, as *mythos*, total creative act."[12] The subordinate symbols do not just point to the comprehensive symbol but are the technological means to its realization, "instruments of mental production"[13] by which nature is reduced to a substance. The rhetoric of demystification in such

10   Northrop Frye, *Anatomy of Criticism: Four Essays* (Princeton: Princeton University Press, 1957), p. 71.
11.   Ibid., p. 119; see also pp. 112–13. See also A. C. Hamilton, *Northrop Frye: Anatomy of His Criticism* (Toronto: University of Toronto Press, 1990), pp. 114–15.
12   Frye, *Anatomy of Criticism*, p. 121.
13   Northrop Frye, "The Instruments of Mental Production," in *The Stubborn Structure: Essays on Criticism and Society* (Ithaca: Cornell University Press, 1970), p. 3.

phrases as "instruments of mental production" and "the goals of human work," far from cutting the symbol off from its roots in romanticism, exposes the more radically egotistical appropriation of nature from which romanticism springs. Nature in Frye is not the awful shadow of some unseen power; it is a reserve of real, material force to be captured and harnessed for utopian ends. Frye's image of the cosmos completing itself in the form of a man sets before technology the goal toward which it should strive: the absolute conquest of nature by desire.

Now a thing may be conquered absolutely, cutting off all possibility of revenge, only when that thing is placed inside the body and annihilated there—only when the thing is devoured. The romantic theory of the symbol softens nature up, makes it palatable, by transforming the objective world into a subjective order of meaning, making the object consubstantial with the subject. As is usually the case with movements that consciously oppose each other, the spirit of romanticism only appears to be inimical to the mechanical philosophy of the Enlightenment. Whether nature is conquered by machines or by spirit, whether it is turned into raw materials for extending the body or into symbols for enlarging the mind, it is gradually absorbed into the form of the human. We see the accomplishment of that desire in Frye's theory of the symbol as monad. The theory affirms the principle that every act of critical attention to an isolated part of a literary structure is an act of communion, manifesting in the words of a poem the body that encloses the cosmos. Criticism and technology have the same end.

What is taken into this infinite body, however, is not merely, or not in the first instance, the natural world. It is other bodies. For the anagogic body is in a position to devour the world only when all other bodies— limited, particular selves—have been taken into it first. All selves are infinite and eternal in desire and recognize all other selves as being the same. Every self wants to be the macrocosm. The self can annihilate this symmetrical desire in the other only by enclosing the other before it is itself enclosed. If the apocalyptic image of a single man enclosing the cosmos is the goal of human work, it is a goal that lies on the other side of an impassable barrier: the absurdity of mutual devouring, allelophagy.

It appears, then, that the theory of the symbol reaches its conclusion not in an apocalyptic body but in the technological drive for absolute mastery of the other, which ends in mutual devouring. It also appears that literary history reaches its conclusion not in the triumphal vindication of the mind of Europe as the mind of Man but in the political conflict of self-separating traditions and cultures. Seen from close up, the critical visions of Eliot and Frye are temperamentally and ideologically opposed. But they move toward the same goal: to construct an allegorical Man whose body encloses nature and whose thought encloses time.

Literary theory in the late twentieth century, after Eliot and Frye, has seen the final consequences of the disintegration of allegory into the theory of the symbol and the practice of literary history. Only the briefest of remarks on this development can be ventured here. The point is to trace the remote antecedents of literary theory in a literary practice, allegory, which shares with this theory the aim of imposing a single, intelligible form on the material remains of the past.

The theory of the symbol has been the occasion for the more technical manifestations of literary theory, inspired by the hope of attaining a general science of signs; it has also been the occasion for the deconstructive critique of the metaphysical grounds of such hope. Romanticism, the rhetoric of subjectivity, has had an afterlife in anthropology, where entire cultures are treated as subjects, and in the new criticism. These have provoked an intense scrutiny, notably in the work of Paul de Man, of the radical autonomy of figural language with respect to consciousness and conscious intention, indeed with respect to the human. For the idea of the human appears, from this radical perspective, to be grounded in the inhuman power of language as an array of rhetorical effects—chiefly the allegorical figure of personification, or, in Greek, prosopopoeia.[14] The symbol is raised up out of the inhuman otherness of figurative language by means of a schematic ordering, polysemy, that is based on the assumption of a single, underlying truth. The symbol approaches the inhuman sameness of allelophagy when it attempts to imagine that truth as a body. For it finds, in place of one glorified body, two bodies that are absolutely opposed, each obeying the truth of its own will to totality. The symbol begins in polysemy and ends in irony.

14 See Paul de Man, *The Resistance to Theory* (Minneapolis: University of Minnesota Press, 1986), p. 96, explicating *reine Sprache* in Walter Benjamin and eliding, a little sensationally, "the inhuman" with the "non-human character of language." For de Man's most sustained discussion of prosopopoeia, see "Shelley Disfigured," in *The Rhetoric of Romanticism* (New York: Columbia University Press, 1984), pp. 93-123. See also Ian Balfour, "Reversal, Quotation (Benjamin's History)," *Modern Language Notes* 196 (1991): 644-45, and Cynthia Chase, "Literary Theory as the Criticism of Aesthetics: De Man, Blanchot, and Romantic 'Allegories of Cognition,'" in *Critical Encounters: Reference and Responsibility in Deconstructive Writing*, ed. Cathy Caruth and Deborah Esch (New Brunswick, N.J.: Rutgers University Press, 1995), pp. 74-75.

As for literary history, it reaches its spiritual apogee at mid-century in the great work of E. R. Curtius, who personified, as much as anyone could, Eliot's ideal of the mind of Europe. Curtius's *European Literature and the Latin Middle Ages* was written in internal exile in Nazi Germany, as an affirmation of the humanist tradition of the West, at the center of which is the ideal of the historically conscious, universal man, represented by Virgil, Dante, and Goethe.[15] I observed that at the end of the twentieth century the project of literary history has reached an impasse in the contest of traditions and cultures that are in revolt against that which sustains them: the affirmation of universal value in the human. The end of the theory of the symbol in the irony of allelophagic desire and the end of literary history in the disintegration of the ideal of European culture are the last stages of a process that began in the Enlightenment, when allegory ceased to function historically.

It might well be supposed, therefore, that a broader, historical being may be assigned only to allegories of the period from late antiquity to the Enlightenment. We saw that within that span of time allegories could exploit widely accepted and densely articulated contexts of meaning; and the remains of the past could be taken up into those contexts as signs. Enlightenment allegories are, in the broad sense of the term, mathematical, the product of a self-contained calculus for linking the already known to the also already known rather than to a transcendental unknown. Although allegories may appear after the Enlightenment, as in Rilke's tenth Duino elegy, they no longer have, or belong to, a history.

To proceed in this manner, however, even if the conclusions we reach are correct, is to fail to confront the problem of allegory and history directly. It is to equate historical process with a static, anthropological concept of culture and to ignore the fundamental processes that generate change. We need to look deeper. To do so it will be necessary to abandon what periodizing models implicitly take as their ground: abstract, chronometric time. Far from being inimical to the model of history as a succession of relatively discrete cultural periods, or phases (the Renaissance, the Enlightenment, and so on), chronometric time is the basis on which such a model may admit temporality. For when historical change is measured against a homogeneous temporal scale, works of art may

15   Ernst Robert Curtius, *European Literature and the Latin Middle Ages*, trans. Willard R. Trask (1953; reprint, Princeton: Princeton University Press, 1973), p. 397.

be analyzed as reflections of a similarly homogeneous cultural space, a "period." But there is no clock in the forest, no universally determining, abstract time. There is only the dynamic temporality of change as it is established in each struggling thing, although the forest—to hold to the analogy for the moment—is its own independent temporal system. Just as the underlying concept that enables us to think temporally about forest cycle is not time but growth, with its strenuously competitive interlocking rhythms, so the underlying concept that will enable us to think historically about allegory is not culture but poiesis, or making. Poetic making is the ground on which real relations between allegory and history stand: the production of new things from the material remains of the past. To affirm this is not to commit oneself to exploring the psychology of the creative process, which would be no more likely than an anthropological model of culture to penetrate to the essence of historical change in the arts. A more radical reflection on principles is necessary.

Typically, historical study in the arts passes over the problem of making to ground investigation in more abstract hypostases of change. We saw that of these the most familiar is the concept of tradition, *traditio*, a "handing down" or a "handing on" of something through time. Tradition is based on the practice of education, a leading out of the young from the confinement of the present into an awareness of the past as movement directed *at* the present. Creative work is supposed to conform to this movement. Beneath every act of making we see a hand reaching back into the past to receive what is handed to it before extending itself forward to release what it holds to the future. The making that belongs to tradition moves forward in time, toward the conquest of nature. But the things that are made also afford moments of ecstatic arrest, when the mind is illuminated and raised up above history, prophetically anticipating history's end. The figure of cultural change as the work of the hand suggests both a carrying forward and an anagogic raising up. In the frame of tradition technology and theology are bound strangely together in thought, like Yeats's mummy-cloth. Everything made expands the power we have over nature; and everything made raises our thoughts above nature.

Behind the Latin word *traditio* is the Greek *paradosis*, which also implies education but is associated more directly with this theological movement, specifically with ritual practices concerning the gods. The practices surround material objects having a memorial function: the temple property, the commemorative tablet, the scepter. *Paradosis* is a key theological term in the great theorist of Christian symbolism, Dionysius the Areopagite, for whom what is handed on through time, the liturgy and the sacraments, is a body of ritual actions—actions he refers to as "material" and "symbolic"—for attaining transcendence. Such mediating and elevating practices are, as he says, "less material" (*abyloteron*) than the scriptures. As written, material signs, the scriptures contain no inherent movement toward a higher, spiritual realm. They are a ladder that the mind must ascend.[16]

The thought of Dionysius, having subsumed Neoplatonism and recast it in Christian form, underwent a long process of translation, assimilation, and expansion (many of the major theologians in the Latin West wrote commentaries on him) to become the world picture for the culture of the sign, into which the classical and biblical contexts of meaning could be readily inscribed. Although Dionysius is unconcerned with nature, his reception into the Latin West, beginning with his first translator and commentator, John Scotus Erigena, entailed the expansion of his system into a complete explanation of nature in terms of a metaphysics of light. For Erigena material things are spiritual lights emanating from, and directing the mind back to, the fountain of light.[17] Although the Scholastic theology of the later Middle Ages is in many technical respects at variance with the Neoplatonism of Dionysian thought, substituting for mystical light the more conceptually efficient idea of form, at the most fundamental level Scholastic theology builds upon the Dionysian gathering of being as hierarchical transference. However automatic the concept of tradition becomes, it preserves this ritually repetitive theological core, enacting the continuity in time of a desire for what is not in its essence in time.

The status of the work within the frame of tradition is threefold. The work is a treasure, a monument, and a mirror. In its most immediate, physical manifestation to sense—for example, as the oldest, Byzantine manuscript of Homer (the text surrounded with commentary, much of it already over a millennium old) or as flakes of pigment adhering to the wall of a cave or a church—the work is a treasure, a thing that must be hidden away and preserved. But this immediate, physical existence

16 René Rocques, *L'Univers dionysien: Structure hiérarchique du monde selon le pseudo-Denys* (Paris: Aubier, 1954), pp. 178 n. 2 and pp. 227–33. See also Jean Pépin, "La Théorie du symbolisme dans la tradition dionysienne," in *La Tradition de l'allégorie de Philon d'Alexandrie à Dante* (Paris: Etudes Augustiniennes, 1987), pp. 200–201.

17 *Celestial Hierarchies*, in *Patrologiae cursus completus . . . series graeca*, ed. J. P. Migne (Paris, 1889), vol. 3, *S. Dionysii Areopagiticae opera omnia quae exstant* 1.121 cd. 35–41. For Erigena, see *Expositiones in ierarchiam coelestium*, ed. J. Barbet (Turnholt, 1975), 1:76–77.

of the work is, as Hegel said of sense-certainty, its poorest, most abstract truth.[18] We come closer to the work when it is allowed to enter into the realm of reproduction, which is also the realm of perception, where the monument is contemplated by subjects as a thing worthy of being remembered, transmitted, and taught. The monument is worthy of being remembered in itself, but it is also a memorial, as a perennial flower is a memorial—a *monumentum*—of the sorrow of Venus for the death of Adonis.[19] Like memory, the monument implies repetition. The monument is perceived in itself as a thing, but in that act of perception something other is called. In the Middle Ages that other is truth; in the modern world it is value; but in either case this calling to mind is accomplished by repetition: one keeps returning to the monument to be reminded of something for which it supposedly stands.

The work as a monument has its basis in the re-presentation of the work from the evidence supplied by its standing as treasure, a re-presentation in the edited text, in the restored or reproduced picture, in the performance and the recording. The monument subsists in the relations between these re-presentations and their perception by cultural subjects. Such complex underlying relations constitute the work's substance, the matrix in which it appears, its monumentality. By virtue of this substance the work opens a space for itself in the crowded arena of things that are made. Only when the work achieves sufficient monumentality is it substantial enough to enter into tradition and to be transmitted forward in time—or to be torn by a hand reaching back into it from the future. From Eliot's point of view (on the threshold of metaphysics) the existing monuments in this arena form an ideal order. But from another point of view (on the edge of the forest) the monuments are held in complex, interlocking rhythms of struggle. Earlier, we saw how the work, as a transmitted object belonging to a tradition, becomes a kind of mirror in which the mind of a culture contemplates itself in the values reflected therein. This self-reflection is called interpretation. To summarize: the work as it appears in the frame of tradition is an object of sense (a treasure); it is an object of perception for cultural subjects (a monument); and it is an object of self-consciousness, in which a culture that is a sub-

18   G. W. F. Hegel, *Phenomenology of Spirit*, trans. A. V. Miller (Oxford: Oxford University Press, 1977), p. 58.
19   Ovid, *Metamorphoses* 10.725.

ject reflects on itself. The work is preserved as a treasure, reproduced as a monument, and interpreted within a tradition.

What we call "the allegorical tradition" may be easily confused with the history of the "West," or Eliot's "mind of Europe." This confusion is accompanied, not surprisingly, by an inclination to regard any work of literature as at least potentially allegorical, inasmuch as the work (as a reminder, a monument) goes beyond itself to say something "other."[20] Both kinds of confusion find their way into the influential *Preface to Chaucer* by D. W. Robertson Jr.:

> As a matter of fact, there is a continuous tradition of allegorical theory and practice extending from the sixth century B.C. well into the eighteenth century. During these centuries, of course, the tradition underwent many modifications, adapting itself to a wide variety of stylistic and cultural changes. The most important of these changes was the introduction of Christianity, which brought with it an allegorical method of its own. During the course of the Middle Ages, literary allegory, although it remained a distinct entity, became closely associated with the allegorical interpretation of the Scriptures.[21]

Plausible as this masterly summary is, with its easy commingling of allegorical interpretation ("theory") and allegorical making ("practice"), the existence of a continuous allegorical tradition from the sixth century B.C. well into the eighteenth century is by no means a matter of fact. It is at best a serviceable hypothesis, allowing the investigator to imagine a continuum of handing on, into which changes, even ones as radical as Christianity, are introduced as mere "modifications" to progress. The grounds for this kind of philological scholarship are not in philology but in a sort of moral utilitarianism about culture itself.

Criticism of such grounds may be said to have had its own tradition, going back to Nietzsche's *Unmodern Observations*. But polemical condemnation is perhaps less useful now than the patient work of historical understanding, which alone can make a permanent change in our view of

20   Martin Heidegger, "The Origin of the Work of Art," in *Poetry, Language, Thought*, trans. Albert Hofstadter (New York: Harper & Row, 1971), pp. 19–20.
21   D. W. Robertson Jr., *A Preface to Chaucer: Studies in Medieval Perspectives* (Princeton: Princeton University Press, 1962), pp. 289–90; cf. p. 365.

the past. Melioristic perspectives on culture—telling us how very far we have come since the Greeks—invariably seek to make culture useful, as a moral substitute for religion or as a handmaid to politics. But this desire to make culture move forward in time must repress any real knowledge of creative work, which is, as Baudelaire shrewdly observed, the enemy of progress.

In the frame of tradition, creative work is understood as the imposition of a form (for example, the medieval fourfold structure of meaning) on a relatively indifferent substance, the "tale of a fox, or of a cok and hen."[22] Making moves forward in time with tradition, borne up by the underlying activity of many hands. When examined more closely, however, the activity of the hand in tradition is not so innocuous as it first seems, generously proffering what has been made in the past. The hand also reaches forward to grasp the unappropriated substance of nature, drawing it back to the mouth. When the otherness of nature is reduced to an object set before a subject for use, as what Heidegger called a "standing reserve,"[23] that otherness has already been gathered into the subject, which correspondingly enlarges itself in order to occupy all. Nature is the future of making: where nature is, there making shall be.

Among the abstract forms with which nature is grasped the most common, in literature, is what we call *genre*. Although the word *genre* is derived from the activity of *genesis* or production, it passes over the actual labor of making. Thus the ode, but not any particular ode, is handed on from Pindar to Horace to Jonson to Shelley, taking its content from what has not yet been absorbed into making, from life. If, however, we look behind the term *genre* to its roots in genesis and genealogy, we discover a more violent scene: the perennial assault of the generated on what is established before it in time, on that which has given it substance. The thick texture of allusion in the language of *Paradise Lost* (to speak of making with respect to a nonallegorical work) is at the most fundamental level uninterpretable. What we call allusion is in truth capture, the process by which a work achieves monumentality by taking its substance from the realm of the previously made.

This retrogressive movement is the key to understanding how allegories function historically. I said earlier that when allegories no longer

22 Geoffrey Chaucer, "The Nun's Priest's Tale," l. 4629, in *Works of Geoffrey Chaucer*, 2d ed., ed. F. N. Robinson (Boston: Houghton Mifflin, 1957).
23 Martin Heidegger, *The Question concerning Technology, and Other Essays*, trans. William Lovitt (New York: Harper & Row, 1977), p. 17.

existed within a common culture of meaning they no longer belonged to a history. This loss of temporal relatedness among allegories and, more generally, of relatedness to previously made works, was accompanied by a loss of vitality. For rather than being involved in complex relations with other works, each allegory stood alone in its relation to a prescriptive aesthetic theory. There is a great difference between the theoretically correct allegories of the Enlightenment and the robust encyclopedism of Jean de Meun, the vast synthesis of Dante, and the associative erudition of Spenser. By "vitality," however, I do not mean to evoke a sentimental attachment to undifferentiated life as an essence. The vitality of allegories in their historical relations with works that have been previously made is more like the struggle of the living to survive and prevail. New works capture their monumentality from works that have already established themselves in the realm of the made. The temporal dynamic of the genre of allegory, when "genre" is taken as a properly historical term, is disclosed in the savage, Hesiodic struggle evoked by the term "genealogy." As historical genre, allegory may be likened to the tale of Cronos, who overthrew his father, Ouranos (the sky), by castrating him and throwing the testicles—the Platonic forms—into the sea, whence the goddess Aphrodite was born. The tremulous undulations in the veil of allegory are the turbulence that remains after the work's violent creation.

The question concerning allegory and history may be posed, therefore, as follows. How does an allegory, striving to be a memorable thing, a monument, make room for itself in the crowded arena of things that have already been made? To pose such a question is to raise matters that are more disturbing than anything we are likely to meet with when accounting contextually for artistic change, according to the hypothesis of the culture of the sign. It is to raise, in a word, the matter of violence, which in the classical sense of the term means the forcing of something out of its predetermined, natural course. Allegory is produced out of a violence against the monumentality of previous works which is similar to the violence it directs against bodies. Allegory improvises with what it rips off.

The three principles constituting allegorical poiesis are parallel with, while differing fundamentally from, the triad of matter, negation, and form: monumentality, violence, and improvisation. The substratum that is prior to any creative event is in the realm of things that have already been made, orienting the work of poiesis toward the remains of the past. Making moves backward in time. When we think of art in these terms, we understand why the language of the Homeric poems was not taken from any one dialect of archaic Greek but was an amalgam of dialects forming an exclusively poetic language. The linguistic substratum of the poem must not be any natural language but a thing that has already been absorbed into making. We see much the same principle at work in the language of *The Faerie Queene* and in that of *Paradise Lost*. Even the deliberately natural poetic diction of Wordsworth is, in moments of intensity ("Rolled round in earth's diurnal course"), quarried from a Latinity that is, by Wordsworth's time, largely an artifact.[24]

The third principle, improvisation, has obvious relevance to the example of Homeric diction, as it does to the combinative dexterity of spontaneous composition in music. Far from being a deviation from the norm in the arts of the West these practices disclose what is essential to making. In even the most rigorously classical composition order is achieved by working with chance. A structure is developed gradually out of the chaotic interactions between the mind of the artist and the materials at hand, that is, the fragments of previous works. At the most fundamental level, poiesis is a schematizing of fragments of the previously made. Through a complex process of struggle among layered revisions, these fall into a pattern that cannot be foreseen but only revealed as it emerges in time.

The concept of improvisation appears in Aristotle's *Poetics*, where it denotes the unskilled, haphazard manner of working which was gradually displaced by the poets as they developed their art.[25] At the beginning of Western aesthetics the technological theory of making is founded on the conception of improvisation as amateurish, ignorant making. The verb "to improvise" is *autoschediazein*, implying the self-development of an external form, a *schema*, as one proceeds, rather than working with a preexisting idea according to a preexisting rule. While the word was generally used in a pejorative sense, it has a positive application in complex systems that change over time, compelling one to rely on instinctive impulse rather than on rules. In Thucydides and Xenophon improvisation is associated with political and military genius, with a sure sense of timing and of touch, nourished by experience, empathy, and talent. These

---

24 William Wordsworth, "Poems of the Imagination," no. 11, "A slumber did my spirit seal," in *Poetical Works*, ed. Thomas Hutchinson and Ernest de Selincourt (Oxford: Oxford University Press, 1936).
25 Aristotle, *Poetics* 1448b8; 1449a14; cf. *Politics* 1326b19. The word is used in a positive sense in Thucydides, *History* 1.38.3, and Xenophon, *Spartan Constitutions* 13.5. I am grateful to J. Robert Connor for drawing these positive uses to my attention.

are of course the very qualities we associate also with lasting achievement in the arts. Now allegory is unusual among the older literary genres in being a more openly improvisatory form. It therefore provides us with an occasion to reflect on the wider significance of the two models of artistic production being considered here: technological making, the imposition of form on indifferent substance, and schematic, or improvisational, making.

In its essential outline, the technological model of poiesis is more clearly reflected in the analysis of change in Aristotle's *Physics* than it is in the *Poetics*. For the analysis in the *Physics* includes, together with matter and form, the crucial principle of "lack" or "privation": "If things which naturally have a quality lose it by violence, we say they have suffered privation."[26] The formal configuration of the substance must be negated by privation—we would now say, by the introduction of disorder, or noise—so that the substance may receive a new form. In this manner the wood of a tree is removed from its standing in growth—such that the form of the tree is destroyed—when it is made into planks for a ship. The violence of making, which begins in the purely mental act of reducing the forest to wood ("board feet"), is seldom brought to consciousness in Western art. But the awareness can happen at boundaries, as in *The Epic of Gilgamesh*, where a great forest is destroyed, or in Homer's description of the fashioning of Pandaros's bow, which begins with the hunting of the wild goat from whose horns it is made.[27] A disclosure of this kind happens suddenly—in perhaps no more than a half-line of verse—in the Old English poem "The Dream of the Rood." The dreamer is addressed by the wood of the cross, but the wood speaks with the voice of a tree, remembering when it was hewn in the forest and removed from its roots, "astyred of stefne minum."[28] The otherness of this voice is not the transcendental other of allegory; it is not a goal for us, nor are we a goal for it; it is something to which we can only attend, in the brief moment when incommensurate ways of being encounter each other. Such an encounter

26 Aristotle, *Metaphysics* 1046b35; cf. 1011b29 and *Physics* 191a15.
27 *Iliad* 4.105–8.
28 "The Dream of the Rood," l. 30, in *Bright's Old English Grammar and Reader*, ed. Frederic G. Cassidy and Richard N. Ringler (New York: Holt, Rinehart & Winston, 1971), p. 312. For Erysichthon, who for destroying a forest is punished with unappeasable hunger, see Chapter 5, note 40. See also Robert Pogue Harrison, *Forests: The Shadow of Civilization* (Chicago: University of Chicago Press, 1992).

recalls the legend of the trees sharing an immemorial wisdom that is largely inaccessible to us, however far we journey into the forest. For this wisdom is not objective information, the sort of thing that can be reproduced in the mind of a subject. It is a way of being for trees, as prudent, empathetic restraint, *sophrosyne*, is a way of being for humans, one that allows us not just to tolerate but to delight in other ways of being. Such wisdom would decline to regard with approval the anagogic image of man enclosing the cosmos.

We are not likely to find an idea less like the legend of the wisdom of the trees than the mathematical doctrine that is first encountered at the end of Plato's *Republic:* the music of the spheres.[29] The music of the spheres is the clearest imaginative expression of what would become, after Descartes, the doctrine of universal subjectivity: that being is based in the subject. When the universe becomes a Platonic-Pythagorean machine—literally, a musical instrument—it is harnessed to a single purpose: to please its ideal perceiver. But we saw that even in this subservient condition nature will not be irrevocably in the power of the subject until it is made of one substance with the subject, that is, until it is devoured. Such is the transition from microcosm to macrocosm: the form of man, as microcosm, comes to look increasingly like the form of the cosmos. Behind the apparently innocuous microcosm-macrocosm analogy, subject and world are joined in an allelophagic conflict wherein the form of the being that will rise from their encounter is left in some doubt. It may be worthwhile to consider what conception of making emerges at the other end of the digestive tract, when the artist is turned toward what has been left behind in the past: monuments and waste, that which we try to remember and that which we try to forget.

The image of the universe as a body raises as many problems as the image of the universe as a machine. A body is the scene of exchanges between inside and outside, between the interior of the organism and its environment. The organism has a direction given to it in its environment by its need to capture energy and excrete waste. It is oriented along the axis of its digestive tract, moving toward what it devours and away from what it excretes. From this movement the organism also derives the material basis of its existence in time. That toward which it moves is its future (nature is the future of making) and that which it excretes is its past. When we speak of putting the past behind us the power of the ex-

29 See S. K. Heninger Jr. *Touches of Sweet Harmony: Pythagorean Cosmology and Renaissance Poetics* (San Marino, Calif.: The Huntington Library, 1974), pp. 179–89.

pression is derived from its metaphorical connection to waste. And when reference is made to the irrelevance of old works of literature or art to the way we live now, that opinion derives its appeal from the same, unconscious metaphor. Indeed all works of art have this tang of the excremental about them, having taken for their sustenance what has already been left behind in the past. Interpretation is largely an effort to conceal this fact.

In its utopian progress toward the goal of technology the microcosm takes the world into itself until there is nothing left to devour, at which point microcosm and macrocosm are one, the terms of the analogy coinciding. But enclosure need not be the end of the struggle. For the world that is devoured by Man escapes him as waste, as that which he has failed to convert into himself, and this waste is the substance of history, of a past that the analogy of microcosm and macrocosm cannot absorb. The material remains of the past are the evidence of our failure, which is already inevitable, to coincide with the world. As the microcosm increases in size, however, this evidence is squeezed into the narrowing space between the limits of the body and the limits of the real, until the evidence is brought around in front of our mouths. Like waste that washes up on the beach, what this man has left behind in the past eventually comes around to confront him, as the contradiction of what he is trying to do. The violence of allegorical making cannot be entirely absorbed in the result, as meaning; nor can it be entirely expelled into the past. It clings to the system at its boundaries, defiling the order that allegory strives to perfect. Therein lies the value of allegory to us: it teaches us to reflect on the past as the real.

8

Spenser's *Mutabilitie* and
the Authority of Forms

In his *Birth of Tragedy* Nietzsche describes the contradictory function of the image in the Apollonian spectacle in words that can
stand as an account of how the allegorical image at once invites
and resists our looking beyond it: "The intense clarity of the image . . .
seemed to hide as much as it revealed, and while it . . . seemed to invite us to pierce the veil and examine the mystery behind it, its luminous
concreteness nevertheless held the eye entranced and kept it from probing deeper."[1] What is actually concealed in this spectacle, according to
Nietzsche, is the truth that the unity radiating from behind the veil is a
projection of human consciousness. The inner mystery, therefore, is not
the rule of nature but the human exception to the rule, and a limitlessly
painful exception when recognized as such. The image does not refer
back to a unifying mystery in nature, a mystery that we can think of as
real because it is, as in allegory, veiled. The truth is that the image conceals an imponderable otherness that is subjectively experienced as pain
and as ecstatic release from the cause of that pain, which is consciousness. The fate of this consciousness is accounted for by Nietzsche in the
story of King Midas, who, having captured the satyr Silenus, compels

---

[1] I have used Francis Golffing's translation of this passage from Friedrich Nietzsche's
The Birth of Tragedy, in *"The Birth of Tragedy" and "The Genealogy of Morals"* (New York:
Doubleday, 1956), p. 141, rather than the more literal translation of Walter Kaufmann, in
Basic Writings of Nietzsche (1966; reprint, New York: Random House, 1968), pp. 139–40.
Further references are to page numbers in Golffing's translation.

him to reveal the secret of what is to be valued most in life—a question presupposing, typically of Midas, that there is one thing in life to which absolute value may be fastened. Laughing, Silenus answers that the best thing for man is never to be born and the second best thing is to die soon.[2] When one possesses this secret it seems that all one can do—short of dying soon or avoiding the mistake of being born in the first place—is to resign every effort to justify the world to individuated consciousness and to surrender, through experience of the Dionysian rites, to ecstatic communion. This is perhaps the deepest meaning, in Spenser's *Mutabilitie*, of the gnomic remark addressed by a goddess of Nature to a goddess of Change: "Thy decay thou seest by thy desire."[3]

There is, however, another recourse open to consciousness less drastic than resignation to ecstasy and death. Allegory is the most satisfying imaginative expression of this alternative, and idealism is its most rigorous intellectual expression. It is simply to decide to imagine the forms, giving them the metaphysical authority to stand as a basis for action and thought. Desire is thus alienated from the realm of the subject, from feeling, so that it may reestablish itself as an object to strive for, the Good. The Good is then imagined to be hidden behind, even as it resonates through, a cosmic arrangement of visual forms. This is the road taken by Western metaphysics, which is grounded in the notion of an objective *idea*, or "thing seen," subjectively contemplated from a position of unassailable detachment—a position, that is, from which one is safe from what one observes. The truth will not reach out to lay hold on us, as the god Saturn lays hold on his children, or as the Titans—whose name Hesiod derives from a verb meaning "to stretch"—reach out to take hold of the heavens.[4] The religious precursor of idealism is the luminous spectacle of the Olympians as they are seen, for example, at the close of the first book of the *Iliad* or in the Farnesina gallery in Rome,

2 Nietzsche, *The Birth of Tragedy*, p. 29.
3 *Faerie Queene* 7.7.59. Spenser's *Two Cantos of Mutabilitie*, published posthumously as the seventh book of *The Faerie Queene*, has been regarded as a separate work, as a portion of some future, uncompleted book of the uncompleted *Faerie Queene*, and as a coda offering a "retrospective commentary" on the project as a whole. For this last, see William Blissett, "Spenser's *Mutabilitie*," in *Essays in Literature from the Renaissance to the Victorian Age*, ed. Millar MacClure and F. W. Watt (Toronto: University of Toronto Press, 1964), p. 26. For a review of these perspectives, see S. P. Zitner, "*The Faerie Queene*, Book VII," in *The Spenser Encyclopedia*, ed. A. C. Hamilton et al. (Toronto: University of Toronto Press, 1990), pp. 287–89.
4 Hesiod, *Theogony*, l. 207. See Anne Lake Prescott, "Titans," in Hamilton et al., *The Spenser Encyclopedia*, p. 691.

eternally happy. But the spectacle conceals the horror of what the gods have escaped in their past: Saturn's reaching hand and open mouth. In the conceptual frame of idealism, however, the positions of the Apollonian veil and the Saturnian mystery are reversed. The forms of the gods are not understood as something through which the eye looks in order to contemplate the flux of becoming. They are understood as something discerned inside that flux as its law. Nature thus stands revealed in its secret interior as an order of visual forms or, as in Spenser, a pageant.

For Nietzsche the authority of this revelation depends on our forgetting its production in the subject as a veil through which one can contemplate life without being overwhelmed by its pain. In terms that resonate unmistakably with Spenser's *Mutabilitie*, Nietzsche describes the veil of forms as the "glittering dream-birth of the Olympians" and what it conceals as "the titanic powers of Nature,"[5] powers which, when contemplated raw, only convince us that it would have been better not to be born. The aura surrounding the forms is created by the power of what those forms have to block out, and the aura is encoded in myth as the anxiety of the Olympians concerning the Titans. By decoding this anxiety in *Mutabilitie* we do not simply discover what the images in the poem mean, for they mean, trivially, what we are told they mean. We discover what it is that the images have to block out in order to appear as a celebration of life. We also discover what is at issue when, at the last, they are contemplated by the poet with loathing.

What is chiefly at issue is the priority of metaphysical concerns over all other kinds of concern—for example, politics, which idealism would reduce to a science of utopian forms. The entire project of *The Faerie Queene* may be described as an improvisatory quest for the formal patterns of relationship which sustain judgments of value in human affairs. Commentary on the poem has understood its task, therefore, as adjudicating the claims of optimism and pessimism on it. The issue raised by *Mutabilitie*, however, lies deeper, in a questioning of the very basis for such judgments of value. Is that basis to be found in a metaphysics promoted by the authority of visual forms or in something else for which that authority is a pleasing but illusory veil? This other thing, which allegory discloses in its negative moments, is the experience of the body, in the clearing or *agora* of political life, living under the threat of destruction. Spenser's *Mutabilitie* evokes this experience by diverting our

5 Nietzsche, *The Birth of Tragedy*, pp. 29–30.

attention from metaphysics to genealogy, from the contemplation of the universe as an order of forms, a cosmos, to the memory of its violent emergence in time.

The Faerie Queene is an allegorical epic loosely constructed around the declared plan of representing in twelve books "the twelve private morall vertues, as Aristotle hath devised."[6] Notwithstanding this abstract plan, the poem is broadly concerned with political matters, which are expressed on three levels of increasing generality and idealization. On the first level there are thinly disguised allegories of contemporary, and for the most part violent, events in England, Ireland, and the Low Countries. On the second level is the promulgation of the historical fiction with which Henry VII (the grandfather of Elizabeth I) legitimated his claim to the throne, ending the genealogical violence of the Wars of the Roses: the Arthuro-Trojan genealogy of the Tudors. On the third level is the poet's extravagant praise of Queen Elizabeth herself, "the most high, mightie and magnificent empresse renowned for pietie, vertue, and all gratious government . . . by the grace of God queen of England Fraunce and Ireland and of Virginia, defendour of the faith & etc." This is the language of the 1596 dedication, but the queen is at the imaginative center of the poem as Gloriana, the Faerie Queene of the title, from whose court the knights proceed on their quests. And her qualities — those abstract ideals that are to be seen preëminently in her: holiness, temperance, chastity — are reflected allegorically throughout the narrative in what the poet calls "colourd showes" (3.proem.3). On this level, from which struggle and subversion are purged, the metaphysical order of the cosmos is reflected in the political order under Elizabeth, "Mirrour of grace and Majestie divine" (1.proem.4).

The prominence of this metaphysical order over genealogical concerns is inverted in *Mutabilitie*, bringing into view something that had been kept out of sight in the preceding books of *The Faerie Queene*. What is brought into view is the truth that genealogy and metaphysics are not just alternative means of legitimating power. For while metaphysics is relatively inert when not used, genealogical discourse is a positive menace that must be coopted, lest it awaken alternative genealogical claims. This distinction between genealogy and metaphysics, while extremely impor-

6 "Letter to Raleigh," in Spenser, *The Faerie Queene*, ed. A. C. Hamilton (London: Longman, 1977), p. 737.

tant, is not absolute, for they originate together in violence. At the most fundamental level genealogy is expressed in a savage, Hesiodic narrative in which the happiness of the Olympians emerges from a history of cannibalism, mutilation, and capture. Nor is this violence merely a thing of the past. Genealogical discourse transmits the violence out of which the authority of the Olympians emerged and from which that authority continues to gather its luster. As long as memory survives, violence is a thing of the present, ready to be awakened by alternative genealogical claims or subtly at work, suppressing such claims, in the narcotic of Olympian splendor. The Jove who at the end of *Mutabilitie* is "confirmed in his imperiall see" (7.7.59) represents this authority, by which all change is assimilated to the rhythms of recurrence: the cycles of nature and of the heavenly bodies. Even the circular motion of the planets, which bear the names of the gods, belongs to the work of suppressing the past. The observed irregularities in that motion, notably in the planets Saturn and Mars—irregularities to which the poet alludes in the proem to book 5, and which Mutabilitie repeats before Nature (7.7.52)—are evidence of a struggle taking place behind the veil of Olympian order. In repetitive, circular motion the spaces left in the memory by suppressing the past are at once forced open and filled by the recurrence of what has survived. Every circular motion in the heavens displaces a memory of violence and pain. And every irregularity in that motion is evidence of the continuing struggle of what has been repressed to return from oblivion.

The metaphysical order of the Olympians is thus challenged by an alternative order that would expose such ideal recurrence as part of becoming, as something that has emerged out of struggle rather than as something that has existed forever. Genealogical discourse operates subversively within the authoritative order of forms as an anxiety that that order is trying to keep down, or a memory that it is trying to suppress, or a truth, like that of Silenus, that it is trying to block out. Mutabilitie's claim against that authority has been thought to be contradictory because she aspires to the very dominion that her discourse subverts.[7] How

7 See C. S. Lewis, *The Allegory of Love: A Study in Medieval Tradition* (Oxford: Oxford University Press, 1938), p. 356; Northrop Frye, "The Structure of Imagery in *The Faerie Queene*," in *Fables of Identity: Studies in Poetic Mythology* (New York: Harcourt, Brace & World, 1963), pp. 72 and 74; Sherman Hawkins, "Mutabilitie and the Cycle of the Months," in *Form and Convention in the Poetry of Edmund Spenser*, ed. William Nelson (New York: Columbia University Press, 1961), pp. 82 and 87; S. P. Zitner, ed., *The Mutabilitie Cantos* (London: Nelson, 1968), p. 16; Blissett, "Spenser's *Mutabilitie*," pp. 40–41; James Nohrnberg, *The Analogy of "The Faerie Queene"* (Princeton: Princeton University Press, 1976),

could change rule? This line of argument misses the point that Mutability would naturally advance a contradictory claim, since logic, which is circular motion (not mere circularity) in argument, is at the heart of what she would subvert. At the origin of everything for her is a cosmogonic struggle, a Heraclitean *polemos* undermining the stability of logical and metaphysical foundations. Causing, from her very onset, an eclipse of the moon, Mutabilitie throws the shadow of politics over the realm of recurrence. It is the style of Jove's rule that Mutabilitie challenges: rule without struggle. She asks Jove, "Where were ye borne?" (7.7.53), because the circumstances of his birth are inseparable from the struggle he would have us forget. Authority, especially under an absolute regime, is the power to compel the public forgetting of what is privately remembered; it is hegemonic amnesia. Memory, therefore, is the stumbling block of the Olympians, opening up to our view what we may call, to adapt Fredric Jameson's phrase, the political unconscious of universal order.

Genealogical concerns are raised in *Mutabilitie* on at least six occasions, which fall into three distinct contexts.[8] These contexts are the mythological, in which Mutabilitie asserts her claim as a descendant of Titan; the political, in which the logic of succession and of uncontrolled growth subverts an aesthetically legitimated order of forms; and the philosophical, in which metaphysics, the study of things with independent being and freedom from change,[9] is shown to have emerged from something other than itself which it subsequently tries to forget, or at least to contain. To the six occasions on which genealogical concerns are raised we should perhaps add one that is less direct than the others but still highly suggestive. I refer to the poet's comparison of the gathering on Mole to the gathering of the gods at the marriage of the nymph Thetis to the mortal Peleus (7.7.12). The union was arranged by a Jove anxious about the prophecy that Thetis would have a son who would be

---

p. 742; and Donald Cheney, *Spenser's Image of Nature: Wild Man and Shepherd in "The Faerie Queene"* (New Haven: Yale University Press, 1966), pp. 246–47.

8   See (1) the narrator's introduction (*Faerie Queene* 7.6.2); (2) Jove's anticipation of what the disturbance is about (7.6.15 and 20); (3) Mutabilitie's initial address to the Olympians, recounting her lineage (7.7.26–27); (4) the initial debate, including Jove's reference to Mutabilitie's claim as another effort of the Titans to "touch celestiall seates with earthly mire" (7.6.29) and Mutabilitie's pointed reference to him as Saturn's son (7.6.29–34); (5) the beginning of Mutabilitie's closing argument, repeating her genealogical claim (7.7.15–16); and (6) the close of that argument, in which Jove is asked where he was born (7.7.53–54).

9   Aristotle, *Metaphysics* 1026a19–20.

greater than his father, which she eventually does in bearing Achilles. Thus Achilles—himself a figure of circular motion when he pursues Hector around Troy—holds the place of an unborn half brother who, by being greater than Jove, would have opened the Olympian realm to genealogical terror.

It will be seen from these remarks that in my judgment the traditional interpretation of *Mutabilitie* as the culmination of Spenser's metaphysical concerns is mistaken. For Spenser is in this poem undoing an illusion that is as necessary to allegory as it is to Renaissance social and political theory: the priority of metaphysics to all other concerns, including politics. This reversal of priority was prepared for, I contend, by the project of thought undertaken in the fifth and sixth books of *The Faerie Queene*, which are deeply theoretical responses to the practical exigencies of Elizabethan policy, chiefly in Ireland. My argument is based on two assumptions about Spenser: first, that he was sensitive to the nuances of social and political life in a more immediate way than was the case even with Dante or Milton; and second, that he was not primarily a narrative poet but a poet whose main concern was to think. He thought in subtle, allusive, indirect, and intuitive ways about problems too complex to be dealt with by entirely rational means, problems we might describe as demanding an associative rather than an algorithmic approach. Spenser takes us into areas of theoretical inquiry the existence of which Milton hardly suspected, or never found a vehicle flexible enough to explore. We may find more congenial, more modern, and certainly more tidy than Spenser's strange relay of virtues Milton's division of human problems into questions of political, religious, intellectual, and domestic liberty. But no reader of *The Faerie Queene* can fail to appreciate Spenser's more nuanced understanding of the complexities of human relations. These are Spenser's strengths. Notable among his weaknesses is his lack of an imaginative grasp of the problem of history. Indeed it is likely that this one deficiency in Spenser is responsible for the neglect into which he has fallen in comparison with Milton. But in *Mutabilitie* Spenser addresses himself to concerns—in particular, to what Nietzsche would call the will to power—that bear profoundly on the theory of history.

I have mentioned these aspects of Spenser's character as a poet—that he is political, and he thinks—to suggest the place *Mutabilitie* has in a project of thought. *Mutabilitie*'s inversion of the relation of metaphysics to what is traditionally derived from it—value, politics, struggle—is not an anachronistic imposition of Nietzschean thought on the poem but something Spenser achieved. Nietzsche and Spenser were both preoccupied with the metaphysical authority of visual forms, Nietzsche as an outright antagonist and Spenser, with the irony that comes with the ability to take complexity seriously, as a quiet apostate. If *Mutabilitie* is the culminating achievement of literary allegory, its greatness depends to a very considerable degree on its undermining the metaphysical basis of allegorical expression. For allegorical expression depends on the belief that natural growth stands within the order of meaning and that the experience of the body in time has value only within the frame of a cosmos that exists out of time.

Spenser's defection from metaphysics, which is completed in *Mutabilitie*, was prepared for by the most important event in his poetic career: the movement, in the middle books of *The Faerie Queene*, from an essentially cosmic perspective to one that foregrounds explicitly social and political concerns. In the fifth book Spenser tried to apply an abstract theory of justice to a society (Ireland) that was profoundly divided, although to describe it as a society rather than a military occupation is to view the matter from the English point of view. That Spenser formulated the problem in legal terms may be seen in his *View of the Present State of Ireland*, where he is concerned to show how the flexible principles of the Brehon law are incompatible with the absolute values embodied in his own legal tradition.[10] Given what he saw as the slipperiness of the Irish, which may be likened to the resistance of matter to the imprint of form, the only solution Spenser could envision is the one that is demonstrated repeatedly in the fifth book: to enforce absolute principles by means of unrestrained violence. Although Spenser supported this solution and its military instrument, Lord Grey, the spectacle of blood and despair raised in book 5 must have indicated something forgotten. He therefore began to think about human aggregation on a deeper level than that on which an abstract principle is imposed on its embodied, recalcitrant, vulnerable subjects. Accordingly, book 6 is not a relief from the concerns of the fifth, a descent, in C. S. Lewis's persistent formulation, from a stony plateau; it is a more radical approach to the same problems.

Spenser found this more radical approach in the theory of *courtesy*, a concept that would translate approximately into our terms as "culture." Courtesy for Spenser is an expression of the fundamental desire for com-

10 Edmund Spenser, *A View of the Present State of Ireland*, ed. W. L. Renwick (Oxford: Clarendon Press, 1970), p. 47, but cf. p. 54.

munity, without which there can be no law. In book 6 he made what was for him an enormous leap from the thought that whatever is right in the abstract must be forced into being, at any cost in blood, to the thought that where there is not in the first place a desire for community none of the higher structures of social concern, such as law, can be erected. Spenser achieved this insight in the extreme circumstances of Ireland, where others of his class—indeed, he himself—had thought unrestrained violence the only possible solution. That courtesy has the potential to undermine the authority of forms may be seen in the image chosen for it in the proem to the sixth book: a seed planted in earth, growing upward from its "lowly stalke" into the higher manifestations of culture.

Prompted by this image, we may discern a gradual progression of thought from idealism to care, from the abstract justice of book 5 to the embodied desire for community that is explored in book 6, and finally to a concern for the body itself in book 7, where Jove declines to "strive with flesh yfere" (7.6.31) and Faunus, in the interest of perpetuating the race of the wood gods, is spared the punishment of castration. This development would appear to be initiated by the Knight of Justice's sword, which Jove used in his great battle with the Titans (5.1.9), and which would eventually be laid aside in favor of legal debate.[11] Such debate, over time, would become less abstract and increasingly attuned to the inherent nature of the life it confronts. Thus courtesy, grounded in the recognition of the other as other, would replace law. But this seamless progression suggests that the search for political foundations in nature can proceed, so to speak, from the top down, descending from the realm of the forms into the lower world of natural processes and historical change. The thought of *Mutabilitie* is more radical than any such progression implies. Giving up the search for stable foundations to human concerns, whether in nature or in the heavens, the poem exposes all such apparent foundations as consequences of struggle. In *Mutabilitie*, allegory and violence are thought of together at last.

Mutabilitie has occasioned some of the more exemplary achievements of Renaissance literary criticism. Yet many of the questions traditionally asked of the poem now seem either banal, such as those concerning the significance of the analogy of subplot to main plot, or incapable of being advanced beyond present formulations of their undecidability, such as

11 See Balachandra Rajan, *The Form of the Unfinished: English Poetics from Spenser to Pound* (Princeton: Princeton University Press, 1985), pp. 58 and 62.

those concerning the precise relation of the text to the rest of *The Faerie Queene*. *Mutabilitie* has seemed too obvious in its metaphysical program, too affirmatively Neoplatonic, perhaps even too beautiful, to make the prospect of its deconstruction anything other than wearying to contemplate. But perhaps the weariness we feel has been deliberately induced, as if by a narcotic, to prevent us from examining what the poem is up to. Something in Spenser—simple prudence, perhaps—intended us to make the mistake we have made.

Two classic essays from the early 1960s seem to have done much to assist him, although one of them, by turning to politics, opens the way for an antimetaphysical reading. The first essay is Sherman Hawkins's learned and elegant reading of *Mutabilitie* as an expression of the cosmic optimism of Renaissance allegory, based on what Hawkins calls the "symbolic center of the Cantos" in "the pageant of the months and the seasons." The second essay is William Blissett's more tough-minded reading of the poem as an expression of the "alienated consciousness" of the later 1590s to which the proper response is not stargazing but prayer.[12] But such prayer is not, as it is in Dante, the culmination of an ascent through the heavenly spheres. In Spenser the motion of the spheres, driven by "the ever-whirling wheele / Of *Change*" (7.6.1), provokes nausea and loathing. The final prayer is an act of rejection.

Hawkins's reading leads us into the higher reaches of what Northrop Frye called "metaphysical comedy," the realm, as Aristotle said, of the theological.[13] According to this reading, *Mutabilitie* is the culmination of a tradition that began with allegorical councils of the gods in the likes of Apuleius and Martianus Capella. In Blissett's reading, on the contrary, metaphysical comedy is undermined by political concerns. Interestingly enough, this subversiveness restores *Mutabilitie* to the course of literary and cultural history. It situates the poem in the historical development extending from the Renaissance use of the gods for the purpose of legitimating princely authority to the more openly contestatory use of the gods in eighteenth- and nineteenth-century political cartoons. (Mutabilitie's reaching out her hand to pluck Cynthia from her chair is a scene worthy of James Gillray; see Figure 12.)

Hawkins's positing of metaphysical hierarchy as the central concern

12   Hawkins, "Mutabilitie and the Cycle of the Months," p. 76; Blissett, "Spenser's *Mutabilitie*," p. 27.
13   Aristotle, *Metaphysics* 1026a19–20. For discussion, see *Aristotle's Metaphysics*, ed. W. D. Ross (Oxford: Clarendon Press, 1924), 1:lxxviii.

Now all the horrors of the heav'ns he spies,
And monstrous shadows of prodigious size,
That, deck'd with stars, he scatter'd o'er the skies.

Th' astonish'd youth, where-e'er his eyes could turn.
Behold the universe around him burn:
The world was in a blaze!
— Ov. Metamorphos.

PHAETON alarm'd!

12. James Gillray. *Phaeton Alarm'd*. 1808. Art Gallery of Ontario, Toronto, Gift of the Trier-Fodor Foundation

of the poem is the initially more attractive approach and has continued to set the terms of discussion even when its limitations are felt.[14] His

14 See Isabel MacCaffrey, *Spenser's Allegory: The Anatomy of Imagination* (Princeton: Princeton University Press, 1976), p. 428; Russell J. Meyer, " 'Fixt in Heavens Hight': Spenser, Astronomy, and the Date of the *Cantos of Mutabilitie*," *Spenser Studies* 4 (1984): 127; and Elizabeth Bieman, *Plato Baptized: Towards the Interpretation of Spenser's Mimetic Fictions* (Toronto: University of Toronto Press, 1988), p. 5. Kenneth Gross, in *Spenserian Poetics: Idolatry, Iconoclasm, and Magic* (Ithaca: Cornell University Press, 1985), p. 235, remarks that in some respects it is order, not its opposite, which is regarded by Spenser as potentially "catastrophic." Sean Kane, in *Spenser's Moral Allegory* (Toronto: University of

reading stands or falls on the finality of Nature's judgment, the very brilliance of which obfuscates the political character of the acts following upon it: "putting down," "silencing," and "confirming" (7.7.59). These acts, suitably obscured, are understood as epistemological in nature, as expressions of a correct understanding of the hierarchy of the cosmos. From the perspective opened by Blissett, however, such acts are essentially political and are of a piece with the shocking representation (especially shocking in the late 1590s) of Mutabilitie threatening Cynthia's chair. They arouse in the poem a spirit of metaphysical rebellion which strikes through the veil of cosmic order at the disintegrating regime of a lady (the phrase is Walter Raleigh's) whom time had surprised.[15] Criticism has yet to come to grips with *Mutabilitie*'s being not only unpublished in Spenser's lifetime but unpublishable in Elizabeth's.

Such a conclusion should not be taken, however, as an invitation to indulge in nugatory allegorizing, to see Faunus as the earl of Tyrone, Molanna as the Irish populace, and the apples and cherries she receives as the promises of sovereignty and the return of the Catholic liturgy.[16] Nor will it suffice to appropriate Mutabilitie to the nineteenth-century concept of entropy, which belongs to calculation and physics. Mutabilitie is an expression of something more forceful, more thrusting, as is indicated in the headings to the two cantos, in which she is called "Bold *Alteration*" and "Proud *Change*." In Elizabethan political code this is highly charged language, evoking revolutionary possibilities and extravagant, genealogical claims. It is language that applies equally well to the return to Roman Catholicism under Mary, to the revolt of the northern earls, and to the climate of discontent in the late 1590s, from which the Essex rebellion would spring. "Bold Alteration" and "Proud Change" belong to the discourse of genealogy.

We may at first find the violence of such discourse difficult to hear because in modern society the institutions of rule are legitimated by

---

Toronto Press, 1989), pp. 211–25, sees Mutabilitie and Jove as "the subjective and objective factors respectively in the classical paradox of power," the latter generating "an abstract and paranoid hallucination of order" (p. 212).

15 Blissett, "Spenser's *Mutabilitie*," p. 33, citing Willard M. Wallace, *Sir Walter Raleigh* (Princeton: Princeton University Press, 1959), p. 206. Raleigh used the phrase at his trial in 1603, which was held on November 17, the late queen's accession day.

16 See Judah L. Stampfer, "The 'Cantos of Mutability': Spenser's Last Testament of Faith," *University of Toronto Quarterly* 21 (1951–52): 153–55. For Molanna as Arabella Stuart, see Zitner, *Mutabilitie Cantos*, pp. 23 and 24n; and R. N. Ringler, "The Faunus Episode," *Modern Philology* 63 (1965–66): 12.

the universalist claims of the Enlightenment. These claims are drawn by analogy from Enlightenment science, in which a hierarchy of cosmic value, an aristocracy of objects, is replaced by a democracy of things and a physics of force. It is easy for us, therefore, to underestimate the impact of genealogical discourse, which in the succession crisis of the late 1590s was as pervasive in the Elizabethan political arena as its public expression was anxiously suppressed. The Arthuro-Trojan genealogy of the Tudors, vigorously promoted in the earlier books of *The Faerie Queene*, is more than ingenious flattery. Contrived a century before *The Faerie Queene* was written, it served to co-opt a genealogical discourse that originally occasioned, and continually renewed, the bloodshed of the Wars of the Roses. It was likewise the genealogical discourse of the church of Rome that occasioned, and continually renewed in Elizabeth's reign, the threat of civil war and foreign invasion. The unity of these political menaces for Spenser is evident in his belief that the campaign in Catholic Ireland against the earl of Desmond, Gerald Fitzgerald, was the conclusion of the Wars of the Roses; for the Fitzgeralds had been Yorkists and the Butlers, led by the earl of Ormond, Lancastrians.[17]

Speaking more generally, we may say that genealogical discourse is an incentive to titanism, the ceaseless mounting of challenges to any authority that declares itself to be permanent. Titanism was repeatedly displayed before the public as a source of fascination and ideological terror, notably in Shakespeare's popular plays of Henry the Sixth, not to mention the extravagantly violent *Titus Andronicus*, and in the revived popularity of revenge tragedy around the turn of the century. Hamlet himself is enjoined to "remember" and promises to do so, "whiles memory holds a seat / In this distracted globe."[18] Memory itself is identified with revenge, revenge being memory in action. Metaphysical discourse, by contrast, as exemplified in a poem such as Sir John Davies's *Orchestra*, has its basis in willful forgetting of how the present order of the world came to be.

It is of course memory that Mutabilitie attempts to awaken in those whom she addresses. For memory, as every authoritarian regime knows, is the only form of intellectual discipline that can subvert the anaesthetic contemplation of power, as when we see the representatives of world order, like the Olympians themselves, raining fire on chthonic forces

---

17 See Spenser, *A View of the Present State of Ireland*, p. 173 n.
18 *Hamlet* 1.5.96–97, in *The Riverside Shakespeare*, ed. G. Blakemore Evans (Boston: Houghton Mifflin, 1974).

below. The "putting down" of the Titaness is gentler, but is essentially the same act of flattening that was borne by the Titans and the giants before. If as readers we acquiesce in this conceptual flattening, the blocking out of memory, we miss what is most important in the thought of the poem. I refer to the thought that is evoked when the poet allows the noise of genealogical struggle to be heard behind the spectacle of Olympian forms. We may hear it, however, by putting our ear to the place hollowed out in *Mutabilitie* by the removal of something that had been crucial in the earlier books of the poem: the Trojan genealogy of the Tudors. The most important structural fact about *Mutabilitie* is the absence of that particular political myth. It is the Trojan genealogy that is thrown into obscurity when Mutabilitie claims Cynthia's chair. There is no positive evidence in the text for this claim; to know it is absent, we have to remember.

The blocking of memory occurs in the three contexts in which genealogical discourse operates in the poem: myth, politics, metaphysics. In the mythical context the concern being blocked is the problem Mutabilitie raises: the legitimacy of Jove and the Olympians, which is called into question by an indecorous, Hesiodic beginning. Mutabilitie forces Jove to recall that his rule was established "by Conquest of our soveraine might" (7.6.33 and note). The political context is immediately invoked by this statement, since it asserts what Spenser claimed for the English in Ireland: the right of conquest, that is, of violence pure and simple. That oxymoronic right, which must recognize the legitimacy of every challenge to it, is precisely what Tudor ideology was designed to efface, so that an unimpressive family history would be occluded by the most impressive one imaginable, overwhelming alternative (and better) genealogical claims. Finally, the authority of visual forms as representatives of the truth hidden in nature depends on our ability to block out the memory of the struggle from which the forms have emerged—the struggle of the mind to objectify and alienate, as a beautiful spectacle, the pain it endures in its organic substratum.

In all these contexts Mutabilitie herself bears a strange relation to the singularity, the conventional point outside the system to which everything in the system refers. Were the singularity to be forcibly drawn into the system and somehow kept from overwhelming the signal throughout, and if it were then personified and given a narrative role, it could appear only as it does in *Mutabilitie:* as the figure of absolute opposition and absolute change. Mutabilitie's vitality and beauty, even her mobility from one part of the cosmos to another, indicate that she is always on the point of being reversed, of actually becoming whatever she opposes. I have already noted the error of supposing this to be a meaningful contradiction—that Mutabilitie, as change, seeks permanent rule—because the charge of contradiction against her can be formulated only within the discourse of recurrence, to which logic belongs. Yet even within the confines of logic such a charge will not do her much harm. For nothing is more logical than for Mutabilitie to try to be what she is not, whatever her prospects of success. Her claim is neither logical nor illogical but a continual oscillation between sense and nonsense, polysemous hierarchy and ironic contradiction. She thus represents the power of genealogical discourse to bring about historical change by taking apart, from the inside, the discourse of homeostatic recurrence.

Turning to Mutabilitie's role as personifying change, we see that that concept too must be understood in the most radical, unsettling terms. Change is not merely the fluctuation of what is but the transformation of one existing thing into another and, most radically, the emergence of a thing from not-being into being. In literary terms, the degrees of change are reflected in mimesis, metamorphosis, and theogony. We see the second in Diana's pseudo-transformation of Faunus, a comic allusion to the fate of Actaeon, and in Molanna's being both the stream in which Diana bathes and one of the nymphs attending the goddess. But when we contemplate the third and most extreme sense of change, Mutabilitie seems capable of terrifying amplification as everything that does not exist struggles to emerge from inside her, from inchoateness. She contains every world that would struggle to displace this actual world were her genealogical power released, spawning worlds by the tens of thousands, like roe. Mutabilitie is the road of not-being which Parmenides warns us against even contemplating.

If we reflect on Mutabilitie as change in the first, and most limited, sense, she represents such things as the migration of birds, the swarming of fish, and the movement of grass in the wind. If these are contemplated on their own terms, however, instead of as examples of a class, they can be seen to contain the most radical ontological struggle between alternative worlds, although this struggle is known to us simply as the struggle for life. Events in the realm of physis—swarming, migration, and growth—are not instances of a higher, more comprehensive truth but independent, and urgently real, moments in the struggle for life, moments in which, for each organism, nothing less than the whole is at stake. The struggle for life is the struggle of each organism to escape from not-being into being and to enclose its environment in itself, thus to become a cosmos unto itself. A blade of grass grows to escape its not-being, which, in a way, it remembers; for its not-being pursues it through existence, like Saturn's reaching hand and open mouth, causing it to grow. The circumambient world—the air, the earth, the moisture, and the light—is an extension of this growth. For the blade of grass, the world is a large blade of grass.

This is the thought that exposes the lie in the magnificent pageant of seasons and times: that everything that has been lost in the past can be recovered again within a larger, cosmic design. Being marshaled by "*Natures* Sergeant," "Order" (7.7.4 and 27), the pageant has always been taken to be a positive affirmation of life and a decisive refutation of the Titaness's case. Nature herself looks up, after contemplating its meaning at length, "with chearefull view" (7.7.57). But the beauty of the pageant proceeds from an awareness of the painfulness of life, and its artistic courage lies in the energy with which the poet transmutes the pain into beauty.[19] It is like the splendor, in Homer, of a stream cascading over the face of a black rock. The darkness, however, is not easy to find in the splendor. It is not enough to assert that the pageant renders picturesque, as in Milton's "L'Allegro," the harsh round of agricultural labor and, more generally, the experience in each of us of bodily decline, even as the seasons return. To point out the distortion is essentially Mutabilitie's strategy in arguing her case; but the strategy is inadequate, as we see when Nature gives judgment. It is the judgment itself that must be judged. We may begin to do so by paraphrasing Nature's statement in terms we may imagine her addressing to us: "It seems to you as if your body is changing, and changing for the worse, and more obviously so with every enlargement of the scale of time—each day, each season, each year. But appearances are deceiving. For all things, including your body, have their origin in a perfection from which they are now in decline but to which they will eventually return. What you see as a ground of dark pain against which the pageant of times brilliantly stands out is only more deeply grounded in joy, the very joy that you find in contemplating the pageant's individual forms."

19   See Harry Berger, "The *Mutabilitie Cantos:* Archaism and Evolution in Retrospect" (1968), reprinted in *Revisionary Play: Studies in the Spenserian Dynamics* (Berkeley and Los Angeles: University of California Press, 1988), p. 267.

We may hear in this speech the narcotic effect that we have heard in the crooning of Spenser's Despair, the allegorical twin of Bad Faith. But if we object with Mutabilitie, "But what we see not, who shall us perswade?" we will be answered, as she is implicitly in the language she uses, by 2 Corinthians 4:18: "The things which are not seen are eternal" (7.7.49 and note). The accusation of naïveté being equally plausible from either side, no mere insistence on the painfulness of life and no invocation of loathing—not even, as it happens, the poet's—can escape the grasp of Neoplatonic emanationism, which is the strategy of metaphysical optimism and the largest circle drawn by the discourse of recurrence. The entire structure of cosmic regeneration is a projection of a wish that one may allow oneself without shame only by disguising it as a statement about the cosmos instead of the body. This strategy cannot be countered by insisting on what the pageant conceals, for such observations may always be included in the logic of widening circles, the widest of which Nature draws at the end. The only escape is to remain in place and to awaken the past. This is why the microcosm-macrocosm analogy is the master metaphor of allegory. What genealogy tells us, however, about emergence and succession pulls the terms of this metaphor apart, exposing, in images of unspeakable horror, a brutal and primitive struggle for life from which every system has emerged. For the assembled Olympians what is most alarming about Mutabilitie is not her rapid ascent to the heavens but her ability to demonstrate that she has always been there in their midst—a "beast of strange and forraine race" (7.6.28)—as the repressed memory of their origin in violent struggle.

It is by a similarly alarming exposure of the foundations of his allegorical art that Spenser discloses in *Mutabilitie* a genealogical disruptiveness that has always been there in his affirmative images of life, making them glow with an inner light. The singularity to which these images refer stands revealed in Mutabilitie herself as the monstrous totality of the possible, out of which order is won by the exertion of force—by Jove's thunder. In its later stages Jove's violence is manifest only as that compulsory forgetting by which visual forms are used to conceal the past. The forms are persuasive as truth because they give pleasure, relying on the most seductive assertion that can be made in the ideological realm: that beauty and truth are the same.

It is by the pleasure that we take in the things seen in the pageant of seasons and times that we are convinced of their sharing in truth, such that they "raigne over change" (7.7.58). We saw in Chapter 1 how allegory provides imaginative solutions to the absurdities of classical idealism, saving the phenomena by drawing a veil of forms over chaos. For one manifestation of chaos is precisely the infinite regression of the Third Man, such regressions being the manner in which "steep Tartaros," as it was called, appears to a logical mind. The veil of allegory is an aesthetic, or perceptual, solution to this logical problem, a saving of the things that appear by attending delightedly to their individuated forms. We will read Spenser differently when we see his allegorical imagery not as striving to return to an origin in the One but as struggling to escape Saturn's devouring maw.

The path to this way of reading Spenser, however, must pass through the strongest affirmation of the authority of forms. We find it in the concluding chapter, "*The Faerie Queene*," of C. S. Lewis's great work, *The Allegory of Love*. As that title may indicate, and as the brilliance of the writing suggests, Lewis's chapter aims to complete what Spenser, or a part of him, was trying to do: to see human life in the frame of a cosmos, governed by abstract ideals. As we read Lewis's cadenced description of *The Faerie Queene*, it is impossible not to desire to assist him in the rhythmical work of forgetting, so that the sound of the violence may continue to shine:

> The clashing antitheses which meet and resolve themselves into higher unities, the lights streaming out from the great allegorical *foci* to turn into a hundred different colours as they reach the lower levels of complex adventure, the adventures gathering themselves together and revealing their true nature as we draw near the *foci*, the constant reappearance of certain basic ideas, which transform themselves without end and yet ever remain the same (eterne in mutability), the unwearied and seamless variety of the whole—all this is Spenser's true likeness to life.[20]

In the sentence following this one Lewis discloses the provenance of his vision of Spenser in the Hegelian metaphysics of process and totality. If Lewis understates Hegel's influence on him (he had taught Hegel's philosophy), it is partly because he wishes to distance himself from a youthful enthusiasm of which he thinks himself cured:

---

20 Lewis, *Allegory of Love*, p. 358. See also Lewis's discussion of Mutabilitie in *Spenser's Images of Life* (Cambridge: Cambridge University Press, 1967), pp. 74-78.

It is this which gives us, while we read him, a sensation akin to that which Hegelians are said to get from Hegel—a feeling that we have before us not so much an image as a sublime instance of the universal process—that this is not so much a poet writing about the fundamental forms of life as those forms themselves spontaneously displaying their activities to us through the imagination of a poet.

There follows what, in English literary criticism, must be among the most impressive descriptions of total art, of the cosmos itself as *Gesamtkunst*, in which every opposition nourishes the hierarchy of being: *The Faerie Queene* "reaches up to the songs of angels or the vision of the New Jerusalem. . . . It reaches down to the horror of fertile chaos beneath the Garden of Adonis and to the grotesque satyrs who protect Una or debauch Hellenore with equal truth to their nature."[21] "Clashing antitheses," "the horror of fertile chaos": such are the forces out of which the poem is raised and from which its forms draw their beauty.

Lewis does not shy away from the social import of this vision, which is recommended "to our own troubled and inquiring age." But his emphasis falls on its effect on the individual, who will benefit from "the complete integration, the harmony, of Spenser's mind." This is not an empty promise, but neither is it altogether free of collective significance. For the private experience to which he refers is derived from a social vision that Lewis is recommending, somewhat desperately one supposes, in the polarized climate of the 1930s. It is the vision of an organic, Burkean community that will turn from the extremes of the left and the right in order to grow upward, erecting a hierarchy in which, as Lewis says of *The Faerie Queene,* "there is a place for everything and everything is in its place. Nothing is repressed; nothing is insubordinate. To read [Spenser] is to grow in mental health."

It is not easy to judge the extent to which Lewis's account of Spenserian hierarchy is a meditation out of its time, as he intended. That it may be a little more of its time than he would have acknowledged is apparent, however, in the *things* referred to in the sentences just quoted, which are not vague places but allegorical persons, bodies imprinted with meaning. To objectify bodies as things in a more general scheme, a cosmos, is useful to ideologies in which meaning is imposed on individuals according to class or to race and in which masses of individuals are

21 Lewis, *Allegory of Love,* p. 359.

formed into signs. To grow in mental health reading Spenser through Hegel is to grow into a totalitarian vision in which all things are equally manipulable and equally expendable, including our bodies. It would be as pointless as it is untrue to suggest that Lewis was in some way attracted to these ideologies; he did everything he could intellectually, which was a great deal, to keep clear of them. And it was to that end that he sought to complete the task on which Spenser had embarked: to give a comprehensive vision of moral life, governed by the abstract authority of visual forms. But because those forms have their genesis in "clashing antitheses," they exhibit the same tendency to unrestrained totalization that we have observed in the fundamental image of allegory: Man enclosing the cosmos.

Nietzsche taught that through the Olympians the Greeks represented to themselves the wisdom of Silenus in an opposite form, thus producing the ideal picture of their existence.[22] What I have been saying about *Mutabilitie* is an unfolding of the consequences of that teaching in the last, and the most self-aware, of the great allegorical poets. I believe that such a reading of Spenser has more to say to us now than does a political reading of Milton, who was too original and too impatient a thinker to work within a long tradition of conventional thought. That is why Milton was not an allegorical poet. Spenser, although always an original poet, was not an original thinker at the outset, for it is of the very essence of allegorical practice to capture and reorganize the material remains of the past in an ideological frame that belongs to the present. Not until book 3 does Spenser consistently make his way into areas of thought that were largely unexplored in his time—and that are not much more familiar now. The neglect into which Spenser has fallen is partly due to a style of thinking that proceeds gradually, almost archaeologically, through a dense medium of accumulated learning. Instinctively conservative, Spenser grew into the challenge of original thought, becoming increasingly radical as he sent his roots deeper into the remains of the past. As Spenser's final poetic statement, *Mutabilitie* is a wiser, though a more secretive, enterprise than the previous six books of the poem. But the wisdom that does not appear in those books was being earned by writing them. That is the most important sense in which *Mutabilitie* both belongs to and stands apart from the creative project called *The Faerie Queene*.

22 Nietzsche, *The Birth of Tragedy*, p. 29.

The liveliness Lewis speaks of as characterizing *The Faerie Queene* does not proceed from the cyclical rhythms of emanation and return, whether in the seasons or in the stars. It proceeds from a feeling of uncanniness that cannot be located in the poem, except in occasional disturbances, which are as unsettling to our faith in its order as the erratic motions of the planet Mars were unsettling to faith in the order of the heavens. It is the feeling we have when we read Spenser's pageants, or the great symbolic centers of which *Mutabilitie* is the most peculiar and risky, that something is being blocked out so that everything on the surface of the poem may shine. We feel as if something alien is about to tear open that surface from within and, like Saturn's reaching hand, thrust itself at us. This thing will belong not to an allegorical center but, like Mutabilitie herself, to a threatening, alternative past. Spenser saw that past lying ahead of him, in our own time.

INDEX

abstraction: and gender, 22-23; the gods as, 47-48, 50, 78-82; and historical change, 158; limitations of, 25-29; and personification, 13-14, 18, 21-22, 33-37; in politics, 124; progression from idealism to care, 176

absurdity, 7, 11, 14, 46, 90

Adams, Robert M., 135-36

Addison, Joseph, 23, 58, 100-102

Aelius Theon, 122n.2

Africa, 117-21

agency, 33-34, 37, 54

agora (forum): and enclosed bodies, 124-30, 132; as political space, 122-24, 134, 138; voice in, 133, 146

Alan of Lille, 20, 22, 38, 105

Allegories and Visions, 100-101

allelophagy, 8, 10, 14; allelophagic desire, 114-15, 117, 120; logic of, 130-33, 156-57, 166

Althusser, Louis, 16

anagogy, 7-8, 153-55, 158, 166

analogy, 2, 68, 104n.19, 105, 108

anatomy. *See* body

anthropology, 66, 70-72; and romanticism, 156; model of culture, 157-58

antiphrasis, 56-59, 131; assimilation of, 72-76; and disruption, 63-65; and the sacred, 61-62. *See also* irony; polysemy

Apuleius, 44, 100, 177

Aquinas, Thomas, 18, 20n.26

Aristotle, 5, 15-16, 30, 47n.28, 50, 69-70, 177; *Physics*, 20, 165; *Poetics*, 164-65; prime matter, 19

Auerbach, Erich, 11n.9

Augustine, Saint, 33n.2; *City of God*, 51; gods as devils, 52-53; and medieval intellectuals, 48-50; on proliferation of gods, 35-37; and uses of classical culture, 43

authoritarianism, 140, 187; communist, 127. *See also* fascism

Bacon, Francis, 47, 78, 83-84, 105, 107; and classical myth, 87-93; as skeptic, 100

Baudelaire, Charles, 63-64, 115, 148-49, 162

Beattie, James, 101

Berkeley, George, 102-3

Benjamin, Walter, 4, 12-14, 64, 69

Bernardus Silvestris, 20, 112

Bible, 49, 51, 148, 159

Blake, William, 101-2, 109, 149, 154

Blisset, William, 177

Boccaccio, Giovanni, 28, 71

body: and allelophagy, 8, 10, 114-17, 132-33, 155-56; bowels, 111; collective, 124-26, 142, 144-47; and culture, 72, 151-55, 167, 175-76; gendered, 19; and Homeric epics, 39; imprinted by ideology, 124, 146; as instrument, 84; material, 25-26; and personification, 21-22; and pleasure, 84, 107; of the

Douglas, Gawin, 71n.28
"Dream of the Rood," 165–66
Dryden, John, 99
Dubos, Abbé, 97n.21, 98
Dubrow, Heather, 78n.3
Dürer, Albrecht, 12

Eliot, T. S., 150–53, 157, 161
Elizabeth I, 85, 171
encyclopedism, 108–9, 163
Enlightenment, 98–100, 107–10, 115, 163, 180
Epicureanism, 47, 107
Erigena, John Scotus, 49, 159
Euripides (*Bacchae*), 81
event, historical, 58–59, 70–71
excrement, 114–15, 166–67

family, 16
fascism, 125–26, 138, 141, 143–45
Father, 15–18, 75–76
feminine, the, 15–23
Ficino, Marsilio, 82n.6
figural realism, 11
figurality, 60, 74
Fletcher, Angus, 10n.9, 35, 132
Fletcher, Phineas, 93–94, 110–12
force, 5–6, 9–10, 24–25, 55, 82. *See also* violence
forest, 13, 30, 73, 148, 158, 166; as substance, 64. *See also* nature
forgetting, 184–85. *See also* memory
form(s): authority of visual, 169–71, 176, 181–82, 184–85, 187; classical theory of forms, 14–15, 36, 40; and matter, 15–23, 131, 165; scholastic conception of, 159
forum. *See* agora
Freccero, John, 24, 26–27
Freud, Sigmund, 35, 63, 69n.20, 75–76, 139–41. *See also* Wolf Man
Frye, Northrop, 7–8, 10, 153–56, 177

Garin, Eugenio, 78n.3, 82n.6
Geertz, Clifford, 70n.24
genealogy (and violence), 170–74, 179–82
gender, 15–23, 140. *See also* Father; feminine; masculine
genre, 10, 162–63
Gilgamesh, Epic of, 165
Girard, René, 8, 81
gods, 9, 14, 177; and Care, 142–43, 145; changing conceptions of, 32–39; decay of, 71–72; in Enlightenment, 107–8, 117–20; ideological use in Renaissance, 53–55, 78–83, 84–97; as spectacle con-

cealing violence, 81–82, 169–74, 181, 184; in Yeats ("Leda and the Swan"), 138–41. *See also* divine; mystery; numinous; sacred
Goethe, Johann Wolfgang von, 149n.2, 150
Goldberg, Jonathan, 78n.3
Grafton, Anthony, 78n.3
Green, William M., 33n.2
Greenblatt, Stephen, 78n.3
Gross, Kenneth, 178n.14
Grosseteste, Robert, 20n.26
growth (*physis*), 13, 17, 183. *See also* nature
Guido de Columnis, 20n.26
Guillory, John, 152n.8

Halmi, Nicholas, 36n.8, 106n.23
Hankins, James, 82n.6
Hartley, David, 103, 104n.19, 107, 109
Haug, Walter, 10n.11
Hawkins, Sherman, 177
hedonism (and science), 107–8
Hegel, G. W. F., 60, 160, 185–87; and risk, 145–46
Heidegger, Martin, 161n.20, 162; allegory of Care, 143–45; and Nazism, 144–45
Heraclitus the allegorizer, 32n.1
"Hercules at the Crossroads," 145
hermeneutics (interpretation), 2, 46, 49, 122
Hesiod, 34n.4, 40, 50, 87, 90, 169
hierarchy, 4, 101, 177–79, 186–87
hieroglyphics, 124
history, 148–67; and capture, 29–30; freedom from, 112; and power of the collective, 124–26, 139–41; as rotting of the gods, 76; and temporality, 51, 69, 157–58
Hobbes, Thomas: on the gods, 80; title page of *Leviathan*, 127–31, 146
Hölderlin, Friedrich, 78, 132n.19
Hollander, Robert, 27–28
Home, Henry, Lord Kames, 98n.1, 104
Homer, 2, 3, 10, 159, 183; Bacon on, 87–92; interpretation of, 39–40, 43–45; personification in, 34, 40–43; 169–70; and poiesis, 163–65; theomachia and psychomachia, 44, 69. *See also* Prudentius
homunculus, 6–7, 114, 117. *See also* participation
Horace, 48
Hugh of Saint Victor, 49
human, the (and the inhuman), 156–57
human rights, 145. *See also* body; voice

Index   191

Hume, David, 101
Hyginus (fable of Care), 142–45

iconography, 71, 76, 80, 82, 86, 88, 148
idealism, 13–14, 170; classical, 15, 36–37, 71, 142–43, 185; as a cultural force, 16–17
ideas, 69, 102–4, 112
ideology, 10; and allegory, 62, 132–33, 187; and the gods, 81–88; and irony, 69; Nazi, 144; as a practice, 16–17; Roman and Christian, 51–52; totalitarian, 187
images, 170
imagination, 7, 102–3, 149
improvisation, 163–65
individuation, principle of, 17
interpretation: as aesthetic effect, 4; allegorical, 32, 46–51, 54–55; and ideology, 16; performative, 64; and polysemy, 65, 68, 72
Ireland, Elizabethan policy in, 174–76, 181
irony: antiphrasis and polysemy, 56–58, 72–76, 182; and belief, 88–92; as disruptive force, 67–69, 132; and negation, 59; relation to allegory, 59–63; and trope, 59–60; as zero, 74. *See also* antiphrasis; polysemy
Isidore of Seville, 56n.1, 61

Jameson, Fredric, 2n.2, 173
Jardine, Lisa, 78n.3
Jauss, Hans Robert, 11n.11
Jerome, Saint, 43n.23. *See also* Christianity: Church Fathers
John of Salisbury, 48
Johnson, Samuel, 23, 42, 99, 101; "Allegory of Criticism," 94

Kane, Sean, 178n.14
Kant, Immanuel, 114
Kantorowicz, Ernst H., 125n.8
Keats, John, 1–3
Kelly, Vera Veronica, 103n.14
Kerrigan, William, 77n.1
Kierkegaard, Søren, 61, 68
knowledge, 7, 17, 109, 133; and power in "Leda and the Swan," 138–41

labyrinth, 3
lack, 165
Lamberton, Robert, 32n.2, 47n.28
Langland, William, 45
Le Brun, Charles, 97, 117
Lenaz, Luciano, 49n.27
Lévi-Strauss, Claude, 94–95
Lewis, C. S., 38n.12, 109; on *The Faerie Queen*, 175, 185–87

liberty, concept of, 129–30
literal, the, 6, 23, 43, 45, 98–99
literary history, 150–53; and theory of the symbol, 152–57; and tradition, 158–63
literary theory, 151–52; theory of the symbol, 149–50, 152–57
Livy, 127–30
Locke, John, 58, 98, 101–4, 107
logic, 12; and personification, 21–22; problems of, 37, 68–69, 74, 114; recurrence, 172, 181–82, 184
logos (and logocentrism), 5, 11, 32, 57, 73, 151
Louis XIV, 83, 85, 97
love, 27
Löwith, Karl, 144n.37
Lubac, Henri de, 49n.38

Machiavelli, Niccolò, 82–83, 88, 134–39
macrocosm and microcosm: and allelophagy, 131, 155–56, 166–67, 182–84; in Coleridge, 106–7, 154; eclipse of, 68, 103–4, 111–17; master metaphor of allegory, 6–8, 67, 83–85, 130–31, 184, 187
making (poiesis), 153, 158, 163–64
masculine, the, 17–21, 23. *See also* Father; gender
mannerist allegorical painting, 149
Martianus Capella, 45–46, 48n.36, 109, 177
masochism, 141
mathematical, the, 105, 157
matter (and substance), 12–14, 39–40, 46, 155; and gender, 15–23; and light, 159; material remains of the past, 53, 69, 92, 153, 167; in motion, 101; resistance of, 29–31
Mazzotta, Giuseppe, 27–29
meaning: Benjamin on, 12–14; and the body, 121, 123; contexts of, 148, 159; instability of, 63–64; instrumental, 2; labyrinth of, 119–20; location of, 39, 93–95; and matter, 19, 155; and narrative, 23–25, 33, 99–100; and poetics of allegory, 5–6, 175
mechanical psychology, 109, 111, 155. *See also* Hartley, David; Locke, John
Medici, Cosimo de', 85
memory (and revenge), 180. *See also* forgetting; genealogy
Menenius Agrippa, 127–29
Menippean satire, 109
metaphor, 56, 60, 73, 100, 104
metaphysics, 31, 133, 169, 184; and genealogy, 170–74; in Heidegger, 142–43; and history, 68; and literary history, 150–

metaphysics (*continued*)
52; metaphysical decay, 58, 68, 76; and politics, 177–79, 186; and sexuality, 15–16; Spenser's defection from, 175; and substance, 69
method, 104–6
Michelangelo, 84
microcosm. *See* macrocosm and microcosm
Middle Ages, 33, 46
Milton, John, 96, 110, 129n.16, 174, 187; "L'Allegro," 183; language of *Paradise Lost*, 164; *Nativity Ode*, 37–38, 54; "On the Platonic Idea," 15; Sin and Death in, 36, 42, 99
mind: of Europe, 150–52, 161; and feedback relations, 52, 94–95; location of, 93, 98–99; mechanics of, 101–2, 104, 108–9; of the poet, 151. *See also* consciousness
Minucius Felix, 51
mirror of nature, 49, 86–87
mode, allegory as, 10, 11
monad, 153–55
Montagu, Charles, Lord Halifax, 99n.2
monuments, 148, 151–53, 159–61, 166
morphological homeostasis, 152
Murrin, Michael, 123
music of the spheres, 166
Mussolini, Benito, 126. *See also* fascism
mutual devouring. *See* allelophagy
mystery, 1, 33, 65–66, 87–88, 95; and irony, 61–62; and symbol, 148–50; and unveiling, 123. *See also* divine; numinous; sacred
myth: ancient interpretation of, 32, 47–48, 122–23, 148; Bacon on, 87–95; expulsion of the sacred from, 96; Lévi-Strauss on, 94–95; as material remains of the past, 92

narrative, 5; and agency, 54–55; in Enlightenment allegory, 99–100; and historical crisis, 35; and irony, 68, 73–75; struggle of narrative and meaning, 23, 33, 99–100; and temporality, 68, 150. *See also* history
Nashe, Thomas, 68
nature, 7, 155; goddess of, 38; as growth, 13–14, 17, 183; mirror of, 49, 79–80, 86–87; as substance, 69, 154–55; as symbol, 149–50, 154–55. *See also* forest
Nazism, 124, 144–45. *See also* fascism
neoclassicism, 100
Neoplatonism, 17–18, 45, 76, 112, 143, 159; and Romanticism, 105–6

new criticism, 156
Newton, Isaac, 102–3, 107
Nietzsche, Friedrich, 24, 57, 92, 161; *Birth of Tragedy*, 5, 168–70, 187
noise, 6, 23, 57–58, 62–64, 66, 75
numinous, the, 50–51, 65–66, 149. *See also* divine; gods; mystery; sacred

object, 66–69
Onians, Richard Broxton, 39n.14
Origen, 49
Other, 5, 66–67; negative and positive, 6–8, 55
Ott, Hugo, 144n.37
Ovid, 38–39, 115n.40
Ovide moralisé, 49

pageant, 170, 183–85
pain, 181, 183
paintings, allegorical, 13, 117–20
Panofsky, Erwin, 36n.9, 78n.3
paradosis, 158–59
participation, 40–41; and the "Third Man," 14–15, 30, 114, 185
Pater, Walter, 71
Patterson, Annabel, 78n.3
Pépin, Jean, 32n.2, 49n.39, 90n.12
performative, the, 64, 70; and performance, 74–75
persona (mask), 22–23, 153
personification, 3, 14, 35, 72, 148, 156; in Enlightenment, 100, 103; and the gods, 32–33; of Justice, 14, 17, 21; and substance, 21–31; and violence, 18–19
Pfeiffer, Rudolph, 46n.28, 57
philology, 11, 48, 92, 96, 161
philosophy, 30, 32
physis (growth), 13, 17, 183. *See also* nature
Pico della Mirandola, 106n.23
Piero della Francesca (*Triumph of Federigo da Montefeltro*), 97
Pietro da Cortona (*Pallas Stripping Venus*), 85
Pilgrim's Progress, 1, 25
Planetary Rooms (Pitti palace), 85, 93
Plato, 14–20, 46n.28, 47, 68, 141; *Parmenides*, 14–15, 182; *Republic*, 90n.12, 166; *Timaeus*, 15–17, 20–21
Platonic Academy, 82
Plotinus, 47n.28, 50
Plutarch, 47, 54n.48
poetics, 5, 8, 30, 66, 72
poetry, 109–12
poiesis. *See* making
political cartoon, 97, 130, 177
political discourse, 123, 132, 146